BUILDING A COMMUNITY:

THE STORY OF JAPANESE AMERICANS IN SAN MATEO COUNTY

DESIGN
Mari Nakamura Design

PRINT PRODUCTION
West Coast Print Center
Oakland, California

PUBLISHER
AACP, Inc.
PO Box 1587
San Mateo, California 94401

ISBN NO. 0-934609-10-1

BUILDING A COMMUNITY:

THE STORY OF JAPANESE AMERICANS
IN SAN MATEO COUNTY

gayle k. yamada ▪ DIANNE FUKAMI

EDITED BY
DIANE YEN-MEI WONG

To Pam—
I hope this inspires
you to do more oral
histories and preserve
your family's stories.
gyle

Dear Pam—
Don't lose track of
your own history!
Dianne Fukami

Contents

Acknowledgments

A community story is by definition the work of many people. This book has been conceived, conceptually shaped, and refined by the dedicated and untiring work of the History Committee of the San Mateo Chapter of the Japanese American Citizens League: Yasuko Ito, the devoted and determined chair who shepherded this project along; George Ikuta, Yoneo Kawakita, Yoshi Mizono, Richard Nakanishi, Jere Takahashi, Tazu Takahashi, and Wells Wadleigh; and deceased members Sam Ota and Ernest Takahashi. Jere's experiences teaching in the Department of Ethnic Studies at the University of California, Berkeley, and as an author himself helped guide us. Wells, also a published author and history teacher, gave considerable input in the editing stage.

Early chapters of this book drew from the first book, *1872-1942: A Community Story*, published in 1981 by the JACL History Committee.

The members of that committee were William Enomoto, Yasuko Ito, Andrea Kuroda, Yoshi Mizono, Richard Nakanishi, Bill Nosaka, Tomiko Sutow, Ernest Takahashi, Jere Takahashi, and Tazu Takahashi.

The genesis for this book began with Yasuko's desire, as president of the San Mateo Chapter of the Japanese American Citizens League, to leave a legacy of Japanese American oral history. Former City Manager Richard DeLong recommended that she apply for funding from the City of San Mateo. A committee was formed to raise funds and to begin gathering material to write the book. Richard Nakanishi conducted many of the interviews in the late 1970s and was hired to write the first manuscript that became the book that preceded this one, while Shazie Tabata was the translator for early interviews conducted in Japanese. In 1993, then-general manager of San Mateo public television KCSM, David Hosley, encouraged Yasuko to initiate a companion book to television documentaries on Japanese Americans that KCSM was producing.

No book can be completed without financial support. For that we thank the Peninsula Community Foundation, the California Civil Liberties Public Education Program, the Atkinson Foundation, the Civil Liberties Public Education Fund, the JACL Legacy Fund, the Jeanette Nakahara Memorial Contribution, the American Express Matching Fund, the San Mateo JACL Ikoi-no-Tomo, the Chrysanthemum Growers Association, the Henri and Tomoye Takahashi Charitable Foundation, and George and Yoshi Mizono, as well as many other individual donors in the community.

Friends and family were swept up by this project as well. The sharp minds and eagle eyes of Aiko Herzig-Yoshinaga and Jack Herzig, and their extensive knowledge about the Japanese American experience were especially helpful in the passages about Executive Order 9066 and the eviction of those of Japanese descent from their homes on the West Coast. Attorney Dale Minami, lead counsel in Fred Korematsu's legal challenge of his forty-year old conviction, advised us on the legal technicalities of the Korematsu case and that of Mitsuye Endo. Haruko Sakakibara and Junko Ito, both Japanese by birth, answered numerous questions about the Japanese language and terminol-

ogy. Carol Peterson, archivist at the San Mateo County History Museum, and her assistant, Joan Levy, helped with research on the early days of San Mateo. Yon Kawakita, Jim Mori, and Shig Takahashi provided details about the pioneer Japanese Americans. Thomas V. Mukai and Robert Mukai obtained materials and photographs. San Francisco newspaper columnist Annie Nakao was generous in the time she spent going through her archives to track down information for us. Diane Matsuda, Program Director of the California Civil Liberties Public Education Program, and her able assistant Lisa Turgeon-Staggs, were instrumental in acquiring archival photographs and information.[1]

Thanks to those who provided us with photographs and artwork, including Hiroshi and Yasuko Ito, Kimi Kodani Hill, Ibuki Lee, Yon Kawakita, Rusty Kimura, Yoshi Mizono, Kyoko Mukai, Irene Nim, Bill Nosaka, Kaoru Ruth Saito, Sei Sakuma, Tad Sakuma, Tony and Fusako Sato, Shig Takahashi, and Hasuko "Hobs" Watanuki.

A special note of thanks to the many interviewees whose names are in the bibliography at the end. We were fascinated by their stories, and their generosity in sharing their memories and experiences was much appreciated.

The committed work of two individuals made writing this book much more enjoyable. Tracy McDonough researched the early years of

---

[1] The California Civil Liberties Public Education Program (CCLPEP) was created by state legislation in 1998 authored by Assembly member Michael Honda of San Jose, Calif. The goal of CCLPEP was to create and provide resources to inform the California community about the Japanese American experience during World War II. CCLPEP was administered by the California State Library under the direction of State Librarian, Kevin Starr, Ph.D.

the Japanese in San Mateo County. In checking factual details, Jolene Nakao's ability to sift through hundreds of footnotes and bibliographical sources as well as text was a blessing. Beyond that, their can-do attitudes made the going easier.

Without the graphic artistry and eye of Mari Nakamura, this book would not have been the same. Her mother, Yoshimi Nakamura, helped obtain photographs through old friends. We would like to thank Suzie Sakuma, who took many of the old photos we used, and applied her artistry and scanning skills to improve their quality. We gratefully acknowledge Marian O'Brien and Keith Whitaker for their guidance, expertise, and attention to details in the printing of this book.

Diane Yen-Mei Wong, editor extraordinaire, spent countless hours going through numerous versions of this book. Her camaraderie, friendship, and unending kindness added an extra dimension.

Our families were extraordinary. Heather Yamada Hosley cheerfully handled many of the clerical details. David Hosley offered his academic expertise coupled with practical knowledge of the Japanese American community in San Mateo. Many thanks as well to Janet Soto Mukai who often took care of the details of life while we were writing. The continued moral support of Gerry, Lindsay, and Hillary Nakano enabled us to spend countless hours researching and writing.

Most of all, we want to thank our parents, Junzo and Mitzi Fukami and Gordon and Kiyo Yamada. Without their experiences that shaped who we are, and their love and support over the years, this book could not have been written.

This book is primarily an experiential history of Japanese Americans in San Mateo County, located just south of San Francisco. In the beginning, the Japanese in San Mateo formed a relatively small group of immigrants. For the most part, they did not keep journals or diaries in either Japanese or English, and the majority has passed away, so their words and experiences are not available to us. Instead, we must rely on secondary sources, that is, written histories and second- or third-hand oral accounts, to tell the early story of the San Mateo Japanese community. Memories and anecdotes collected by the History Committee of the San Mateo Japanese American Citizens League and the authors over the past twenty-five years give a richer picture of the lives of these pioneers in the 1910s, '20s, and '30s.

This history takes us from the initial immigration of the Japanese, through their forced removal and eviction during World War II, and into the early years of returning to San Mateo and beginning life again after the war. It is not meant to be an all-encompassing history. Rather, it allows the reader to experience a different time and place, and to understand the struggles and triumphs of some of America's pioneers. Through this understanding, we can build on the strengths of our forebears.

Throughout the book, we refer to those of Japanese ethnicity, whether immigrants or their American-born children, as "Japanese." "Japanese Americans" refers strictly to those born in the United States and who thus are American by birth.

The War Relocation Authority (WRA) camps where people of Japanese descent were confined during World War II are not referred to by the government euphemism, "relocation centers," and instead are called "incarceration camps," "imprisonment camps," or "concentration camps" since the Japanese were held against their will behind barbed wire fences with armed guards patrolling them. The people who lived there are referred to as "prisoners" or "inmates."

The term "internment camps" is technically correct only for those imprisoned in the U.S. Department of Justice internment camps such as Crystal City Internment Camp in Texas or Santa Fe Internment Camp in New Mexico.[1]

Many immigrants took on western names, gave their children both a Japanese name and a western one, or called their children by a shortened version of their Japanese names. On first reference, we have identified people by both their Japanese and western names but, on second and subsequent references, we have dropped the formal name and used the more informal name. Married women have their maiden name in parentheses, unless they use it in their married name, so the reader will be able to clarify relationships. An example of that is Yoshiko "Yoshi" (Sato) Mizono. The full formal name is cited in the footnotes, bibliography, and index.

Many people interviewed for this book were not originally from San Mateo County but, because they were incarcerated at the Tanforan Assembly Center, they lived in San Mateo County at the order of the U.S. government and thus became a part of the county's history.

This story has been an intellectual odyssey for us. The History Committee of the San Mateo Chapter of the Japanese American Citizens League commissioned this book to document the history of Japanese Americans through the lives and recollections of San Mateo County residents. Determining how this history should be told and what it means to be a community story were the subjects of many debates as we decided on the approach, what to include, what to omit, and why. We were given the opportunity to see life then through the eyes of the people we interviewed as they shared the stories of their lives with us. Like an artist who creates beautiful artwork by stitching together pieces of old kimono, their individual accounts become a new fabric that, together, is the collective history of our America.

---

[1] Soon after the Japanese attacked Pearl Harbor, leaders of the San Mateo Japanese community, primarily men, were forcibly taken to U.S. Department of Justice camps while their families were forced from their homes into temporary assembly centers and, eventually, into permanent concentration camps for the duration of World War II.

Introduction

The story of Japanese on the San Francisco Peninsula is a story of pride, perseverance, and progress despite prejudice. It is the story of a people who are overcoming discrimination, racism, and fear to claim their share in the American dream. Why these San Mateo pioneers came to America, how they built their lives and homes, and what their hopes and dreams were–all these questions are similar to those of Japanese who immigrated to other parts of the country.

The uniqueness of the San Mateo story lies in its proximity to San Francisco, for these Peninsula immigrants had one of the earliest "suburban" experiences in the United States. The first jobs at which the Japanese worked did not require fluency in English. They worked as domestics for wealthy San Franciscans who had country homes in San Mateo County and, encouraged by the climate, they began farming, both inland and along the

coast. They established their own businesses and found ways to own land despite laws forbidding such ownership. In the process, they laid the economic and cultural foundations for an American life that retained many of the qualities and ways of the homeland they left. With time, as their ideas about settling in America changed, they created a Japanese American community here that, though it had constant reminders of Japan, was undeniably western.

Japan had largely isolated itself from the rest of the world for 200 years. In 1853 Commodore Matthew Perry brought a proposal from U.S. President Millard Fillmore requesting permission for American ships to dock at Japanese ports for supplies. Because he was aware of the strength of America and the West, in 1854 the Tokugawa *shogun*, or "military leader" at the time, signed the agreement. Displeased with the signing of this agreement, the *samurai* class rallied behind the Japanese Emperor Meiji, who previously had been mostly responsible for religious duties. In 1868 the restoration of the Emperor as Japan's ruler, along with a parliamentary government, spelled the end of the *shogun* era.[1]

Emperor Meiji's regime was known as one of "enlightened rule," for he believed modernization and an open-door policy to Western countries would best protect Japan from future attempts at European colonization. This new openness to the West included sending students abroad to learn about western ways and to bring that knowledge back to Japan. So it was in 1860 that the first Japanese embassy in the United States was established and, a decade later, Japan opened a consulate in San Francisco. It is here our story begins.

---

[1]One exception to this isolationism was the annual arrival of a Dutch merchant ship for limited trade.

CHAPTER 1

STARTING OUT:
EARLY HISTORY AND THE PIONEERS

Island soul of me
Cast off to cross the ocean.
Ah, the world is big!

— ISSA[1]

The first known Japanese in San Mateo County were part of a delegation led by Ambassador Tomomi Iwakura in January 1872. The Ambassador had stopped in San Francisco to witness the signing of a contract between Japan and the San Francisco Assaying and Refining Works to refine Japanese gold coins. In his group were forty-eight officials and fifty-nine students. During the trip, the Iwakura delegation was invited to the Belmont home of William C. Ralston, a major owner of the San Francisco Assaying and Refining Works as well as co-founder and director of the Bank of California.[2]

Members of the 1872 Iwakura Delegation were some of the first Japanese to visit the Peninsula. *Courtesy of Manchester Boddy Collection*

[1] Kazuo Ito, *Issei: A History of Japanese Immigrants in North America*, trans. by S. Nakamura and Jean S. Gerard (Seattle: Executive Committee for Publication of Issei, 1973), 51.

[2] The first Japanese diplomatic mission to the United States arrived in San Francisco aboard the *Kanrin Maru* on March 17, 1860. It went on to Washington, D.C., where members of the party met with President James Buchanan. Brian Niiya, ed., *Japanese American History: An A-to-Z Reference from 1868 to the Present* (New York: Facts on File, 1993), 26; Ria Elena Dewing, *Heritage of the Wooded Hills: A Belmont History* (Belmont, Calif.: Wadsworth Publishing Company, 1977), 19-24; and Hal F. Marks, "Ralston and the Imperial Mint," Vol. VIII, no. 2, as cited in San Mateo Chapter, Japanese American Citizens League, *1872-1942: A Community Story* (Palo Alto, Calif., 1981), 5.

The first Japanese women to visit San Mateo County came to the Peninsula as part of the Iwakura delegation in 1872. *Courtesy of Manchester Boddy Collection*[3]

"The Belmont," the country estate of William Ralston south of San Mateo had a bowling alley, gymnasium, Turkish bath, greenhouse, tennis courts, a carriage house, and stables – much more space than Japanese estates offered. The servants' quarters, on the left, were called "Little Belmont."[5]

Among the first Japanese to arrive in the continental United States following the Iwakura delegation to the West Coast were three types of students. The first were elite students, sent abroad by the Meiji government to study. They went mainly to Europe but also to America, especially New England, expecting to return and serve Japan. A second group, financed by private means, also studied primarily on the East Coast. The third category, the *dekasegi-shosei* or "student-laborers" who worked their way through school, were among the first Japanese to settle permanently in the continental United States, including San Mateo County, where they laid the foundation for Japanese immigrant society.[4]

The Belmont School for Boys, which the first Japanese students in San Mateo County attended, was the former servants' quarters of the Ralston estate and was called "Little Belmont" in Ralston's day. *San Mateo County History Museum*

Most of these student-laborers came to America intending to learn English and other useful skills, make their fortunes, and return to Japan.

---

[3] San Mateo Chapter, JACL, *A Community Story*, 7.

[4] Yuji Ichioka, *The Issei: The World of the First Generation Japanese Immigrants, 1885-1924* (New York: Free Press, 1988), 7; Ronald Takaki, *Strangers from a Different Shore: A History of Asian Americans* (Boston: Little, Brown, 1989), 46. Also, Roger Daniels, *Asian America: Chinese and Japanese in the United States since 1850* (Seattle: University of Washington Press, 1988), 104.

[5] Dewing, *Heritage of the Wooded Hills*, 21.

A handful of Japanese students came to San Mateo in the 1880s to attend the Belmont School for Boys, an exclusive semi-military school established adjacent to the Ralston estate in 1885 by William T. Reid, a former president of the University of California.[6]

The common name for these student-laborers was "school-boys," a term credited to Belmont School headmistress Mrs. Reid. During the day, they were free to attend school. Before classes and in the evenings, they provided domestic duties for a family in exchange for lodging, board, and a small monthly wage. Though primarily students, they were the first Japanese to serve as domestics in America.

No official figures exist detailing the number of Japanese students who came to San Mateo in this first wave. Most of the immigrants who came to America and to San Mateo County in the 1880s were from four prefectures in southwestern Japan, all among the poorest: Hiroshima, Yamaguchi, Kumamoto, and Fukuoka. Many were contract laborers who came to California by way of Hawai`i, chosen for their ability and willingness to work under the grueling conditions of the Hawaiian sugar plantations. A disproportionate number continued to come from these prefectures because they were encouraged by friends and family already in America. This established an emigration pattern by the time the contract labor system ended around 1900.[7]

From the 1900s on, the number of Japanese immigrants to the United States grew. Some emigrated because changes in Japan's law requiring military service eliminated many prior exemptions, including heads of households, sole sons, and those who could afford to pay a fee instead of serving. The exemption for students living abroad remained in effect, however, making emigration to study in America even more attractive to those who wanted to avoid the draft legally.

Famine, poverty, large families, and Japan's traditional practice of primogeniture, that is, inheritance by the eldest son, were other reasons for leaving Japan. Younger sons inherited no property and formed separate households upon marriage. A saying among farmers reflected thoughts about their children: "One to sell, one to follow, and one in reserve." The "one to sell" was the daughter, who would marry and leave her

---

[6] Dewing, *Heritage of the Wooded Hills*, 29.

[7] Between 1891 and 1900, Japanese immigrants numbered 20,826. From 1901-1910, 62,432 Japanese immigrated. Yamato Ichihashi, *Japanese Immigration: Its Status in California* (San Francisco: The Japanese Association of America, 1913), 7. More than half of the Japanese population in the United States in the early 1900s lived in six California counties: Los Angeles, Sacramento, Fresno, San Francisco, Alameda, and San Joaquin. San Mateo is not among them, but its Japanese population has been influenced by its proximity to San Francisco, for many Japanese worked for the wealthy San Franciscans who had country homes in San Mateo. Yamato Ichihashi, *Japanese in the United States: A Critical Study of the Problems of the Japanese Immigrants and Their Children* (Stanford, Calif.: Stanford University Press, 1932), 97-100. Also Roger Daniels, *The Politics of Prejudice: The Anti-Japanese Movement in California and the Struggle for Japanese Exclusion* (Berkeley: University of California Press, 1962), 5-6.

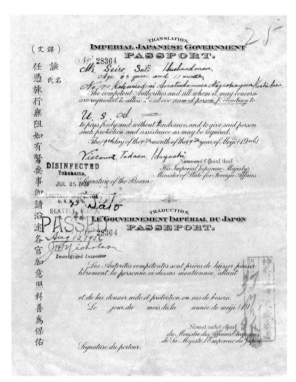

Seiro Sato's passport, dated August 13, 1906. An eldest son, Sato arrived in the United States in 1890 and settled in the Stockton, California area, where he became a successful farmer. He returned to find a wife in his prefecture of Kochi, Japan, where he made a big impression with his relative wealth. He married Masao Hara. She became pregnant, so Sato returned to Stockton alone on August 13, 1906 and she came later. The Sato family moved to San Mateo in 1928, after Mrs. Sato died of cancer.[8]
Passport courtesy of Yoshiko "Yoshi" (Sato) Mizono; photo by gayle k. yamada

family. The "one to follow" was the eldest son, who would inherit the family property and care for his parents. And the "one in reserve" was the younger son who would not inherit anything but who was like insurance for the family: in case the first son died, he would inherit the land and carry on the family name. So while sometimes the eldest son went to the United States to earn money before he had to care for his parents, generally it was the younger sons who left home.[9]

These first immigrants were known as Issei, or first-generation. Most were *dekaseginin*, or "sojourners." After the Chinese Exclusion Act of 1882 banned Chinese workers from the United

---

[8] Yoshiko "Yoshi" (Sato) Mizono and Sue Sato Okamura, interview by Richard Nakanishi and Shizu "Shazie" (Yamaguchi) Tabata, San Mateo, Calif., May 15, 1978; and Yoshiko "Yoshi" (Sato) Mizono, telephone conversation with gayle k. yamada, December 10, 2001.

[9] Takaki, *Strangers from a Different Shore*, 49.

States, the Japanese eagerly filled the demand for cheap labor. They had no intention of staying permanently but wanted to send money home to Japan or return home wealthy. Many sailed the ten-day trip to Hawai`i to work on the sugar plantations; others endured the fifteen- to twenty-eight-day voyage to the mainland. The arduous trip did not dampen their enthusiasm.[10]

County real estate records show that Tomi-suke Ito was one of the early Japanese residents of San Mateo. Although he had attended Kobe Commercial College and had worked for the Mitsui Company, a large and well-known company in Japan, he had to settle for work as a domestic servant when he moved to San Mateo in 1891, after spending three years in San Francisco.[11]

On May 13, 1903, Ito became the first Japanese to purchase land in San Mateo County. He bought three lots between Grant and Fremont Streets, a subdivision that was part of the estate of Agnes Bowie, wife of Henry Bowie at the time of her death in 1893. On one of the Fremont Street lots, Ito and his friends built a four-unit apartment building that he rented to other Japanese immigrants. A crude, one-story building made of plank redwood lumber, fronted by four garages, with no

Ito's property. The far left building was for storage, next to it was the *nagaya*, and straight ahead was the social gathering place. The Itos' home was on the right. The two children are Hiroshi and his older sister Tomiko, children of Tomisuke Ito, *circa* 1918. *Courtesy of Yasuko "Ann" (Ishida) Ito*

heating or insulation, it was nicknamed the *nagaya*, or "longhouse."[12]

For many years, the *nagaya* at 112 North Fremont Street was a way station for many Japanese families who stayed until they found other housing. In the early days, the *nagaya* became the unofficial community gathering place for the Japanese immigrants. Meetings, parties, and celebrations took place there, and the property

---

[10] In the word, "Issei," "*i*" means "first" and "*sei*" means "generation" in Japanese. The literal translation of *dekaseginin* is "go-out-to-earn people." Also Dorothy and Thomas Hoobler, *The Japanese American Family Album* (New York: Oxford University Press, 1996), 23.

[11] Hiroshi and Yasuko "Ann" (Ishida) Ito, interview by Richard Nakanishi, San Mateo, Calif., March 17, 1978.

[12] Tomisuke Ito's land purchase is on file at the Office of the Assessor-County Clerk-Recorder, San Mateo County; Henry Bowie helped found the Japan Society in 1905 in the San Francisco Bay Area and spent much time in Japan. Unbeknownst to his San Mateo friends, Bowie had a Japanese wife there whom he married in 1898 and with whom he had two sons. Michael Svanevik and Shirley Burgett, "Henry P. Bowie: The Man Who Loved Japan," *The* (San Mateo, Calif.) *Times*, July 23, 1993; and Katsuko "Susie" (Endo) Oshima, conversation with Yasuko "Ann" (Ishida) Ito, San Mateo, Calif., October, 2001.

It looked just like a long barn. There was totally no insulation, so if you lived in that long barn, it was like living in a basket. It was really like a shack; and in the wintertime you froze, in the summertime you roasted. No air conditioning, no insulation, no nothing. Just a cheap, single shingle roof…The place was all cut up into small portions of rooms where one family would [live], and we had a common lavatory for the whole nagaya. And, of course, the Japanese were very meticulous about cleanliness—boy, I tell you, they really kept the place clean! There was a great deal of pride in that because they knew which family was to take care of the lavatory in turn. They didn't want to be outdone by anybody else! They really kept it clean!

— WILLIAM NOSAKA

who lived in the San Mateo nagaya as a teenager [13]

eventually included a teahouse and bathhouse. Washing and dressing facilities were available for residents and other immigrants who wanted to enjoy the traditional Japanese *ofuro*, or "bath."

The *nagaya* in San Mateo, *circa* 1920. *Courtesy of H. Ito Collection*

The *nagaya* was a community social gathering place where friends and family members could relax after a hard week of work. *Courtesy of H. Ito Collection*

---

[13] William Nosaka, interviews by Dianne Fukami, July 19, 1994 and gayle k. yamada, November 12, 1998, both in San Mateo, Calif.

Saturday was community *ofuro* night–a night for bathing and socializing.

Another early property owner was Tomezo Yoshida, who arrived in 1895 and also did domestic work. After he married in 1916, he began looking for property to buy in San Mateo. Daughter Haruko (Yoshida) Sugishita recalled that her father was employed by several wealthy Hillsborough families and received twenty-five dollar tips in gold coins. With the help of San Mateo attorney J.E. McCurdy, on August 23, 1917, Yoshida paid three hundred dollars in gold coins to purchase the property next to Tomisuke Ito's on the old Bowie estate.[14]

Yoshida needed McCurdy's services because the Alien Land Law, passed in California in 1913, prohibited those ineligible for citizenship from owning land and permitted only limited leases of three years of agricultural land to aliens. U.S. naturalization laws did not allow Asians to become citizens, and thus the Japanese could not own property, at least in their own names. To circumvent this, they registered property titles under the names of their American-born children who were citizens by birth, or they turned to trusted Caucasian friends such as McCurdy, who registered Yoshida's land in his name until he could legally

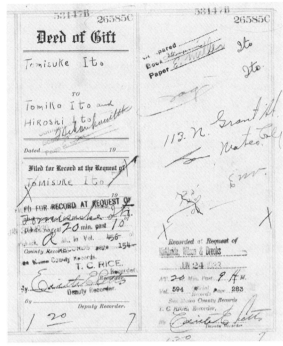

One of the first Japanese to buy land in San Mateo, Tomisuke Ito instructed Dr. Benner to transfer property to his American-born children, Tomiko and Hiroshi, in 1929, when they were eighteen and thirteen years old respectively, to be held in trust by Dr. Benner until the younger Itos were age twenty-one. *Courtesy of Yasuko "Ann" (Ishida) Ito*

sign it over to the Yoshida family. Even Tomisuke Ito, who bought his property prior to the passage of the Alien Land Law, placed ownership of the *nagaya* in trust with Dr. Alan Benner after the law was passed.[15]

---

[14] Haruko (Yoshida) Sugishita, interview by Richard Nakanishi and Shizu "Shazie" (Yamaguchi) Tabata, San Francisco, Calif., January 31, 1976, as cited in San Mateo Chapter, JACL, *A Community Story*, 14.

[15] California was the first state to enact an Alien Land Law. Also Mortgage Documents, no. 52154, Tomezo Yoshida to M.E. [*sic*] McCurdy, August 23, 1917, California Pacific Title Company, 117, San Mateo County Records (now Office of the Assesor-County Clerk-Recorder, San Mateo County), Redwood City, Calif., as cited in San Mateo Chapter, JACL, *A Community Story*, 14. Texas and Washington both enacted similar Alien Land Laws. Texas Legislature. *General Laws, 1921 Regular Session, on Aliens–Amending Act Relating to the Rights, Powers and Disabilities of* (Austin, 1921), 261-263; and Washington Legislature, *Session Laws, 1920 Extraordinary Session, on Aliens* (Olympia, 1921), 156-160.

The Japanese also faced other forms of discrimination. In San Mateo, as early as 1869, there was an American Protection Association, an anti-immigrant, anti-Catholic organization. Its activities on the Peninsula, however, apparently were not "vigorous." The first large anti-Asian mass meeting in the nation took place in July 1870 in San Francisco and featured anti-Chinese speeches. This sentiment continued through the 1870s, perpetrated largely by labor organizations that felt threatened by Asian immigrants who were willing to work for lower wages. A response to this was the passage of the Chinese Exclusion Act of 1882, which prohibited Chinese immigration to the United States.[16]

As the number of Japanese immigrants increased, so did the perceived threat. Caucasian laborers in 1900 urged Congress to extend the Exclusion Act beyond the 1902 expiration date and to include the Japanese. There was not enough popular support to expand the law to ban Japanese immigration.[17]

Then, in early 1905, a series of anti-Japanese articles came out in the *San Francisco Chronicle*, calling Japanese immigration the "problem of the day." Press headlines included, "Japanese a Menace to American Women," "The Yellow Peril–How the Japanese Crowd Out the White Race," and "Brown Artisans Steal the Brains of Whites." The first anti-Japanese pressure group, the Asiatic Exclusion League, largely an organization of members of labor groups and unions, formed in May of that same year. Under pressure from the league, the San Francisco Board of Education in 1906 ordered Japanese schoolchildren–ninety-three of them–to attend a segregated school to which Chinese students had already been sent. This decision caused an international incident that changed the course of Japanese immigration to the United States.[18]

Although the San Francisco press did not report on the board's action, Tokyo newspapers did, and the news eventually made its way back to the United States. After protests by the Japanese government, President Theodore Roosevelt stepped in to defuse the situation diplomatically. Earlier, in his annual message in December 1905, he stated his views: "[I]t is unwise to depart from the old American tradition and to discriminate for or against any man who desired to come here as a citizen…We cannot afford to consider whether he is a Catholic or a Protestant, Jew or Gentile; whether he is Englishman or Irishman, Frenchman or German, Japanese, Italian, Scandinavian, Slav, or Magyar." He seemed to say that Japanese immigration would not be

---

[16] Mitchell Postel, *San Mateo: A Centennial History* (San Francisco: Scottwall Associates, 1994), 76.

[17] According to the 1870 U.S. Census, fifty-five Japanese lived in the entire country. By 1890, that number had increased to 2,039 and, ten years later, to 24,326. Ichihashi, *Japanese Immigration*, 7.

[18] Niiya, *An A-to-Z Reference*, 103-104; *San Francisco Chronicle*, February 13-March 13, 1905, as quoted in Daniels, *Asian America*, 116.

viewed in the same negative light as Chinese immigration.[19]

So President Roosevelt in 1907 signed an executive agreement with Japan. Under the terms of this "Gentlemen's Agreement," which took effect in the summer of 1908, the Japanese government agreed to stop issuing passports to Japanese laborers en route to America. This slowed Japanese male immigration which, in turn, temporarily lessened anti-Japanese activity. The agreement did not, however, pertain to merchants and students, who had made up only a small percentage of the immigrant population until then, or to wives, children, and parents of Japanese men already living in the United States. The U.S. agreed to treat fairly those Japanese immigrants already in America.

Because the agreement also did not preclude wives from immigrating, an unanticipated outcome was the arrival of Japanese picture brides, or *shashin kekkon*, literally, "photograph marriage." Though some women who arrived had married conventionally before their husbands left Japan or while their husbands were on trips home, many married by proxy. A go-between facilitated negotiations between families of the prospective bride and groom in Japan. After an arrangement was concluded and the bride's name entered into the husband's family's registry, the couple was officially married, at least in Japan. Because the United States did not recognize the legality of such marriages prior to 1917, mass wedding ceremonies were held when the brides' ships docked in America and the couples met–usually for the first time.[20]

In addition to immigration laws, an 1880 California statute prohibiting the "marriage of white persons with Mongolians" had also limited the number of families in the Japanese community. Picture brides meant the beginning of families with children who were American by birth. They represented stability and permanence in the United States.

The Gentlemen's Agreement changed immigration patterns and the Japanese population dramatically. In 1900, there were 958 Japanese women, or four percent of the Japanese population in the United States, compared to 27,082 men. After the Gentlemen's Agreement went into effect, women accounted for more than fifty-five percent of all Japanese immigrants. By that same year, the number of immigrants dropped immediately, too, from 9,544 in 1908 to 3,111.[21]

Ishiye (Baba) Takahashi's feelings about coming to San Mateo in 1906 reflected those of many other picture brides:

---

[19] Though he did not state it, Roosevelt was also conscious of Japan's military strength at the time; Japan had just soundly defeated Russia. In the same address, Roosevelt also publicly proposed that Japanese be allowed to become naturalized citizens, as cited in Daniels, *The Politics of Prejudice*, 35-39.

[20] Until 1915, the Japanese Consulate required laborers to show solvency by proving they had at least $800 in the bank before they could send for their wives.

[21] Niiya, *An A-to-Z Reference*, 282; and Ichihashi, *Japanese in the United States*, 64-72; and Ichihashi, *Japanese Immigration*, 4, 10.

My father brought me to Kobe from our hometown in Wakayama. After a physical examination, the health inspector found that I had a contagious eye infection. Therefore, I would not be permitted to sail to San Francisco because of the hazardous conditions caused by the devastating earthquake.

I knew that if I returned home to Wakayama, I would never leave Japan. An alternate city for my entry to the United States was Seattle, so a cable was sent to my prospective husband.

I sailed on the vessel *Shunyo Maru* to Seattle, Washington. The passage took two weeks. I was seasick during the entire voyage. Upon my arrival in Seattle, I stayed at the Fujii Hotel to await the arrival of Mr. Tokutaro Takahashi to take me to San Mateo. While waiting for him, the owner of the Fujii Hotel took me shopping for western dresses because I had brought only Japanese clothing with me.[22]

Picture brides arriving at Angel Island immigration center in San Francisco Bay, *circa* 1915. *National Archives*

William Nosaka's parents, Koyo Katamoto and Kiyoto "George" Nosaka, were married in 1912, in San Francisco. Katamoto arrived in the United States in 1911 but, unlike the typical bride of the time, she knew her husband from Japan. Her shipmates were picture brides meeting their intended spouses for the first time.

Some were disappointed with their new partners. Many brides found their grooms were not as wealthy, good-looking, or young as their photographs and letters had indicated, while many men found their brides not hardy enough for the difficult lives they would lead. The women were often more educated than their husbands and not prepared for the rough life they faced in America.

Despite the economic and social forces working against them, most couples stayed together. Their marriages, following traditional Japanese values, were based not on love and affection but on *giri* – "duty and responsibility." The desire to honor the obligation and to establish families in America convinced most to live by the

---

[22] Ishiye (Baba) Takahashi, interview by Richard Nakanishi and Shizu "Shazie" (Yamaguchi) Tabata, San Mateo, Calif., November 16, 1977.

Kiyoto "George" Nosaka and his bride Koyo (Katamoto) Nosaka, in a wedding photograph, 1911. "It took three months [in 1911] to come by boat. My mother was seasick practically the whole way. She was very seasick because, you know, being a country girl, she had never been on a boat like that," said William Nosaka.[23] *Courtesy of William Nosaka*

Tomo Kamiya Kawakita, *circa* 1914. *Courtesy of Yoneo "Yon" Kawakita*

My mother [Tomo Kamiya Kawakita] was a picture bride and married my father in 1915. I remember my mother telling me that when she received my father's picture in Japan, she thought, "My, what a handsome man!" When she saw my father for the first time in person, she was quite disappointed. My mother was about five feet three inches tall and my father was only four feet nine inches.

— YONEO "YON" KAWAKITA[24]

philosophy of *gaman* – "*perseverance*" – and to overlook the imperfections. They would make sacrifices "*kodomo no tame ni,*" that is, "for the sake of the children."

---

[23] W. Nosaka, interview by yamada.
[24] Yoneo "Yon" Kawakita, "The Incarceration of Yoneo 'Yon' Kawakita" (unpublished memoir, San Mateo, Calif., 1997).

The era of the picture bride ended on February 25, 1920. With rising cries against Japanese immigration in the United States, the Japanese government stopped issuing passports to picture brides. By that time, however, thousands of Japanese women had already settled in the United States, bringing with them a significant change in the hopes and dreams of the Japanese living in San Mateo and across the United States.

The Kawakita family, *circa* 1930, at Coyote Point in San Mateo County, known in the 1930s as Pacific City. *Left to right:* Sister Miyo, Yon, father Sahioye, sister Satoye, and mother Tomo. *Courtesy of Yoneo "Yon" Kawakita*

CHAPTER 2

BUILDING AN
ECONOMIC FOUNDATION

Illusion and I
Travelled over the ocean
Hunting money-trees.

– KIJO[1]

For the Japanese, San Mateo was an area ripe with opportunity. The way they conducted business reflected the values by which they lived: *gaman*, or "perseverance;" *giri*, or "responsibility;" *enryo*, or "reserve;" *on*, or "obligation;" and *kodomo no tame ni*, or "for the sake of the children." While becoming westernized, they retained many Japanese practices that helped them start their businesses and preserve their strong social connections. It was a balancing act between the two cultures, and the Japanese who settled in San Mateo exemplified this.

The first Japanese who came to America had intended to earn money to pay off family debts back home or to make their fortunes and return to Japan. But after the Gentlemen's Agreement of 1907-1908, many began to quit thinking of themselves as *dekaseginin*, or "sojourners," and to adopt the attitude of settlers instead.[2]

The town of San Mateo was becoming increasingly popular with Caucasian families, as evidenced by the growing census numbers. Warm weather, sprawling lands, and railroad service between what is now Palo Alto and San Francisco combined to lure the wealthy, who built estates for summer and weekend recreation. Their names are memorialized on streets, buildings, and public places in modern day San Mateo, among them, John Parrott, who gained success in commerce and banking; Charles Polhemus, who made his

---

[1] Kazuo Ito, *Issei*, 51.

[2] Frank S. Miyamoto, "Views from Within" (paper presented at symposium on the Japanese American Internment Experience," University of California, Berkeley, Berkeley, Calif., September 20, 1987); Ito, *Issei*, 34; William C. Smith, *Americans in Process: A Study of Citizens of Oriental Ancestry* (Ann Arbor: Edwards Brothers, Inc., 1937), 163. In his survey of Issei men, "Tradition and Opportunity: The Japanese Immigrant in America," 163-168, John Modell found that only fifteen percent of those who entered before 1907 intended upon arrival to stay in the United States permanently, and that thirty-six percent of those who arrived after 1909 came with intentions of settlement, as cited in Takaki, *Strangers from a Different Shore*, 52-53.

money in real estate; William H. Kohl, who made a fortune in the Alaska fur seal trade; and horse breeder Stephen B. Whipple.

The proliferation of estates and wealth created its own industry in San Mateo–merchants, tradesmen, skilled craftsmen, domestic laborers, gardeners, and landscapers. Most Japanese immigrants found work as domestics, gardeners, and landscapers. Despite any education they may have had in Japan, their inability to speak English often precluded them from jobs requiring more skill. Daily life was tough, and the Japanese were viewed by many as second class. They faced racial discrimination as well; even those who could speak English often were not hired for skilled work. As long as Japanese were content to be hired hands for agricultural work, they were welcomed by growers. But as they began to lease and even own land, they became increasingly unpopular. In the coming years, their success in farming was a growing cause of friction with some competitive Caucasian growers in parts of California.[3]

The most common occupation for the first Japanese students who arrived in San Mateo was as "school-boys." One who worked for Judge David Bixler in San Francisco, Yuya Fujita, recalled, "My duties as a 'school-boy' were to wait on the table at breakfast and dinner and to clean up. For the dinner service, I wore a white coat and apron that was given to me. I attended a Christian church school and studied conversational English during the daytime." He later became the owner of Yokohama Laundry in San Mateo.[4]

Other immigrants were domestic workers. Married couples, such as Kenzo Higashi and his wife Etsuko, often lived and worked together in an employer's household in San Mateo, Burlingame, or Hillsborough, with the wife assigned housekeeping or other domestic chores while the husband served as butler, chauffeur, or gardener. This live-in arrangement often resulted in close relationships between the immigrants and their employers that developed into lifetime employment and friendship.[5]

Another kind of domestic service was "day work" which did not involve living in. Instead, workers were paid on an hourly or daily basis to perform domestic duties in private homes. Chores included general housecleaning, gardening, laundering, cooking, and serving food.

Around 1908 domestic workers and gardeners in San Mateo County formed the *Rodo Kumiai*, literally the Labor Association. It served as a job referral agency, wage mediator, and problem-solving center for its many members.

The Association purchased supplies in bulk as needed for jobs through the *Rodo Kumiai* and made them available to its members on a cooperative basis. In 1952, the group evolved into the San Mateo Gardeners' Association.[6]

---

[3] Ivan H. Light, *Ethnic Enterprise in America* (Berkeley: University of California Press, 1972), 9, 72-73.
[4] Yuya Fujita, interview by Shizu "Shazie" (Yamaguchi) Tabata, San Mateo, Calif., November 18, 1977.
[5] Kenzo Higashi, interview by Yasuko "Ann" (Ishida) Ito, San Mateo, Calif., November 9, 1994.
[6] "History of the San Mateo Labor Association" (San Mateo, Calif., 1998), 1.

By 1910, some Japanese gardeners were already working at the Bessie Boston Dahlia Farm in San Mateo. Japanese gardeners soon gained quite a reputation in the county for developing and maintaining the beautiful gardens on the estates in San Mateo, Burlingame, and Hillsborough.[7]

Sankichi Ono was the first Issei to be employed by San Mateo County and became the foreman for the county's mosquito abatement program in the early 1900s. Ono bred fish and placed them in stagnant waters throughout San Mateo where they would eat the mosquito larvae.[8]

A group of Japanese worked at the Casey Rock Quarry and lived at a nearby camp on Half Moon Bay Road, southwest of San Mateo. Jubei Miyachi, who arrived in San Mateo in 1906, remembered seven other Japanese men working at the quarry. Miyachi himself worked there for three years, crushing, sorting, and loading rocks onto horse-drawn wagons. He earned $1.50 per day for nine hours of work.[9]

The salt industry in San Mateo County also employed Japanese immigrants. The county's

THE LIST OF NAMES AND THE MAIN BUSINESS OF THE MEMBERS OF LABOR ASSOCIATION OF SAN MATEO, CAL.

Marks beside the names show their main work, and the new rates of wages, namely:

(X)   Gardener—$5.00 up per day; $3.00 up half day.
(O)   House and Laundry Work $5 up per day; $2.50 up half day.
(A)   Cook and Waiter, $1.00 up per hour.
(-·-) Dish Washing, 75c up per hour.

BUSINESS	NAME	PHONE	RESIDENCE
	Harry Aoyagi	S. M. 1320-R	110 North F
	Charley Adachi	S. M. 1112-J	141 North G
	Frank Bando	S. M. 1282	St. John's Lane
	Faji Fujihara	S. M. 1457-J	113 North E
	Harry Hosokawa	S. M. 822	112 North F
	George Hama	S. M. 651	106 C
	George Higashi	Burl. 695	140 Clarendon Road
	Tokyo Hosoume	S. M. 1316	142 North Railroad
	Harry Hirata	S. M. 256	517 Second
	Ishi Ishihashi	S. M. 857	37 Grand Blvd.
	Sada Ishihashi	S. M. 273-W	234 North D
	Frank Ito	S. M. 822	112 North F
	Ino Inouye	Burl. 695-B	140 Clarendon Road
	Yewi Kariya	S. M. 636-M	206 South D
	Komaru	S. M. 645-J	616 Fourth
	Frank Kato	S. M. 1365-R	240 South H
	James Kato	S. M. 1003-J	512 Second
	Kageshima	S. M. 397-J	100 St. Matthews
	Kura	S. M. 822	112 North F
	Kono	S. M. 512	16 North C
	Mori	S. M. 1033-R	250 North D
	Matsu Matsushita	S. M. 651	106 C Street
	George Monji	S. M. 512	16 North C
	Henry Nomura	S. M. 857	37 Grand Blvd.
	Frank Nakamura	S. M. 1241	Homestead
	George Nosaka	S. M. 798-R	112 North F
	Onishi	S. M. 1334	339 North D
	Ota	S. M. 512	16 North C
	George Saiki	S. M. 1274	113 North D
	Saki Sakuma	S. M. 919-J	30 Ellsworth
	Saki	453-J	328 Grand Blvd.
	Frank Shimizu		
	Shoji	S. M. 512	16 North C
	Ben Suiki	S. M. 1292	141 North F
	Arthur Tomita	S. M. 1457-W	112 North F
	Kay Tsubokura	S. M. 1319-J	310 Indian
	Take Taketomo	S. M. 512	16 North C
	Frank Takeda	S. M. 1190	714 Tilton
	Frank Takahashi	S. M. 314-M	254 North D
	Tani	S. M. 651	108 South C
	Takara	S. M. 767-J	500 Second
	George Takahama	S. M. 822	112 North F
	Frank Yoshida	S. M. 1353	112 North F
	Aida	S. M. 978	
	Harry Nakashima		

An early – probably pre-1924 – list of the *Rodo Kumiai* shows members were gardeners, house and laundry workers, cooks, waiters, and dishwashers. *Courtesy of Yasuko "Ann" (Ishida) Ito*

---

[7] The Bessie Boston Dahlia Farm was located at El Camino between Tilton and Mt. Diablo Avenues. Masae Sakuma, letter, March 22, 1978; and George Tsukushi, interview by Richard Nakanishi, Redwood City, Calif., March 29, 1978.

[8] Hamae Miyachi and Masao Segi, interview by Richard Nakanishi and Shizu "Shazie" (Yamaguchi) Tabata, San Mateo, Calif., November 11, 1977.

[9] Jubei Miyachi, interview by Richard Nakanishi and Shizu "Shazie" (Yamaguchi) Tabata, San Mateo, Calif., November 11, 1977.

The Redwood City Salt Company has commenced operations on their works. A force of 35 Japanese are [sic] building their embankments and the company is advertising for 25 white men to work.

— *PENINSULA PENNANT*
April 27, 1901 [10]

Work at the West Shore Salt Works has begun this week. 40 men including a number of Japs [sic] are employed reconstructing levees and erecting buildings. Work will be rushed so as to be ready to take off a crop of salt this summer.

— *REDWOOD CITY DEMOCRAT*
March 6, 1902 [11]

location on San Francisco Bay made it ideal for harvesting salt by solar evaporation. In 1901, the Redwood City Salt Works began hiring Issei in large numbers.

A year later, A.L. Whitney's father, C.E. Whitney, who started the Leslie Salt Refining Company, bought two hundred acres east of the Southern Pacific Railroad tracks to begin work. Most of his laborers were Japanese. The Whitney family also hired Issei as cooks, gardeners, and domestic workers at their estate, the "Homestead." San Mateo native Yon Kawakita grew up on the edge of the salt ponds. He recalled, "As I was growing up, I had the whole salt works as my backyard, including the salt ponds." [12]

Most of the men who worked at the Leslie Salt refinery were single and worked six days a week, twelve hours a day. At first, they were paid ninety cents a day; later the wage rose to thirty-five cents an hour. Yon Kawakita's father Sahioye began work at Leslie Salt in 1910, tending the boiler. Through the next twenty years of his employment, he witnessed hazardous working conditions that caused electrocutions and other on-the-job injuries. [13]

Like the quarry workers, the men who worked for the salt companies lived in crude,

---

[10] Richard N. Schellens Collection, Section 1, Vol. 8, Pt. 1 (personal clipping file, Redwood City Library, Redwood City, Calif.).

[11] Schellens Collection.

[12] Merrill P. Whitney (C.E. Whitney's nephew), letter. According to Yoneo "Yon" Kawakita, "The Leslie Salt Company property was located from 16th Avenue south to Freeway 92 and from the railroad tracks east to Seal Slough. Part of the salt works' evaporation ponds were located in the same area where the current post office, Shell station, bowling alley, and the 19th Avenue Eichler housing tract are located. The rest of the salt ponds were located east of all these current businesses to Seal Slough." Y. Kawakita, "Incarceration."

[13] Sahioye Kawakita, interview by Richard Nakanishi and Shizu "Shazie" (Yamaguchi) Tabata, San Mateo, Calif., December 8, 1977.

Left to right: Sister Satoye "Sally," sister Miyo, and Yon Kawakita at the family home, *circa* 1930. *Courtesy of Yoneo "Yon" Kawakita*

makeshift labor camps that were sometimes breeding grounds for tuberculosis. The workers put in long hours and, during their time off, many socialized together, drinking, and visiting the Chinese bordellos and gambling houses in town. But Sahioye Kawakita recalled, "I don't remember anyone ever coming back to the salt works with winnings." Still, some managed to save enough to purchase property or to invest in private business.[14]

As with Japanese immigrants elsewhere, the San Mateo Issei began opening businesses catering to members of their own community to provide Japanese food, living accommodations, and services. The experiences many Issei had had running

An early newspaper account shows that, though few in number, the Japanese in San Mateo made their presence known:

"A.L. Whitney, the millionaire salt manufacturer, whose country home is at Homestead, a mile out of San Mateo, chased a burglar through the grounds about his residence Tuesday evening, and after a struggle with his powerful thief in the dark, succeeded in overpowering and making him a prisoner…There were really two battles with the burglar, as he was first discovered concealed in a room by A. Mikami, a Japanese servant. The Japanese attacked the intruder and a lively fight went on in the room. Mikami, being trained in jiu jitsu [sic], used the Japanese methods of attack and despite the fact that he is about half the size of [Tossie] Undrie [the suspect], he hurled his powerful [six-foot tall, two hundred pound] antagonist through the window. Undrie fell twenty feet and was partially stunned by the fall."

— SAN FRANCISCO EXAMINER
Thursday, May 20, 1909[15]

---

[14] Vera Graham, "He Follows a Recipe for Longevity," *The* (San Mateo, Calif.) *Times*, November 19, 1982, interview with Sayohei [sic] Kawakita on his 100th birthday as cited in Postel, *Centennial History*, 140.

[15] *San Francisco Examiner*, May 20, 1909, Schellens Collection.

After fire destroyed our original house, we moved across the road to a small four-room house provided by the salt company. It was our home until internment. Our address was Route 1, Box 124, which was located in the vicinity of where K-Mart Department Store is today on South Delaware Street and Highway 92. The house had running water, but in the beginning we had an outhouse for a toilet in the back yard and took baths in a washtub in the kitchen. Eventually, they built a toilet attached to the back porch, but we still had to take baths in a washtub.

— YONEO "YON" KAWAKITA[16]

their own businesses in Japan contributed to this move to become independent. Discrimination against the Japanese and difficulty in communicating in English also fueled the shift to operate their own businesses. Yon Kawakita recalled an incident when a publicity photo was taken at the Leslie Salt refinery. "This was in an assembly area where they assemble the salt, put labels or whatever on the containers. And according to what [my father, Sahioye] was told, they didn't want him in the picture because he was an Oriental. They wanted all whites."[17]

The clientele of the small businesses later expanded to include Caucasian customers as well. Groceries, merchandise stores, laundries, and other service industries proliferated. San Mateo also had a floral industry unique to its location and attributable to the talent the Japanese showed for gardening. The industry flourished along the coast, and eventually made San Mateo County the "flower basket" of the nation—so much so that, in a 1908 pamphlet, San Mateo was declared "The Floral City—San Francisco's Nearest and Most Beautiful Suburban City."[18]

In order to finance the start-up of these businesses, the Japanese, in San Mateo as in other places, sometimes relied on a system they brought from Japan, *tanomoshi*, an informal rotating credit association through which borrowers received low-cost loans from other members of the community.

[16] Y. Kawakita, "Incarceration;" also Yoneo "Yon" Kawakita, electronic correspondence to gayle k. yamada, December 4, 1999.
[17] Ichihashi, *Japanese in the United States*, 117-118; and Yoneo "Yon" Kawakita, interview by gayle k. yamada, San Mateo, Calif., March 2, 1998.
[18] Schellens Collection, Section 7, Vol. 1, Pt. 1, 196.

The Imperial Laundry was located at 214 First Avenue, next to the Yamanouchi home, and just down the street from the elementary school. "I was helping my mother until the school bell rang in the morning," said Watanuki. "I had to work until 9 o'clock–the bell rings, and then you take your books and go to class!"[19] *Courtesy of Hasuko (Yamanouchi) Watanuki*

Tanomoshi was important because it allowed Japanese to capitalize businesses on their own without having to obtain credit or put up security. Though borrowers made interest payments, as time wore on, these payments were seen more as gifts rather than payment for use of the money. The *tanomoshi* was a friendly financial arrangement based on prefectural ties and social relationships among family and friends.[20]

The first known Japanese-owned business in San Mateo was the Yokohama Laundry, opened in 1900 by Mr. S. Sato and Mr. K. Katoaka [*sic*] at Tilton Avenue and North El Dorado Street in what is now on the outskirts of downtown San Mateo. In 1908, Tetsuo Yamanouchi opened the second Japanese laundry, the Imperial Laundry, renting space from the Wisnoms, a pioneer San Mateo family.[21]

The Imperial Laundry in 1909. *Courtesy of H. Watanuki Collection*

In addition to the family of five children, the laundry also employed as many as seven other people. When Tetsuo Yamanouchi died in 1936, his wife Yoshiko took over the business and successfully operated it until 1963. It was unusual in those times for the wife to take over a business

---

[19] Hasuko (Yamanouchi) Watanuki, interview by gayle k. yamada, San Mateo, Calif., November 19, 1998.

[20] For a more complete discussion of *tanomoshi*, *see* Light, *Ethnic Enterprise*, 27-30.

[21] Kiyoshi Asai, "San Mateo Japanese History" (San Mateo, Calif., 1940), San Mateo County History Museum, Museum Archives. "Katoaka," found in Asai's paper, is not a conventional spelling of the name. The authors believe the spelling could be the more common "Kataoka."

Hasuko (Yamanouchi) Watanuki, Tetsuo Yamanouchi's then fourteen-year old daughter, recalled that in those days, no one slept in a bed sheet that was not ironed. "[W]e didn't have what you call an ironer at our place of business because they're very costly. So we would count the customers' sheets, and maybe there would be 115 for several days. We'd tie them up and put them in the truck, and I'd have to drive the laundry to San Francisco and have it washed at the Pine Street Laundry... Because I was a girl, they were so helpful," she said. "...I'd go to Pine Street, and the fellow would put them on the truck...and then I'd bring it back. And we'd have to take each one of those sheets, and they'd all have a number on them, and we'd have to go and put down where every one should be...It was a very tedious business. But everything gets to be a ritual. It got so I enjoyed my driving!" [22]

Yoshiko Yamanouchi, seen here with her books, kept her desk by the entrance.[23] *Courtesy of Hasuko (Yamanouchi) Watanuki*

when the husband died, but Mrs. Yamanouchi was determined that the laundry would go on. "It was very challenging for her," said her daughter. "And she knew within her heart that she was willing to do it, and she was going to make it."[24]

Konosuke Ito opened the Depot Hand Laundry at 247 Railroad Avenue in 1912. The location was convenient for his customers who commuted daily from the Peninsula to San Francisco. Six years later, Kyusuke Yamaguchi opened the Sunrise Cleaners at 151 B Street in downtown San Mateo. In the meantime, the Yokohama Laundry had changed ownership several times until Yuya Fujita bought it in 1932. Fujita came to San

---

[22] H. Watanuki, interview by yamada.

[23] H. Watanuki, interview by yamada.

[24] H. Watanuki, interview by yamada. The Imperial Laundry was renamed the Blu-White Laundry and Cleaners in 1946, after World War II because the connotation of the word "imperial" brought to mind images of imperial Japan which may have been perceived as negative. It was located at 80 North B Street in San Mateo.

The photograph above is unusual in that it shows the Yokohama Laundry's second operators, Katsuji Endo and Mr. Aoyagi, and their wives in western dress. Yuya Fujita bought the business in 1932. *Courtesy of T. Endo Collection*

Francisco in 1906, two months after the devastating San Francisco earthquake. After first working as a school-boy, he operated the laundry until World War II. At one point he had sixteen employees and a fleet of trucks.[25]

As early as the early 1900s, the laundry and cleaning businesses run by the Chinese and Japanese became targets of discrimination. The Anti-Japanese Laundry League held a convention in San Francisco on December 8, 1908. A member from San Mateo gave a report on the attempts being made to dissuade customers from patronizing

The Yokohama Laundry at Fifth and Railroad Avenues was the first Japanese-owned business in San Mateo. In the San Mateo business directory of 1922-1923, an advertisement for the laundry read, "Yokohama Laundry. First class work – cheapest in the city. Phone San Mateo 270. Special attention to ladies' and gentlemen's goods washed by hand. Orders promptly attended to."[26]

---

[25] Aiko (Inouye) Yamaguchi, interview by Richard Nakanishi and Shizu "Shazie" (Yamaguchi) Tabata, San Mateo, Calif., January 26, 1978; and Y. Fujita, interview by Tabata. After the original owners, S.Sato and K. Katoaka [*sic*], the Yokohama Laundry went to Katsuji Endo and a Mr. Aoyagi. The business changed hands again and was owned by Yashiyoshi Kobori, who died in 1919 when the boiler at the laundry exploded. A fourth operator of the laundry, a Mr. Miyaoi, moved the business to a building on the corner of Fifth and Railroad Avenues. Toshio Endo, interview by Richard Nakanishi and Shizu "Shazie" (Yamaguchi) Tabata, San Mateo, Calif., June 1, 1978; *San Mateo* (Calif.) *News-Leader*, March 22, 1919 and April 9, 1919, Schellens Collection.

[26] Schellens Collection, Sec. 7, Vol. 1, Pt. 1, 55

Kyusuke Yamaguchi of Sunrise Cleaners in 1918. *Courtesy of Kunio Yamaguchi Collection*

Shiro Kashiwagi (right) and two other associates worked at the Hata Merchant Tailor Shop during the early 1900s. *Courtesy of S. Sakuma Collection*

Japanese-owned laundries. The following report of the league's activities was given:

1) People called "trailers" were hired to follow Japanese owners in order to learn the names and addresses of their customers;

2) Letters were sent to the customers, stating reasons for not patronizing Japanese businesses and, at the same time, encouraging them to patronize French and American laundries instead;

3) Attempts were made to get support from local newspapers to maintain the "Yellow Peril" hysteria against the Japanese.[27]

These discriminatory efforts were unsuccessful in shutting down the laundries. For the most part, the businesses thrived even during the Depression and throughout the 1930s. Kyusuke

Yamaguchi of the Sunrise Cleaners purchased land at 233 Baldwin Avenue for a new dry cleaning plant in 1928. Because of the Alien Land Law, he had to put the title of his property in trust with Drs. Norman Morrison and Ernest Sisson. Yamaguchi later opened two more branches of his dry cleaning business, one in Burlingame and the other in San Francisco. Prior to World War II, there were nine known Japanese-operated cleaning or laundry businesses in San Mateo, not including the services that were operated out of homes.[28]

Some Japanese opened tailoring businesses. The Hata Merchant Tailor Shop was originally located at 122 B Street in downtown San Mateo. Tokumatsu Hata opened it in 1901, five years after setting foot in the United States. He returned briefly to Japan to marry Toku Hamada and came

---

[27] "Pacific Coast Convention of the Anti-Jap Laundry League Proceedings," Bancroft Library, University of California, Berkeley, Berkeley, Calif., December 8, 1908.

[28] San Mateo Chapter, JACL, *A Community Story*, 27; and A. Yamaguchi, interview by Nakanishi and Tabata.

back to San Mateo where he picked up an apprentice, Shiro Kashiwagi. Kashiwagi originally had arrived in Seattle, Washington in 1902, then settled in San Mateo the following year. Eventually he became Hata's partner.[29]

The Hata Merchant Tailor Shop was popular within the Japanese community because the Issei were comfortable conducting business in their native language and a demand existed for the tailoring services the shop offered. Most Issei in the

T. M. Hata in front of the Hata Merchant Tailor Shop on B Street between Second and Third Avenues in 1902. *Courtesy of S. Sakuma Collection*

early 1900s could not easily find ready-made clothes to fit them and needed western clothes for their jobs as domestics. They also wanted to look their best in the photographs they sent back to Japan to be circulated among the families of prospective brides.

Because Hata and Kashiwagi were able to speak English, their business, supported by Japanese and Caucasian clientele, was successful. By 1911, however, business may have become too good. Efforts to discriminate against Japanese businesses forced them to abandon their shop's B Street location to a less favorable site at 301 Ellsworth Avenue.[30]

In 1918, Kashiwagi became a certified agent to sell war savings stamps and liberty bonds to support the United States during World War I. Both he and Hata were also members of the American Red Cross. Since both men were ineligible for citizenship, they were not allowed to vote but were still required to pay San Mateo county poll taxes.

Their partnership was dissolved in 1924, and Hata moved to San Francisco. Kashiwagi continued to do tailoring out of his home at 10 North Fremont Street until World War II.

Another pioneering Japanese-owned business was Tokutaro Takahashi's Oriental grocery and merchandise store, which he opened in 1906. Takahashi came to the United States from Wakayama in 1898, at the age of eighteen. At first he

---

[29] Tomoko Kashiwagi and Sei (Kashiwagi) Sakuma (Shiro Kashiwagi's daughters), interview by Richard Nakanishi and Shizu "Shazie" (Yamaguchi) Tabata, San Mateo, Calif., May 17, 1978.
[30] San Mateo Chapter, JACL, *A Community Story*, 25.

worked as a supervisor at the Alvarado Salt Works in the East Bay. After witnessing the growing Japanese population and its need for a grocery store, he opened one on B Street in San Mateo between a blacksmith and a Chinese laundry.

At first, Takahashi drove a horse-drawn wagon loaded with supplies and traveled to campsites and the homes of Japanese workers to conduct his business. His store stocked Asian food items such as rice, *shoyu,* or "soy sauce," and *miso,* or "bean curd paste," along with other staples not available in traditional grocery stores. He also sold merchandise such as shoes, pants, fishing rods, tackle, and bait. Takahashi's brother Genji came to San Mateo in 1914 to help with the business.[31]

The store later moved to the southeast corner of Second Avenue and Claremont Street, then to the opposite corner of the same street. Today, run by the third generation, Gene and Jack Takahashi, it is located at Claremont Street and Third Avenue.

In 1922, Shigematsu Ishizaki opened the Menlo Fruit Market on Santa Cruz Avenue, across from the Southern Pacific train depot in Menlo Park. It was the offshoot of a wholesale business he had begun earlier in which he bought fresh vegetables from Japanese farmers between Palo Alto and San Jose and delivered the produce to

Certificate showing S. Kashiwagi was authorized to sell U.S. War Savings Certificate Stamps and Thrift Stamps. *Courtesy of S. Sakuma Collection*

S. Kashiwagi receipt for State Poll Tax, March 20, 1909. *Courtesy of S. Sakuma Collection*

Tokutaro Takahashi and his son Noboru, pre-1922. *Courtesy of Kenge Takahashi Collection*

---

[31] Ishiye Takahashi, interview by Richard Nakanishi and Shizu "Shazie" (Yamaguchi) Tabata, San Mateo, Calif., November 16, 1977.

Genji and Kamechiyo (Morishita)
Takahashi with their son Moto.
Courtesy of Kenge Takahashi Collection

Menlo Fruit Market, 1922. *Courtesy of Kikue Ishizaki Collection*

grocery stores throughout San Francisco and the northern Peninsula. At first he encountered discrimination when he opened the retail store, but the high quality of his fruits and vegetables attracted customers. Ishizaki later opened two other stores—a second Menlo Fruit Market on El Camino and Oak Grove in Menlo Park and a third store, the Cash Savings Food Shop, across the street.[32]

Kamechiyo (Morishita) Takahashi, the wife of Genji Takahashi, ran a successful business as midwife to Japanese women in San Mateo County. An Issei, she had studied for two years to become a midwife in Japan before coming to America in February 1917. In June of that year, through a Nisei attorney named Okawara, she took an examination to get a California midwife's license.[33]

Takahashi initially bicycled to help laboring mothers. Then she used the family store's car, driven at first by her husband, to make her calls. Takahashi became the first Japanese woman in San Mateo to obtain a driver's license; she later got an old Ford that she cranked up by herself and drove to help women from Pescadero to Mountain View. Eventually, she opened the Takahashi

---

[32] Kikue Ishizaki, interview by Richard Nakanishi, San Mateo, Calif., September 1978. The Ishizakis also founded the Yamato restaurants in San Francisco and Los Angeles.

[33] A "Nisei" is a second-generation Japanese American. In Japanese, "*ni*" means "two" and "*sei*" means "generation." Keiko Nakayama, "Japanese Issei's [*sic*] Contribution to San Mateo County During Early 1900's" (unpublished manuscript, December 11, 1989). Nakayama interviewed Kamechiyo (Morishita) Takahashi on November 11, 1989; also Eileen S. Sarasohn, *The Issei* (Palo Alto, Calif.: Pacific Books, 1983), 98.

Midwife Kamechiyo
(Morishita) Takahashi.
*Courtesy of Kenge
Takahashi Collection*

services; she recalled only three times she was not paid.

Takahashi continued the business until 1930, when she had to quit due to illness. During her midwifery days, more than 350 Japanese babies were born in San Mateo County, most of them under her care. Every baby delivered was normal, and only two women during that period required hospitalization. On two occasions, Takahashi delivered Caucasian babies at the request of mothers who could not afford to go to the hospital. "I was always happy to see the happiness in the faces of the new parents as they carried their child home," she said.[35]

Many Issei turned to businesses in a wholly different area: the floral industry. The Japanese almost single-handedly brought chrysanthemums to the American market. In 1882 a school-boy named Hiroshi Kan Yoshiike began growing chrysanthemums in the backyard of his employer's home in Oakland using stem cuttings he had brought from Japan. Four years later, he began selling the chrysanthemums he cultivated. When the demand for the flowers increased, he bought some land and started raising them commercially, becoming the grower who introduced chrysanthemums to the floral marketplace.[36]

At about the same time, brothers Yonoshin and Kentaro Domoto also began to grow chrysanthemums. They were more successful in the

Clinic of Midwifery at her home on 523 Second Avenue in San Mateo. Mothers were permitted to stay at the three-bed clinic for two weeks, during which time she cooked and served them Japanese food. Many times, when a second child was being delivered, the mother would bring the first child. So, in addition to midwifery duties, Takahashi fed and cared for the older child. She never took a job that kept her away from her family overnight.[34]

Takahashi charged twenty dollars for each delivery, plus one dollar per day for room and board. Often she had to furnish medical supplies and was not reimbursed. Payment might be a long time in coming–one person did not pay her until the child began school; some people paid in installments; still others gave her only a token payment. Rarely was she not compensated for her

---

[34] Shigeharu "Shig" Takahashi, interview by gayle k. yamada, San Mateo, Calif., January 11, 2000.

[35] Kamechiyo (Morishita) Takahashi, interview by Richard Nakanishi and Shizu "Shazie" (Yamaguchi) Tabata, San Mateo, Calif., November 8, 1977.

[36] Japanese Association of America, *Zaibei Nippon Jin Shi (History of the Japanese in the United States)* (San Francisco, 1940), 205-221.

Flower-growing families such as the Egashira and Eto families helped San Mateo County earn a reputation as the "flower basket" of the nation, *circa* 1910. *Courtesy of T. Endo Collection*[37]

wholesale business than they had been in retail, raising various kinds of flowers in Oakland and importing camellia, wisteria, lily, and azalea plants from Japan. In the late 1890s, Kentaro Domoto, along with other Japanese, Chinese, and Italian growers of the time, peddled flowers at street stands in San Francisco, beginning a huge cut-flower industry that flourished throughout the Bay Area for the next thirty-five years.[38]

After the 1906 earthquake, the Domoto brothers spearheaded the formation of an organization called the California Flower Growers Association. Its mission was to locate a suitable market site and, in 1909, the group ended up at 31 Lick Place, in an alley between Kearny and Montgomery

Streets in San Francisco. The growers' association leased floor space to forty-two charter members, including Japanese, Chinese, and Italians, while the wholesale firms of the Domoto Brothers, Sadakusu Enomoto, and E. W. McLellan occupied separate stores at the site. It was a huge step for the growers. Until then, as individuals, they had been unsuccessful in marketing their own flowers because of discrimination from buyers, enabling Caucasian middlemen to charge a huge mark-up. The association successfully allowed buyers the opportunity to eliminate the middlemen.

The increasing number of Japanese flower growers led them to break away in 1912 and incorporate as the California Flower Market, Inc. with fifty-four charter members/shareholders. It started at a location at 440 Bush and St. Anne's Place.[39]

The flower market moved once before settling at its current location at Fifth and Howard Streets in San Francisco in 1924. The market place by 1952 had grown to include approximately one hundred Bay Area growers and flower shippers, including Chinese and Italian growers as well as Japanese.[40]

Japanese flower growers began moving to the Peninsula after the 1906 earthquake, largely because of a better growing climate that still allowed easy access to San Francisco. Sango

[37] Yamato Ichihashi, "Study of the Situation of the Japanese Nursery and Its Related Business in San Francisco and Bay Region" (unpublished manuscript, Stanford University Archives, Stanford, Calif., 1927-1928), 1-4.

[38] Edward Norton Barnhart Papers, Japanese American Research Project (JARP) Collection (Collection 2010), Department of Special Collections, Charles E. Young Research Library, University of California, Los Angeles, Los Angeles, Calif.; Ichihashi, "Japanese Nursery," 1-4.

[39] Gary Kawaguchi, *Living with Flowers: The California Flower Market History* (San Francisco, California Flower Market, Inc., 1993), 32.

[40] William Enomoto, conversation with Richard Nakanishi, January 11, 1981.

As time went on, there were improvements, as far as covering with cheesecloth and black cloth. They call it black cloth because it shaded the plants to fool into [thinking it was] early autumn to shorten the days so that chrysanthemums would form their buds and bloom. But that lengthened the season. So those are the things that I've seen develop as my father was growing flowers.

— HIDEYOSHI "HID" KASHIMA

whose family grew chrysanthemums at Horgan Ranch in Redwood City [41]

Fukushima, Isaburo Adachi, and Takajiro Imai were among those who began to grow carnations in Colma. In Redwood City, land was subdivided into five-acre parcels to lure growers to the Peninsula. Nurseryman and retail florist Henry L. Goertzhain of Redwood City developed a technique using cheesecloth as a shade to create artificial autumn conditions to help chrysanthemums grow—a method soon adopted by the Japanese growers because it was relatively inexpensive and increased yield. For the first time, growers could now produce multiple harvests throughout the year, rather than one crop. [42]

Brothers Eikichi and Sadakusu Enomoto got their start in Redwood City in December of 1906 when they made a deposit of $250 to purchase five acres in Redwood City. They began growing chrysanthemums, one of which became known as the "football mum" because of its shape and enormous size. [43]

By 1910, many of the Japanese gardeners began to take advantage of the expanding flower industry, going into business on their own. The Alien Land Law of 1913 made short leases the only option to people ineligible for citizenship, such as the Japanese. Within the town of San Mateo, they leased fields in the Beresford and Homestead areas to grow flowers, mostly chrysanthemums.

---

[41] Hideyoshi "Hid" Kashima, interview by Dianne Fukami, San Carlos, Calif., July 19, 1994.

[42] "Joseph" Iwasuke Rikimaru, interview, Japanese American Research Project (JARP) Collection (Collection 2010), Department of Special Collections, Charles E. Young Research Library, University of California, Los Angeles, Los Angeles, Calif., September 16, 1967, as cited in San Mateo Chapter, JACL, *A Community Story*, 50. Other personal recollections do not attribute the cheesecloth growing method to Goertzhain. *See* "Redwood City's Contribution to San Francisco," *American Florist*, December 26, 1901, Schellens Collection.

[43] William Enomoto, interview by Richard Nakanishi, Redwood City, Calif., March 2, 1978.

Chrysanthemums flooded the local markets by 1912, so growers like Sadakusu Enomoto began looking into the viability of shipping surplus flowers out of the state. In 1915, he made arrangements to ship California-grown chrysanthemums to New Orleans for the All Saints Day observance. As a result of his success, other out-of-state markets were created.

From 1910 to 1925, the floral industry in southern San Mateo County was booming. Besides Redwood City, chrysanthemums were grown in Belmont and the Hillsdale area of San Mateo. A roster of people contributing to the growth of the Peninsula's floral industry included Nobuo Higaki, Kichisaburo Honda, Kotoharu Inouye, Tamakichi Kashima, Rikima Kitagawa, Komataro Nabeta, Katsutaro Nakanishi, Kaoru Okamura, Matsutaro Tsukushi, and Tadashi Yamane from Redwood City. From Belmont there were Sadajiro Higashi, Chuta Nagatoishi, Taichi and Yujiro Kariya, and the Mori brothers—Shigeru, Tosaku, Yoshiaki, and Torao. In San Mateo Seishiro Mayeda, Tokujiro Tanaka, and Saikichi Yamada started nurseries. The concept of wholesale consignment was started by the Peninsula's Yoshinosuke Kiwata in 1910. Also during this time, Ryosuke Shibuya produced new and superior varieties of pompom chrysanthemums

Before the [chrysanthemum growing] season started, in Redwood City they used to sew it [cheesecloth] into so many strips, and call the neighbors. We'd have a picnic afterwards, after we put the cheesecloth on top. On about three-foot lathes or so, they used to hang it every ten feet. The stake houses were ten-feet-by-ten feet, and they were one hundred feet long. They used to call ten-by-one hundred feet a room. They had all this terminology they would use!

— HIDEYOSHI "HID" KASHIMA[44]

for nationwide markets. To prevent a surplus of mums, growers began to raise other flowers as well—roses, carnations, gardenias, and lilies.[45]

At the 1930 Florist Telegraph Delivery Association's (FTDA) annual convention in San Francisco,

[44] H. Kashima, interview by Fukami.

[45] Hirosuke Inouye, interview by Richard Nakanishi, Redwood City, Calif., March 20, 1978; Nobuo Higaki, interview by Richard Nakanishi, translated by Harumi "Harry" and Sachiko Higaki, Redwood City, Calif., May 4, 1978; "Pioneer Flower Growers Honored After 50 Years," *Redwood City* (Calif.) *Tribune*, February 24, 1959; "Kaoru Okamura Operates Nursery Here 52 Years," *Redwood City Tribune*, August 3, 1961; William Enomoto, conversation with Richard Nakanishi, January 25, 1981; and Kawaguchi, *Living with Flowers*, 113-114.

Growing was a hard business, even if the Japanese had honed their skills at it. "If you had a good crop, it was beautiful. But when business was bad, you could see the stems just leaning over. Some families just left their crop out there because they couldn't sell out. There were times like that. And it was a one-shot deal, too."

— HIDEYOSHI "HID" KASHIMA[46]

The Kashima family, shown here in 1974 with William Turner chrysanthemums the family raised. *Courtesy of Hideyoshi "Hid" Kashima*

the California Flower Market sponsored a "Japan Day." As part of the entertainment, attendees received invitations to tour the Peninsula nurseries. The event was so successful that the next year Redwood City held "the first *Kiku Matsuri* [Chrysanthemum Festival] ever attempted in the United States," from September 28 to October 3. The festival was also Redwood City's contribution to "Fiesta Year," an event celebrated throughout the state that year. Eventually, the Chrysanthemum Festival evolved into San Mateo County's annual Floral Fiesta Festival:[47]

So famous were San Mateo chrysanthemums that Paramount Pictures decided to send a newsreel crew to San Mateo and film the workers in the field cutting chrysanthemums…As they were about to roll, the director realized there was something definitely wrong…He became concerned that there were so many Japanese faces. And at that point, he ordered the workers out of the fields and a number of blonde and brunette Caucasian models went out into the fields and carried a few chrysanthemums each and had their photographs taken surrounded by these giant William Turner chrysanthemums. And that's the newsreel that played across the country. No Japanese face. Needless to say, there had been a great deal of excitement among the Japanese that

---

[46] H. Kashima, interview by Fukami.

[47] FTDA Annual Convention 1930, "Japan Day" program, September 1, 1930, San Mateo County History Museum, Museum Archives, Redwood City, Calif.; "The Story of the Kiku Matsuri," October 1, 1931, San Mateo County History Museum, Museum Archives, Redwood City, Calif.; also Schellens Collection, Sec. I, Vol. 4, Pt. 1, 61.

there was going to be attention, but no one would have ever known it was a Japanese industry.

— *Michael Svanevik, Historian*[48]

In 1931, the California Chrysanthemum Growers Association was formed to unite growers and increase their chances of survival after the stock market crash and ensuing Depression. The Association formed guidelines to regulate production so prices would not drop and so that businesses would not undercut each other. Another objective was to promote and publicize the floral industry on the Peninsula.

In spite of the publicity and attention that the local growers received, however, the California Chrysanthemum Growers Association remained financially unstable, and most of the individual growers worked from sunup to sundown to make ends meet. So in 1932, the Association hired "Joseph" Iwasuke Rikimaru as its general manager. During Rikimaru's tenure, the financial health of the association improved: outstanding debts were restructured and accounts restored to good standing. The work of people such as Rikimaru, Makio Watanabe, Mitsuzo Yamada, and James Bodell, coupled with increased flower yields because of the cheesecloth method, improved the association's cash flow even more, despite the Depression.

Rikimaru also encouraged the Japanese growers who leased land at Horgan Ranch on Woodside Road in Redwood City, to purchase acreage when it became available for sale. Thomas M. Horgan, who had subdivided the land in five-acre parcels to lease to the Japanese nurserymen, owned the ranch. In 1939, the law firm of Albert Elliott and Guy Calden of San Francisco helped the Issei to buy the land.[49]

There were 36 members [in the association]. They were really in financial trouble; some families couldn't afford to buy rice for dinner. They couldn't even pay for their water and electricity bills.

—"JOSEPH" IWASUKE RIKIMARU[50]

---

[48] Michael Svanevik, interview by Dianne Fukami, San Mateo, Calif., July 26, 1994.

[49] "Joseph" Iwasuke Rikimaru, interview by Richard Nakanishi, San Mateo, Calif., January 10, 1978.

[50] "Joseph" Iwasuke Rikimaru, interview, JARP Collection (Collection 2010), Department of Special Collections, Charles E. Young Research Library, University of California, Los Angeles, Los Angeles, Calif., September 16, 1967, as cited in San Mateo Chapter, JACL, *A Community Story*, 54.

Yutaka Yoshifuji on Fordson tractor in 1926. *Courtesy of Chiye Yoshifuji Collection*

Yutaka and Chiye (Shintaku) Yoshifuji, 1936. *Courtesy of Chiye Yoshifuji Collection*

As the effects of the Depression dissipated, markets for the floral industry expanded through the use of refrigerated trains and air transportation. By 1939, San Mateo County was home to thirty-eight percent of the 140 independent Japanese flower growers in Northern California.[51]

Along the coast of San Mateo County, the town of Pescadero became home to several Japanese farmers. The first Japanese, a party of five men, arrived in 1912 from Salinas, to develop a five-hundred-acre hay ranch. The partners were Yutaka Yoshifuji, Tom Yuki, Kumasuke Yuki, Torasuki Shimonishi, and a Mr. Matsuda.

The group leased a ranch and bought a tractor, but the ranch failed. Although the other four men left Pescadero, Yoshifuji stayed behind with his wife Chiye and their family. After that first failure, the family moved inland toward Butano Creek and leased four hundred acres of land on the Marsh Ranch. The area was uncultivated and required extensive preparation for planting. Yoshifuji decided to raise fava beans because they required no irrigation. He and his wife worked hard and helped other Japanese immigrants who settled in the Pescadero area.[52]

Another pioneering Japanese farmer on the Peninsula was Eitaro Kuwahara, who moved into the area from Salinas and worked on the Yoshifuji farm for a short time. Kuwahara later leased his own land just outside of Pescadero and had his son Tsunematsu join him from Japan. Together they operated the Level Lea Farm and grew strawberries

---

[51] San Mateo Chapter, JACL, *A Community Story*, 55.

[52] Chiye (Shintaku) Yoshifuji, interview by Richard Nakanishi and Shizu "Shazie" (Yamaguchi) Tabata, San Francisco, Calif., May 12, 1978.

and a wide variety of vegetables, including peas, lettuce, cauliflower, spinach, corn, and fava beans.[53]

Because of the Alien Land Law, most Japanese farmers moving to Pescadero had only three-year leases. In time, the Japanese farmers cultivated two thousand acres of land, and many became famous for their "Fog Kist Peas." Produce from the farms was transported by truck to San Francisco and by train to Los Angeles. During the height of the season, as many as twenty-one truckloads of produce were shipped out of Pescadero in a single day.[54]

Although most farmers along the coast grew produce, Mitsugoro Morimoto and Einoshin Habu were among several who grew helichrysum straw-flowers, which had been introduced by agriculturist Luther Burbank. Further up the coast were a number of other families who settled in Half Moon Bay. Most grew flowers, but Zenichi Takaha grew Oriental vegetables. Other coastal agriculturists included Moriki Kakimoto, who grew decorative bulb plants, and Seiro Sato, who grew marguerite flowers. With their families and businesses flourishing in San Mateo County, the Japanese continued settling this new land. Like immigrants from many lands before them, the Japanese in San Mateo were making their indelible mark on America and now were calling America their home.[55]

---

[53] Yuku (Miyazaki) Kuwahara, interview by Richard Nakanishi and Shizu "Shazie" (Yamaguchi) Tabata, San Mateo, Calif., October 28, 1978; and Kaoru Yoshifuji, telephone conversation with gayle k. yamada, December 11, 2001.

[54] San Mateo Chapter, JACL, *A Community Story*, 44.

[55] W. Enomoto, conversation with Nakanishi, January 11, 1981; Yoneji Takaha and Mari (Takaha) Tamaki, interview by Richard Nakanishi, San Mateo, Calif., October 3, 1978; and Y. Mizono and S. Okamura, interview by Nakanishi and Tabata.

CHAPTER 3

BUILDING COMMUNITY

Resolved to become
The soil of the foreign land,
I settle down.

— R Y U F U [1]

While building an economic foundation, the Japanese in San Mateo County developed a cultural and social life that reflected their ethnic roots as well as their American experience. The Japanese community struggled, trying to strike a balance between westernizing their children and retaining old world values and social mores. What emerged was a community centered on family, education, and enterprise.

The Issei tried to keep the spirit of their homeland alive in this new land by maintaining Japanese customs and social activities. They sent their children to Japanese language school, to church to learn about Buddhism or Christianity, and to social events organized by Japanese groups. At the same time, these immigrant parents were laying the groundwork for their children to grow up as citizens rooted in America. Organizations such as the Boy Scouts and Blue Jays, and social activities such as annual picnics became regular parts of Japanese American life.

Even with this balance, however, the Japanese still chose largely to socialize among themselves. They faced racial discrimination that was both legal and socially acceptable. There were laws regarding immigration, citizenship, and property ownership; and groups such as the Anti-Japanese Laundry League and the Asian Exclusion League, and those in San Mateo opposed to the construction of a Japanese school.

Though the distance between farms limited social activities among the Japanese families in the Pescadero area along the San Mateo County coast, they still managed to find time to come together. They celebrated *oshogatsu*, or "New Year's Day," and a dozen or so families held monthly potluck dinners. They had picnics on the beach, fished for striped bass and perch, hunted for

[1] Ito, *Issei*, 11.

abalone, gathered *nori*, or "edible seaweed," and watched Japanese films brought in by movie exhibitors.

Many of the boys in Pescadero were members of the Judo Club, which was founded by Tsunematsu Kuwahara, who taught them judo. They learned not only the art of self-defense but also good sportsmanship while they competed in tournaments with clubs from other Japanese communities.

One of the first formal economic, political, and social Issei organizations in the community was the *Nihonjinkai*, or the Japanese Association of America, a federation of local groups. Founded and incorporated in 1900, and headquartered in San Francisco, initially it had chapters in California (including San Mateo), Nevada, Utah, Colorado, and Arizona. Though it was not legally affiliated with the Japanese government, the association acted as a "bureau of information" for newly-arriving immigrants, helping them adjust to American customs and culture and providing resource information on social conduct, interpretation, legal advice, employment, and housing. The national association also advised the Japanese government about problems in the United States that arose for Japanese, even taking on a political advocacy role in the early 1900s, actively fighting discrimination when the Anti-Asiatic League began to spread racist propaganda about the Japanese.[2]

The San Mateo Chapter of the Japanese Association began in 1906, with fifty people attending the initial meeting. Artist Sekko Shimada was elected the first president. He had originally arrived in San Mateo in 1902 as a guest of Henry Bowie, who founded the Japan Society in the San Francisco Bay Area in 1905.[3]

The association was supported largely through membership dues and donations. Additional revenue came from Japanese citizens living in America who paid the association certificate fees when they applied for exemptions from the Japanese military. Japan's conscription law required Japanese men between the ages of twenty and thirty-seven living abroad to register every year. The Japanese Consulate contracted with the association to issue certificates of notification, and the association collected a fee of fifty cents per certificate. When the Gentlemen's Agreement went into effect, the Japanese Association also handled certificates of residence that allowed Japanese to return to Japan for a visit and then easily be re-admitted to the United States.[4]

One of the social highlights for the San Mateo chapter was the picnic it sponsored every summer in the Beresford area, located south of Nineteenth Avenue and west of El Camino Real.

---

[2] Ichihashi, *Japanese in the United States*, 224-225.

[3] Henry P. Bowie, *On the Laws of Japanese Painting* (New York: Dover Publication, Inc., 1952), 5; and Postel, Centennial History, 142; also, Sazanami Iwaya, Introduction to Henry P. Bowie, *On the Laws of Japanese Painting* (New York: Dover Publication, Inc., 1952), v-vi; and Nihonjin-kai, *History of Japanese Living in the United States*, 755.

[4] Ichihashi, *Japanese in the United States*, 226.

The San Mateo Chapter of the Japanese Association and members of the community, 1914. *Left to right, Row 1*: M. Miyaki, T. Ito, Nakahara, T. Takahashi, Sakuma; *Row 2*: Aoyagi, (unidentified), K. Ito, I. Takahama, T. Yamanouchi, S. Kashiwagi, Agari.
Courtesy of H. Ito Collection

Japanese from the coastal communities and as far south as Redwood City would all take a day off to come to the picnic with their families. "It was an annual affair, so everybody looked forward to it," remembered Shizu "Shazie" (Yamaguchi) Tabata, who grew up with the picnics as a regular feature of life in San Mateo County. "My mother used to always make me a new dress for the occasion, and everybody used to make lots of good food...It was a time for gathering of the whole of San Mateo.

Whether you were Buddhist or Christian, it didn't make any difference–they all came to San Mateo."[5]

In addition to an abundance of food, there were games and a masquerade parade. "They had community picnics that were very close knit," remembered Hideyoshi "Hid" Kashima, who grew up on Horgan Ranch in San Mateo County. "We had parades, costume parades, races, and everybody brought their own food. We used to go up to Beresford; it was around this area. It was just an

---

[5] Shizu "Shazie" (Yamaguchi) Tabata, interview by Dianne Fukami, San Mateo, Calif., July 26, 1994.

Beresford picnic, May 4, 1930. *Courtesy of Yoneo "Yon" Kawakita*

San Mateo-born Tomoko Kashiwagi remembered, "At the picnics, I know we took our Japanese *bento* [lunch boxes], *nigiri* [rice balls], and everything. They had races for the children – sack races, egg races. And then at the end, the older people would get costumes and wear them and have a parade...Some of the men would dress like women and put lipstick on and everything, which was kind of fun to watch."[7] *Courtesy of A. Yamaguchi Collection*

open field. And we'd sit around somebody's property, which they, of course, got permission to have the picnic [on]. I remember to this day, after the picnic was finished, the Japanese would clean it better than it looked before they rented it!"[6]

Another type of social organization was the *kenjinkai*, or "prefectural organization." The Issei came from *ken*, or "geographical prefectures," in Japan, and each *ken* had its own characteristic speech, foods, and customs. When they immigrated, these ties were re-established in America, and people from the same area in Japan would frequently settle in the same general vicinity in the United States. The *kenjinkai* held regular meetings and sponsored social activities.

Buddhist and Christian churches became focal points for the Japanese community in the San Mateo area. A meeting was held in 1909 to discuss establishing a Buddhist church in San Mateo. After repeated encouragement from others, Imperial Laundry owner Tetsuo Yamanouchi, who had been educated and trained as a Zen Buddhist priest in Japan, became the church's founding spiritual leader. His wife Yoshiko organized the Sunday School and Women's Auxiliary.

Original church members included Kazo Fukagai, Tomisuke Ito, Seiichi Kaneko, Tokutaro

---

[6] The Horgan Ranch, owned by Thomas M. Horgan, was a ranch off Woodside Road in Redwood City, about two miles west of what is Highway 101 today. When the Dumbarton Bridge was built in the mid–1920s, the water table was contaminated by salt water, and Horgan considered the land ruined for vegetable farming. The ranch was then divided into smaller parcels and used by the chrysanthemum growers. James K. Mori, telephone conversation with gayle k. yamada, February 3, 2002; and H. Kashima, interview by Fukami.

[7] Tomoko Kashiwagi, interview by Dianne Fukami, San Mateo, Calif., July 25, 1994.

The Buddhist Church became a focal point for the Japanese community in San Mateo. January 12, 1933.
Courtesy of H. Watanuki Collection

Takahashi, Mr. Inouye, and a Mr. Yamaguchi. At first, the small congregation held services at the Yamanouchi home at the corner of First Avenue and Ellsworth Street. As the living room began to fill up with more people, however, services were moved to an adjacent store on First Avenue. For many years, Yamanouchi rented this space for the church for forty dollars a month from the Wisnoms, a well-known San Mateo construction and real estate family.[8]

On February 20, 1910, congregation members applied to the San Francisco Buddhist Church for affiliation. By 1929, the San Mateo Buddhist Church had sixty members and began operating independently of the San Francisco Buddhist Church, although the ministers from San Francisco were retained to conduct local services. Four years later, Yamanouchi received the Certificate for Distinguished Service from the Nishi-honganji Temple in Kyoto, Japan, the first time the award was given to a person outside of Japan. Another important event occurred on March 2, 1935, when Gorenshi Shojo Otani, the Lord Abbot Otani from the Nishi-honganji Temple, arrived to perform a confirmation ceremony for eighty-five members of the church.[9]

Many Buddhist ministers came to San Mateo from San Francisco to serve the members of the temple, including Shingetsu Akahoshi, Jitsusho Kitayama, Gijo Motoyama, Shinjo Nagatomi,

---

[8] Buddhist Churches of America, *75 Year History 1899-1974, Vol. I and Vol. II* (Chicago: Nobart, Inc., 1974), 330-335, as cited in San Mateo Chapter, JACL, *A Community Story*, 38.
[9] Buddhist Churches, *75 Year History*, 330-335.

Shozen Naito, Shintatsu Sanada, Hosho Sasaki, Kakue Takahashi, Tansai Terakawa, and Tokiko Yamaori.[10]

The church began to outgrow its First Avenue facilities, so services were moved to the Japanese language school at 504 Second Avenue. In 1939, the congregation began a capital campaign, led by church president Yuya Fujita, to build a church. He managed to persuade members to donate or pledge the necessary funds, resulting in the purchase of lots at Two South Claremont Street on June 27, 1940 for $2,600. Before construction could begin, however, World War II broke out.[11]

In January 1924, several years after the Buddhist Church was established, a few Japanese led by Masazo Shimizu, Hidematsu Tamura, and Tomoko Yamamoto founded a Japanese Christian Church in San Mateo. The first informal gatherings were held at the Tamura home on Grant Street. Later the group held services twice monthly at the Congregational Church on Tilton Avenue with services performed by the Reverend Shokochi Hata from San Francisco.[12]

In 1925, physician Dr. Ernest Adolphus Sturge came out of retirement at the age of sixty-nine to help establish a church in San Mateo. He

Dr. Ernest Sturge was a respected member of the community who moved to San Mateo to help establish a church. *Courtesy of Yasuko "Ann" (Ishida) Ito*

had been the director of evangelism under the Presbyterian Board of National Missions and worked in the Japanese community in San Francisco and other Japanese communities on the West Coast. Sturge also treated Issei in his medical practice and delivered many of the Nisei babies. He and his wife moved from Carmel to San Mateo, and their Elm Street house became a meeting place. The congregation initially called itself the Christian Endeavor Society, but in January 1926, it became an official branch of the Japanese Church of Christ in San Francisco. A year later it

---

[10] Buddhist Churches, *75 Year History*, 18.

[11] Buddhist Churches, *75 Year History*, 331. Also, according to an amendment dated October 24, 1940, filed with the San Mateo Buddhist Temple Articles of Incorporation, the Board of Directors limited membership to U.S. citizens, believing it to be in the best interests of the church. The thirteen board members who voted unanimously for this amendment were: Tomonori Ishida, Kyoji Kashima, Shigeo Kashima, Shigeru Kitagawa, Shigeki Mori, Takashi Okubo, Sadami Sakai, Takeshi Shiba, Sutemi Sugaya, Tomiko Sutow, Sadaichi Suyama, Motoichi Takahashi, and Yoneo Tashiro.

[12] The Reverend Sumio Koga (compiled), *A Centennial Legacy: History of the Japanese Christian Missions in North America, 1877-1977, Vol. I*, 176-177.

Sturge Memorial Cottage, 1944

became the Japanese Independent Union Church of San Mateo.

The congregation was able to purchase property on 25 South Humboldt Street in 1930 and was in the middle of a fundraising drive for a new building when Dr. Sturge passed away in 1934. He willed his home on Elm Street to the congregation. Proceeds from the sale of the house, valued at five thousand dollars, were used for a new building, which was called the Sturge Memorial Cottage. On April 24, 1938, the church held a dedication ceremony. As with the San Mateo Buddhist Temple, further construction on the church was delayed by the start of World War II.[13]

Despite efforts to adjust to life as members of the San Mateo community, the Japanese resi-

dents continually received reminders of how their non-Asian neighbors continued to see them as "different." In September 1930, for example, the Japanese school in San Mateo met opposition from residents when it proposed constructing a new building on Cypress Avenue and Idaho Street, a mostly residential area with a few empty lots. The *Nippon Gakuen*, or Japanese School, had been at its location on Second Avenue for eleven years and needed larger quarters. The fifty-six opponents maintained that they did not object to the construction of a new school, but they did not want it in their neighborhood.[14]

At a San Mateo City Council meeting, area resident Mike Boepple testified that, "if the Japanese were allowed to cut into the sections, they would destroy the district." The council formed a committee to find a more suitable location for the school in what was termed "the Oriental quarter of the city." Although there was no area officially designated as such, bankers and realtors followed an unwritten rule that no Japanese could buy a house or live outside of the area from Fifth Avenue to Poplar and from El Camino to Bayshore. The area was primarily residential, with a few corner neighborhood grocery stores along Bayshore.[15]

---

[13] J.I. Rikimaru, interview by Nakanishi. Sturge Presbyterian Church, *Fiftieth Anniversary*, (San Mateo, Calif., 1973).

[14] Yoneo "Yon" Kawakita, electronic correspondence to gayle k. yamada, November 28, 2001. The Japanese Language School was referred to as "*Nihongo Gakko,*" which means Japanese language school, or "*Nippon Gakuen,*" which means Japanese school. The terms were used interchangeably.

[15] Postel, *Centennial History*, 167; also "Japanese Language School Location Creates Big Stir in San Mateo, New Offer Made," *Burlingame* (Calif.) *Advance-Star*, September 30, 1930. Although rigid ethnic districts had not taken shape in San Mateo, the Japanese, along with Italian residents, tended to live east and north of the town's center. Postel, *Centennial History*, 143, 167; Yoneo "Yon" Kawakita, electronic correspondence to gayle k. yamada, November 21, 2001.

The sting of discrimination was felt outside the boundaries of the city of San Mateo, too. Yoshiko "Yoshi" (Sato) Mizono, who lived in Half Moon Bay, remembered a time when she and her family received different treatment. "When we moved voluntarily from one side of the creek to the other, school officials said that the creek was a boundary line. So my brother and I had to change schools to a two-room schoolhouse in Miramar. My brother only had a half-year to go, and I just had a year and a half. But a Caucasian neighbor that was living on the same farm as we were somehow was allowed to use her grandmother's address in Half Moon Bay and stay at the same school. I felt it was unfair."[16]

Those incidents, however, paled in comparison to what would come during World War II. Still, while the war shook the foundation the Japanese had worked so hard to build, it did not crack it. Thanks to the strength and intimacy of their community organizations, the Japanese in San Mateo County had built a solid base for their lives, allowing their children to survive and mature as Americans while respecting traditional Japanese values.

---

[16] Yoshiko "Yoshi" (Sato) Mizono, interview by gayle k. yamada, San Mateo, Calif., March 25, 1998; and Yoshiko "Yoshi" (Sato) Mizono, telephone conversation with gayle k. yamada, December 9, 2001.

CHAPTER 4

THE EMERGENCE OF A
NEW GENERATION

*It was only natural that we would respect parental
ties and follow the decisions the Issei mapped out
concerning community and social policies at home.
Yet, we were also American citizens in tune with
American things, such as dances, parties,
and independence to marry someone
of our own choosing.*

—TOMIKO SUTOW
*who grew up in San Mateo County
in the 1920s and 1930s[1]*

The dreams and goals of the immigrant Japanese began to change as they established families. As the Nisei children began to grow up, the Japanese community evolved in a way that took the new generation into consideration. Like children of other immigrants, these Japanese American youths had to find a compromise between their parents' roots and their American birthplace. At home, the language, food, and customs were still from Japan, but at school, the Nisei youths tried to appear as American as their classmates.

Between 1904 and 1942 in San Mateo County, 589 children were born to Issei parents.

The highest number of births occurred in the 1920s, more than likely the result of the large number of marriages that occurred before 1924, when the National Origins Act established immigration quotas and barred entry to anyone who was ineligible for citizenship. Since Asians were not allowed to become naturalized citizens, the National Origins Act effectively ended Japanese immigration after that year.[2]

That year also marked the launch of a membership drive in San Mateo for the white supremacy organization, the Ku Klux Klan. An article about the drive appeared on the front page of the *San*

---

[1] Tomiko Sutow as quoted in Jerrold H. Takahashi, "The San Mateo JACL" (unpublished paper written for a Contemporary Asian Studies course, University of California, Berkeley, Berkeley, Calif., 1973), 14-15. Sutow was born October 1, 1920.

[2] San Mateo County, *Index to Births 1866-1965, A-K and L-Z*, Office of the Assessor-County Clerk-Recorder, Vital Records, Redwood City, Calif.

Mateo Times, written in a matter-of-fact manner that could have described a Rotary Club activity.[3]

By the mid-1920s there were three different kinds of people of Japanese descent in the United States—the Issei, or "first-generation immigrants;" their American-born children, known as Nisei, or "second generation;" and the *kibei*, also Nisei, who were born in America and sent to Japan to be educated, and who then returned to the United States.

Non-Japanese Americans often did not accept their Nisei classmates, who looked different and had different cultural backgrounds, customs, and values. Yet the Nisei's strong desire to be seen as Americans fueled their efforts to adapt to the prevalent culture. San Mateo native Yon Kawakita summed up what many of them experienced, saying, "There was a period of rude awakening that you're different than the rest of the fellows because you never get invited to their birthday parties; or these kids would be having fun, and you don't feel like you're one of them." So the Nisei played and socialized mostly among themselves.[4]

A boys' athletic league was formed in San Mateo to sponsor baseball and basketball games between other Japanese communities. The local San Mateo athletic club was called the *Ryusei*, or Meteors. Some boys joined the local Boy Scouts. Troop 115 was organized around 1925, consisting of a mixed group of Italian, Japanese, and other boys attending Turnbull School on North Delaware Street and East Poplar Avenue in San Mateo.[5]

Despite the desire to be seen as "American," many Nisei joined clubs centered around more traditional Japanese activities like martial arts, including *judo*, or "the Way of Yielding," and *kendo*, or "the Way of the Sword," which uses a bamboo sword to teach fencing. Issei parents encouraged their children to take *judo* or *kendo* lessons, sports with which they themselves were familiar and which reflected their own upbringing.

"The Boy Scouts was a real character-building organization, and I really respect that organization," said Harumi "Harry" Higaki. "It was a foundation in my life. They were the character-building years." San Mateo Boy Scout Troop 115, *circa* 1930. *Courtesy of K. Yamaguchi Collection*[6]

[3] The *San Mateo* (Calif.) *Times*, March 8, 1924, 1.

[4] Y. Kawakita, interview by yamada, March 2, 1998.

[5] Shigeki Mori, interview by Richard Nakanishi, San Mateo, Calif., January 11, 1978; and Postel, *Centennial History*, 180.

[6] Harumi "Harry" Higaki, interview by gayle k. yamada, Hillsborough, Calif., November 20, 1997.

San Mateo Kendo Club, 1930. *Courtesy of H. Ito Collection*

Girls could join the Blue Jay Club, unique to San Mateo, which was formed in 1926 by Tomoko Yamamoto, the wife of San Francisco dentist Dr. Tatsuo Yamamoto who, on weekends, brought his family to the Peninsula where he also served as the dentist for Japanese residents of San Mateo County. One of the few Issei who could speak fluent English, Mrs. Yamamoto organized the Blue Jay Club when she saw that immigrants were working so hard to earn a living that they did not have the time to help organize their daughters' social activities. As many as twenty young Nisei girls were Blue Jays. They met every weekend, and, during summer months, they went on camping trips to Pescadero and Ukiah to fish and swim.[7]

I used to ride my bicycle or walk–most of the time I'd ride my bicycle–to [the scoutmaster's] home and the meeting place was held at the [American] Legion Hall. I think it was Troop 48, and their hall was located on East Bellevue between San Mateo Drive and the railroad tracks…And through the scouting movement, you learn all the necessary things like cooking and knot tying…At least I was exposed to this other area of scouting, which I think even today, people–kids–enjoy scouting and do better themselves.

— YONEO "YON" KAWAKITA
Boy Scout, 1935-39[8]

[7] Verlin T. Yamamoto, interview by Shizu "Shazie" (Yamaguchi) Tabata, San Francisco, Calif., December 26, 1977.
[8] Y. Kawakita, interview by yamada, March 2, 1998. Kawakita was the only Japanese American in Troop 48, comprised of students in the Hayward Park area and sponsored by the American Legion.

Former Blue Jay members on their bicycles. *Left to right:* Shazie (Yamaguchi) Tabata, Fumi Imazu Okamura, Nellie Kikuchi Sakuma, Naomi Tanaka Yamaguchi, Martha Tanaka Imai, Yoshi Imazu Ariyoshi. *Courtesy of A. Yamaguchi Collection*

The girls can never forget the traditional first night's dinner at camp that Tomoko Yamamoto would prepare at home—meat loaf and tossed green salad!

— VERLIN T. YAMAMOTO
*son of Blue Jay leader
Tomoko Yamamoto* [9]

The experiences were memorable for many of its members. For one activity, a national "Dolls of Friendship" program, they donated a doll named "Mae San Mateo," one of more than 12,700 little blue-eyed dolls sent to schools in Japan along with a song of its own:

AOI ME NO NINGYO
(THE BLUE-EYED DOLL)

Pretty doll of celluloid
   with lovely eyes of blue,
All the way from U.S.A.
   she came to play with you;
When this little dollie
   first arrived here in Japan,
Her pretty eyes were full of tears,
   and she did cry, "Boo hoo."

Here they speak a language
   that I cannot understand.
I will surely lose my way,
   and then what shall I do?
Listen to me,
   gentle little maidens of Japan:
Play with her, and be as nice
   and friendly as you can.
Play with her, and be as nice
   and friendly as you can.

The club also put on an annual stage production, described by Shazie (Yamaguchi) Tabata:

One year at the local Masonic Temple, we put on a play called *Onabesan,* "The Cooking Pot." Mrs. Yamamoto wrote the

---

[9] V. Yamamoto, interview by Tabata.

play and directed it. All the members actively participated, taking parts in the play; they sang, danced, or played musical accompaniments, or accepted responsibilities to chair committees for getting the production to the public. People came from near and far to view the productions. Local young men helped us with the stage props and scene changes. It was really part of the young people's way of life then. The girls of San Mateo will never forget how much time and effort Mrs. Yamamoto put forth towards our well-being.[10]

48 Mae San Mateo

Mae San Mateo from a 1989 "Return Homecoming Exhibition of Friendship Dolls from U.S.A." pamphlet. *Courtesy of Tomoko Kashiwagi*

"The San Mateo Blue Jays sent a blue- eyed doll named Mae San Mateo," according to Eiko Takeda, author of the pamphlet about the local doll. "Like all the other dolls, Mae San Mateo carried her own passport and visa with a message, 'May the United States of America and Japan always stay friends. I am being sent to Japan on a mission of friendship. Please let me join the Girls' Festival in your country.' These dolls were distributed to schools and kindergartens throughout Japan."[11]

Although Issei parents generally paid little attention to their children's social lives, they considered education of prime importance and a key to getting ahead. In their homeland, teachers were held in the utmost respect. Many of the Issei, educated in Japan but lacking a knowledge of English, were unable to find jobs commensurate with their skills. They were determined to see that their children would not be in the same position, so they made many financial sacrifices to ensure that their children had the best education possible. At the same time, they wanted their children to grow up with a cultural appreciation for Japan, so many paid tuition for their children to attend Japanese language school every day after they finished regular school.

Many Issei relied on Japanese language school, or *Nihon Gakko,* for proper language instruction to ensure their second-generation children learned the Japanese language. In the town of San Mateo, the first Japanese language school opened in 1916, at a building on Fremont Street, relocating in 1919 to the southwest corner of South Delaware and Second Avenue.[12]

---

[10] Shizu "Shazie" (Yamaguchi) Tabata, interview by Yasuko "Ann" (Ishida) Ito, San Mateo, Calif., April 14, 1994. *Onabesan* is an honorific expression for *nabe,* which is a "cooking pot." In Japanese folktales, household items are often personified. Haruko Sakakibara, electronic correspondence to gayle k. yamada, December 1, 2001.

[11] Eiko Takeda, "Return Homecoming Exhibition of Friendship Dolls from U.S.A.," trans. and ed. Minoru Saitoh (pamphlet, Tokyo: GOSP, Publishers, 1989).

[12] Kiyoshi Asai, "History of the Japanese Pioneers in San Mateo" (unpublished paper written for a course at San Mateo Junior College, San Mateo, Calif., 1941), San Mateo County History Museum, Museum Archives, Redwood City, Calif., 5. But *see* Minako Maki, "The History of Japanese Language School in San Mateo County" (unpublished paper written for a California History course, 1993), San Mateo County History Museum, Museum Archives, Redwood City, Calif. which says the Japanese Language School first was established at 512 Second Street in May of 1916 and a drive to buy the facility was launched in 1919.

First site of the San Mateo Japanese School, 1916. *San Mateo County History Museum Archives*

Commonly known as "*Nihongo Gakko,*" or Japanese Language School, in San Mateo. *Circa 1928-1929. Courtesy of San Mateo Chapter, Japanese American Citizens League*

They were taught Japanese music, literature, and art, as well as social customs and conduct. Teachers received about two dollars a month per child in addition to *orei*, which is an honorarium, and other gifts from parents. Some of the teachers were Masako Hirata, Motoko Hosoume, Nui Takahashi, Yoshiko Tsubokura, Shichiro Oida, Tsurumatsu Saiki, and Taiichi Kawase.

Not all the students were as enthusiastic as parents about putting in more study time everyday. Yon Kawakita said:

I wasn't quite eager to learn Japanese. The chore begins when I had to ride my bicycle there. It was a situation you hated, and when you hate something, you don't take that much interest in learning. I used to go there and sit way in the back of the class and hope *Sensei*, or the teacher, didn't call on me...One day I was riding my bicycle by Railroad Avenue, just past Ninth, toward Fifth Avenue, and this [Caucasian] guy with a car stopped about fifty feet in front of me and started walking toward me and said, "Get off your bike and give me your bicycle." And I said, "No, I'm not." And he was a great big mean looking guy, if I recollect. So I picked up my bike and ran across the railroad tracks to get away from him. Of course, I never rode that way after that, but that was a deterrent for continuing my Japanese school![13]

Most other Japanese communities established their own language schools. In Redwood City, a multi-purpose structure was built on the property of the Kichisaburo Honda nursery on Valota Road. It served as both the Japanese language school and community hall. The school in Pescadero was formed in 1930 by some of the pioneers of the farming community there – Yutaka Yoshifuji, Eitaro Kuwahara, and Einoshin Habu. It

[13] Y. Kawakita, interview by yamada, March 2, 1998.

In Pescadero, Japanese language classes were held downtown in a vacant church on land rented by the Japanese community.[14]
Courtesy of Y. Kuwahara Collection

had fifty-three charter students. Teachers in Pescadero included Choko Tsuchiya, the Reverend Gibun Kimura, Guntaro Kubota, and Hiroshi Hashimoto.[15]

As the Nisei grew older and began attending colleges and universities, they became more aware of their second-class status in America. They were American citizens but unable to get equal treatment. Many of the college-educated Nisei had trouble finding work in their chosen career fields and often even encountered blatant discrimination on their job hunts. Between 1925 and 1935, three-quarters of the 161 Nisei graduates from the University of California were unable to find work in their chosen careers.[16]

Saiki Muneno was one of them. Originally from Hawai`i, he attended the University of California, graduating in zoology. He moved to Los Angeles to find a job but was unable to find work in his field because of the racism against those of Japanese ancestry. After a brief stay in Los Angeles, Muneno ended up in San Mateo County, working on his brother's farm in Pescadero. While there, since he was born in the U.S. territory of Hawai`i and was thus an American citizen, his name was used to lease and purchase land for the Issei farmers.[17]

The Nisei felt a need to address questions of citizenship rights and loyalty. In 1918, Nisei in San Francisco attempted to start an organization called the American Loyalty League, and Seattle

---

[14] Kaoru Yoshifuji, conversation with Richard Nakanishi, San Mateo, Calif., date unknown. Also in San Mateo County, Aya (Miyake) Takahashi taught at the Belmont Language School from 1930-1935.

[15] W. Enomoto, interview by Nakanishi. In addition to the interest in Japanese language schools, the growing number of immigrant farmers and their families led to an increase of Japanese students along the coast in public schools. Former Pescadero teacher Katherine (Pitcher) Valentine recalled, "It was a pleasure to be a teacher to the Japanese students because they were eager to learn and willing to study." Katherine (Pitcher) Valentine, telephone interview by Richard Nakanishi, date unknown.

[16] Takaki, *Strangers from a Different Shore*, 218.

[17] J. Takahashi, "The San Mateo JACL," 13.

Nisei in 1922 formed the Seattle Progressive Citizens League.

The creation of a national organization occurred in 1930, when a group of Nisei convened to form the Japanese American Citizens League (JACL), with chapters in Washington, Oregon, and California. People who played a key role included Clarence Arai of Seattle, Thomas Yatabe of Fresno, and Saburo Kido of San Francisco. The group's primary mission was to emphasize loyalty among the Americans of Japanese descent and, secondarily, to focus on dual citizenship issues and the protection of Issei rights. Twenty-one local chapters throughout the country had formed by 1934.

The San Mateo JACL chapter began on May 11, 1935, at a meeting held at the Japanese language school. Members elected Saiki Muneno as chapter president, formally adopted the national JACL constitution, and selected a board of governors. At first there were about fifteen to twenty members, whose average age was eighteen. They initially held their meetings at the language school and then later moved to Sturge Memorial Cottage.[18]

Tomiko Sutow, who retired as a supervising nurse at what was then Mills Hospital, was the chapter secretary in 1940 and remembered that the local chapter provided an emancipating outlet for Nisei who wanted to escape the influence of their Issei parents. A dilemma arose, however. Because of their youth and the Depression, for a while the Nisei-run organization was financially dependent upon the Issei-run Japanese Association. Former chapter president Joe Yamada recalled, "We had a hell of a time getting membership dues, which at that time had only been a dollar a year. It was the Depression, and our parents were not going to give us that kind of money for social things."[19]

Despite the Depression, the San Mateo County chapter remained active. The first inaugural banquet took place at the Benjamin Franklin Hotel in August 1935. The theme was "Americanism and second-generation progress." National JACL President Saburo Kido urged members to "gain friends for the league in order to combat anti-Japanese legislation and to spread an understanding that the American-born are loyal to the United States."[20]

Other gatherings, such as dances, were held at the Benjamin Franklin Hotel, the Kloss Hall of the Congregational Church, and the Masonic Temple. Nisei also had the opportunity to attend JACL District Council meetings and meet Nisei from other cities and towns throughout the country.[21]

---

[18] Muneno, who studied zoology, had been a classmate of Saburo Kido, who went into law at the University of California, Berkeley. Kido was JACL Executive Secretary and served two terms as national president. For a more complete discussion of the San Mateo and national JACL, *see* J. Takahashi, "The San Mateo JACL," 12-22.

[19] J. Takahashi, "The San Mateo JACL," 14.

[20] Schellens Collection, Sec. 2., Vol. 1, Pt. 2, 69.

[21] Schellens Collection, Sec. 2., Vol. 1, Pt. 2, 69.

The San Mateo JACL entered a float in the 1940 county fair parade that consisted of a huge American flag, seventy-by-forty feet, carried by fifty of its members. It received the award for most unique float. *Courtesy of National Japanese American Citizens League*

At the heart of their adaptation to western culture was the Nisei desire to be treated as full-fledged American citizens. Meanwhile, events in the world worked against them. Japan's 1937 invasion of Chinese territory heightened tensions between Japan and the United States, which supported China. That, coupled with the outbreak of war in Europe in 1939, created a growing sense of unease among Japanese Americans. Members of the JACL recognized that war with Japan could adversely affect their own community, so, in 1940, the JACL participated in every civic event possible to highlight the loyalty of the Japanese Americans.

War drums were already sounding. By June 1941, seven Japanese American men in San Mateo were already serving in uniform as part of the peacetime draft instituted by the U.S. Army. A few months later, on September 7, the members of the local JACL took out a newspaper advertisement in the *Burlingame* (Calif.) *Advance-Star,* publicly declaring their loyalty as American citizens.[22]

Any benefits from all those efforts, however, were erased on Sunday, December 7, 1941, when Japan bombed Pearl Harbor.

---

[22] The U.S. Army drafted Nisei until March 30, 1942, when the Selective Service reclassified all Japanese Americans 4-C or "enemy alien."

"Our aim is to let all Americans know that the American citizens of Japanese parentage stand loyally and shoulder to shoulder with Uncle Sam in this world crisis. All of us who have been drafted or volunteered into the service of the United States have attained excellent records. This constant development of San Mateo County, too, is a thing of vital concern to us. We have been and always will be willing to do our bit for the betterment and welfare of this county, and thus, to this our United States of America... We, TOO, are Americans."[23]

[23] *Burlingame* (Calif.) *Advance-Star,* September 17, 1941 (Howard Imada Collection, San Mateo, Calif.).

CHAPTER 5

PEARL HARBOR:
A DAY OF "INFAMY"

These guys came in and said, "Goddamn Japs [sic]
attacked Pearl Harbor!" And I said, "Who do you
mean?" He said, "Japan, your goddamn country!"
And I said, "That is not my country. The United
States is my country…I'm an American."

— WILLIAM NOSAKA
who was in the U.S. Army
on December 7, 1941[1]

"December 7. It was a Sunday," recalled Kaoru Yoshifuji, a *kibei* farmer in Pescadero. "I was working in the field, and then at lunchtime I was coming home, driving the tractor. Sayoko, my second sister, hollered at me, 'Japan, they go to war with the United States!' And I didn't believe that at first…Left the tractor…Stick by the radio… Everybody stick by the radio…Listen to the news. Shock. After that, I don't feel like working anymore."[2]

News of the attack on Pearl Harbor came during breakfast for many in San Mateo County. Kenzo Higashi, cook to the Wisnoms, and his wife Etsuko, their maid, remembered the Wisnoms were upset but did not discuss the bombing. They also kept the Higashis on as domestic servants until just a few weeks before their forced removal to Tanforan.[3]

At the Beresford Country Club, now the Peninsula Golf and Country Club, in San Mateo, a big golf tournament was in progress that morning. Three hundred potential new members had turned out to play golf and raise funds to renovate and rehabilitate the country club and golf course. The tournament had been underway for about an hour when the news came. People who were there remembered the near panic. Everyone suddenly left. Reservists and Guardsmen rushed to join their units; fathers, brothers and sons went home to their loved ones.[4]

---

[1] W. Nosaka, interview by yamada.
[2] Kaoru Yoshifuji, interview by Dianne Fukami, San Mateo, Calif., April 13, 1994.
[3] K. Higashi, interview by Ito.
[4] Postel, *Centennial History,* 217.

A different kind of fear descended on members of the Japanese community, not only fear of enemy attack but fear of reprisal because they **looked** like the enemy. Beginning December 7 and continuing over the course of the next few weeks, in San Mateo County and around the country, FBI agents began arresting Issei leaders and removing them from their communities, fearful they would spy for Japan or sabotage U.S. defense efforts. In a frightening and confusing time, heads of families were suddenly arrested and taken away.

Yoneko (Inouye) Arimoto was working with her father, mother, and brother in the family's greenhouse in Redwood City that Sunday morning. She remembered a group of people, including police officers and a judge, coming into the greenhouse and leading the family out. Confused because they had not even heard the news about Pearl Harbor, they watched as her father was taken to an undisclosed location by authorities. The family had no contact with him for more than two weeks.[5]

Ministers, Japanese language school officials, newspaper workers, employees of Japanese corporations, and leaders of Japanese organizations were all suspect and were whisked away from their homes and families without warning. Harumi "Harry" Higaki, whose family grew cut flowers in Redwood City before the war, remembered, "My

dad was picked up by the FBI in the first wave. So it was within the first few days after Pearl Harbor was attacked that he was taken into detention, and he wasn't given too much time to pack up…Since I was the oldest, I had to take over…It certainly wasn't fair. It certainly wasn't justified – the way it all happened."[6]

The U.S. government froze bank accounts of all Japanese as well as Japanese American citizens, financially crippling many families who had their accounts with them. Throughout Japanese communities along the West Coast, families began destroying or hiding any traces of ties to Japan. They burned or buried books, magazines, and family photographs so no one would question their loyalty to America. Kyoko (Takeshita) Sasano recalled, "My father would bring [our Japanese books and records] outside and burn them, and it would smell, and it smelled so bad. He burned some in the wood stove." Others gave away or stored valuable keepsakes such as heirloom *kimono* and *samurai* swords. Edes (Nakashima) Enomoto, who came from a family of flower growers, recounted, "We had [*samurai*] swords and all that kind of stuff, you know. We had to get rid of those, so we went to Stanford, and we knew a professor there, and he kept them for us."[7]

On Monday, December 8, the first day after the bombing, at the president's request, Congress

---

[5] Yoneko (Inouye) Arimoto, interview by Yasuko "Ann" (Ishida) Ito, San Mateo, Calif., February 11, 1996.

[6] H. Higaki, interview by yamada.

[7] Kyoko (Takeshita) Sasano, interview by Yasuko "Ann" (Ishida) Ito, San Mateo, Calif., January 24, 1994; and Edes (Nakashima) Enomoto, interview by gayle k. yamada, Atherton, Calif., October 21, 1997.

declared war against Japan. Tsukasa Matsueda, a San Mateo High School student at the time, remembered, "We had to listen to the speech given by [President] Franklin Roosevelt. We all went to the auditorium, and that was very, very uncomfortable." Nevertheless, he recounted, a few of the teachers said, "This is a war between nations, not between people." At Sequoia High School in Redwood City, fifteen-year old Jim Hiroshi Nakano recalled there were about fifty or sixty Nisei students. "We also had a Japanese Students Club. We made a public statement stating our loyalty to the United States in spite of all the other propaganda that was going on."[8]

Hideyoshi "Hid" Kashima, a junior high school student in Redwood City, returned to school as usual and, for the first time, realized his Japanese ancestry separated him from his classmates. Up until then, his Caucasian peers had accepted him and invited him to birthday parties and other social functions, but, on December 8, no one would even speak to him and no Caucasian wanted to be his friend any longer. The memory has remained seared in his brain more than fifty years later.[9]

At San Mateo Junior College, student body president Cliff Pierce addressed his fellow students at an assembly, asking them to remain calm and not overreact. He remembered that, in spite of his plea, many students–and many instructors as well–immediately signed up for military service.[10]

Burlingame resident Elizabeth Howat Curtis remembered most what she called "panic" during the days immediately following the attack:

> It was such high level of fear. One of the first things that happened was sandbagging and putting machine guns in placements on each side of the Crystal Springs dam and blocking off Skyline. In those days there was no [I-] 280 [freeway], of course, and Skyline was the main way into the city besides El Camino. They blocked that off because they were afraid of sabotage, and if that dam was ever blown, it would have been devastating because San Francisco and San Mateo counties would have no water. That was our water supply.[11]

Fear of attack and sabotage by the Japanese were rampant. As Frank Stanger of the San Mateo County Historical Association later explained, "In this war, for the first time in over a hundred years, Americans were threatened with foreign invasion and this Peninsula was in the center of the potential invasion coast." Hillsborough resident Paul Fagan personally financed the construction of an observation tower just west of San Mateo on Skyline Boulevard. Called "Fagan's Tower," it was

---

[8] Tsukasa Matsueda, interview by gayle k. yamada, San Mateo, Calif., October 24, 1997; and Jim Hiroshi Nakano, interview by Yasuko "Ann" (Ishida) Ito, San Mateo, Calif., March 7, 1996.
[9] H. Kashima, interview by Fukami.
[10] Postel, *Centennial History*, 217-218.
[11] Elizabeth Howat Curtis, interview by Yasuko "Ann" (Ishida) Ito, San Bruno, Calif., August 1, 1996.

staffed until 1943, with volunteers phoning in every visible aircraft to a screening center in San Francisco. Blackouts were imposed because of worries that enemy Japanese would be able to bomb areas that were visible from the night sky. Schools adopted blackout procedures and conducted air raid drills.[12]

In the Japanese American community on the Peninsula, there was another kind of fear. In San Mateo, high school student Tsukasa Matsueda observed the change. "We perceived ourselves as Americans but, of course, the others looked at us like Japanese. For example, teachers and other students would look at us–though they didn't do anything hostile, there was a definite coolness." Many Japanese American students, overwhelmed by the racism and taunting, finally stopped going to school.[13]

And it was not just at school. Pescadero resident Kaoru Yoshifuji, who was twenty-eight at the time, recalled, "I was going to San Mateo and in Half Moon Bay there was a garage which had a sign, 'No Japs [sic].' In San Mateo, the Fat Boy Barbeque had a sign, 'No Japs [sic].'"

Kimiye Ota's husband Satoru was physically attacked. "When the war broke out, some of the gardeners were told, 'Jap [sic], go home,' and tomatoes were thrown and on the way home in Baywood, tomatoes and eggs were thrown," said Kimiye Ota. "Mr. Ota [my husband] came home covered with eggs and tomatoes." Long-time San Mateo resident Yoshi (Sato) Mizono remembered the son of a prominent leader in Half Moon Bay seeding the driveways of Japanese families there with nails.[14]

Many families still had no idea where the FBI had taken their husbands and fathers. Most worried about the future and especially the fate of the Japanese immigrants who by law had been denied American citizenship. Yon Kawakita, then eighteen years old, voiced those early concerns about his parents, both of whom were non-citizens. Kawakita feared his parents would be imprisoned and even shipped back to Japan. He realized that he, an American citizen, was being treated the same way–"just like an alien!"[15]

The public, including many influential people, began to demand government action against the Japanese. Just two weeks after the attack on Pearl Harbor, the Agricultural Committee of the Los Angeles Chamber of Commerce recommended that all Japanese nationals in the United States be put under federal control. That recommendation mirrored sentiments from both the Western

---

[12] Frank Stanger, Ph.D., as quoted in Postel, *Centennial History*, 217-218; Postel, *Centennial History*, 219.

[13] T. Matsueda, interview by yamada.

[14] Baywood is the area west of El Camino Real, between Crystal Springs Road to the north and Notre Dame Avenue to the south. Also, Kaoru Yoshifuji, interview by Yasuko "Ann" (Ishida) Ito, San Mateo, Calif., March 23, 1995; and Kimiye Ota, interview by Yasuko "Ann" (Ishida) Ito, San Mateo, Calif., March 8, 1994; and Y. Mizono, interview by yamada, March 25, 1998.

[15] Some were taken to county facilities and released after a week or two. Others were taken to Department of Justice internment camps in places such as Santa Fe, New Mexico; or Crystal City, Texas; or other isolated areas, and incarcerated for months or years. Also, Y. Kawakita, interview by yamada, March 2, 1998.

Growers Association and the Grower-Shipper Vegetable Association, which had earlier accused the Japanese of cheap labor and unfair competition. A *Saturday Evening Post* magazine article quoted a Grower-Shipper official as saying, "We're charged with wanting to get rid of the Japs [*sic*] for selfish reasons. We might as well be honest. We do. It's a question of whether the white man lives on the Pacific Coast or the brown man. They came into this valley to work, and they stayed to take over."[16]

As the political anti-Japanese propaganda grew, so did anti-Japanese sentiment on a very personal level. Many Japanese found it increasingly difficult to find employment. Redwood City resident Masako (Hanyu) Iwase, then twenty-two, realized she could not get a job, so she applied for unemployment benefits. "The man who was interviewing me was shocked because he said Japanese as a whole never come to apply for unemployment. Then he said, 'I'm glad you came.' So a bunch of us went together. I got my last check after I went into camp."[17]

Satoye "Sally" (Kawakita) Tanouye, who was about twenty-five years old at the time, remembered the people who worked with her were shocked at how she was treated. "I worked at

the State Board of Equalization in [the] San Jose office, and December 7 was the bombing, and on Monday, December 8 around 9:30 or 10:00 a.m., George R. Reilly of the Board of Equalization from San Francisco came down to San Jose and said to me, 'Since Japan bombed Pearl Harbor, you are no longer employed.' I was fired the day after the bombing, and later I found out that those who were working in Sacramento for the State Department were able to work until shortly before evacuation."[18]

On December 29, U.S. Attorney General Francis Biddle ordered all enemy aliens in the Western states to surrender all contraband, which included radios with shortwave bands; cameras; binoculars; and a variety of weapons, such as guns, swords, and knives.

Civilian Kazuo "Kay" Mori remembered rushing to the draft board along with his Caucasian friends to sign up for the army and fight for his country. He was crushed when his friends were accepted and he was rejected, classified as 4-C. All Japanese American men were classified 4-C, that is, "enemy alien," beginning March 30, 1942.[19]

Those Japanese Americans already in the military were discharged, assigned duties that did not require carrying weapons, put on kitchen police

---

[16] Roger Daniels, Sandra C. Taylor, and Harry H.L. Kitano, *Japanese Americans: From Relocation to Redress* (Salt Lake City: University of Utah Press, 1986), xvi; *The Saturday Evening Post*, May 9, 1942, 66, as cited in Jacobus tenBroek, Edward N. Barnhart, and Floyd W. Matson, *Prejudice, War and the Constitution, Series: Japanese American Evacuation and Resettlement, Vol. 3* (Berkeley: University of California Press, 1968), 80.

[17] Masako (Hanyu) Iwase, interview by Yasuko "Ann" (Ishida) Ito, San Mateo, Calif., February 22, 1994.

[18] Satoye "Sally" (Kawakita) Tanouye, interview by Yasuko "Ann" (Ishida) Ito, Redwood City, Calif., February 21, 1995.

[19] Kazuo "Kay" Mori, interview by Dianne Fukami, San Francisco, Calif., March 8, 1996.

duties, or given menial tasks. William Nosaka, already in the army, said when he first heard about Pearl Harbor, "I was one of the first ones that wanted to go overseas...I was going to fight those 'Japs,' as you call them." But, he said, "The army told me I can't go. And I argued like hell. I said, 'These are my buddies. I can't leave them!' And they wouldn't allow it...because I'm Japanese, and all Japanese are supposed to be traitors."[20]

The momentum calling for removal of the Japanese increased. While the Department of Justice, as late as February 10, 1942, "was unwilling to recommend the evacuation of citizens," the War Department responded to the growing tension. California Congressman Leland Ford of Los Angeles, on January 6, 1942, wrote Secretary of State Cordell Hull, calling for the removal of all those of Japanese ancestry, citizen and alien alike, from the West Coast. California Attorney General Earl Warren called the Japanese situation in his state the "Achilles heel of the entire civilian

defense effort" and warned that, unless something was done, there would be another Pearl Harbor. The California State Personnel Board decided to bar all people of Japanese ancestry from civil service positions and dismissed those already employed.

The Department of Justice, on January 29, designated the first of 135 "prohibited areas"–the San Francisco waterfront area and the Los Angeles Municipal Airport–and ordered German, Italian, and Japanese aliens to vacate them in less than a month. A few days later, on February 4, following the recommendations of General John L. DeWitt, of the Western Defense Command, the Department of Justice designated "restricted areas" for enemy aliens and instituted a 9 p.m. to 6 a.m. curfew, allowing them to travel only to and from their jobs. Additionally, they could not travel farther than five miles from their homes, and anyone disobeying these regulations could be arrested.[21]

---

[20] W. Nosaka, interview by yamada.

[21] The Department of Justice and the War Department disagreed over the call for the eviction of those of Japanese ancestry, whether citizen or alien. While the War Department called for the exclusion of all people of Japanese ancestry, the Department of Justice was unwilling to recommend the removal of citizens. Until February 9, 1942, the Department of Justice implemented all recommendations made by the War Department. But, on February 10, the Department of Justice refused to order that citizens of Japanese ancestry as well as aliens be expelled from Bainbridge Island, Washington. In the end, however, General DeWitt's final recommendation for mass expulsion prevailed. With the signing of Executive Order 9066 on February 19, 1942, President Franklin D. Roosevelt transferred the power to handle all people of Japanese ancestry to the War Department, which resulted in confining all people of Japanese ancestry on the West Coast in imprisonment camps. The order did not target Japanese Americans but was clearly aimed at them. Morton Grodzins, *Americans Betrayed: Politics and the Japanese Evacuation* (Chicago: The University of Chicago Press, 1949), 236-273; Daniels, Taylor, and Kitano, *From Relocation to Redress*, xvi; and Commission on Wartime Relocation and Internment of Citizens, *Personal Justice Denied* (Washington, D.C.: U.S. Government Printing Office, 1982), 85.

Regarding General DeWitt's proclamation restricting movement in and out of specific military zones by German and Italian aliens and all persons of Japanese descent whether citizen or alien, there are memos and transcripts between General DeWitt and Assistant Secretary of War John J. McCloy (or their representatives) in which they come to an understanding

Michiko (Takeshita) Mukai's father, Manzo, a gardener who sometimes moonlighted as a dishwasher at night, had to sneak out of the house in San Mateo, causing his children to be scared for him. "I remember he came home one night or two whenever he did extra jobs doing dishwashing, and he came home one night with his headlights off, and they [security or civil patrol officers] were following him home," she said. "We were so frightened."[22]

In San Mateo, "Joseph" Iwasuke Rikimaru, who belonged to a group of prominent Japanese men that welcomed dignitaries from Japan, was picked up by the FBI just before his daughter's wedding. Groom Shigeharu "Shig" Takahashi asked local minister Reverend Sidney Buckman to try and persuade authorities to release the bride's father in time for the wedding. The minister's attempts were in vain. The bride, Best (Rikimaru) Takahashi, remembered, "He was getting ready to go to our wedding. They [FBI agents] came to our house trying to pin something on him, and they took him away. We didn't know where. After, we went through with the wedding, but we had someone else [a close family friend, Mr. Tamura] stand in my father's place." Shig Takahashi added, "They talk about the Gestapo and all that, but the way they came in, and the way they treated you, you know, the United States can't be very proud, either."[23]

The American Legion chapter in Portland, Oregon, circulated a resolution calling for the removal of all enemy aliens and all Japanese regardless of citizenship. West Coast congressmen, on February 13, sent a letter to President Roosevelt urging the removal of all persons of Japanese ancestry from California, Oregon, and Washington. The next day the Native Sons of the Golden West called for eviction of all Japanese, regardless of citizenship status. On February 16, the California Joint Immigration Committee recommended all Japanese be taken off the Pacific Coast. General DeWitt declared that "a Jap's a Jap," [sic] and strongly urged removal of all Japanese

---

that permits could be issued to Germans and Italians eligible to travel in and out of restricted areas, but not to people of Japanese ancestry and that the proclamation would be worded in such a way so as to appear as though it were constitutional. So those Germans or Italians who were on the FBI list as "potentially dangerous" were not given permits, but those not on the lists could be issued permits. Jack Herzig, electronic correspondence to gayle k. yamada, February 6, 2002; Aiko Herzig-Yoshinaga, electronic correspondence to gayle k. yamada, February 11, 2002, April 3, 2002, and April 9, 2002; and Aiko Herzig-Yoshinaga and Jack Herzig, electronic correspondence to gayle k. yamada, March 8, 2002, March 17, 2002.

Many years later, then-U.S. Attorney General Francis Biddle later expressed regret at the way Japanese Americans were treated. In his memoirs, he wrote, "American citizens of Japanese origin were not even handled like aliens of the other enemy nationalities—Germans and Italians—on a selective basis, but as untouchables, a group who could not be trusted and had to be shut up only because they were of Japanese descent..." Francis Biddle, *In Brief Authority* (New York: Doubleday & Co., 1962), 212-213, as cited in Michi Weglyn, *Years of Infamy: The Untold Story of America's Concentration Camps* (New York: William Morrow and Company, Inc., 1976), 68.

[22] Michiko (Takeshita) Mukai, interview by Yasuko "Ann" (Ishida) Ito, San Mateo, Calif., January 20, 1994.

[23] Best (Rikimaru) Takahashi, interview by gayle k. yamada, San Mateo, Calif., January 11, 2000; and Shigeharu "Shig" Takahashi, interview by gayle k. yamada, San Mateo, Calif., January 11, 2000.

from the West Coast, even though the Justice Department maintained it could identify, locate, and confine individual suspects without forcing a mass removal of the Japanese community.[24]

On February 19, 1942, President Roosevelt signed Executive Order 9066, authorizing Secretary of War Henry L. Stimson to establish military areas that were off-limits to any person who would be viewed as a threat. General DeWitt was given authority to implement the order. This order and DeWitt's role combined to shape the course of Japanese American history. Under DeWitt's direction, Colonel Karl Bendetsen established the Wartime Civil Control Administration (WCCA) and opened sixty-six offices on the West Coast to undertake the removal of all people of Japanese ancestry. This happened despite a congressional committee's recommendation against confinement, even though the committee concluded there was a "military necessity" to force the mass eviction of the entire Japanese community.[25]

On March 2, General DeWitt issued Public Proclamation Number One, which designated military areas along the West Coast. It also stated that certain people may have to be excluded from those areas, which included a broad strip of the coast running from the southern part of Arizona up through the western halves of California, Oregon, and Washington. The proclamation further stated that, if the situation required it, German and Italian aliens, or any person of Japanese ancestry, alien and citizen alike, could be excluded.

At first it was a shock to the people of Japanese ancestry that the eviction orders would include the Nisei, that is, American-born citizens. There was a degree of understanding that the foreign-born Issei may have to be removed, but many Nisei never felt their own loyalty and citizenship would be questioned. Tsukasa Matsueda, born a U.S. citizen, said, "Issei took [eviction] as a matter of course—'We are the enemy aliens.' They understood. For us here, it was hard to believe, you know, because why are we being evacuated?"[26]

It soon became clear that the exclusion order would not be enforced against German and Italian aliens, only against those of Japanese ancestry, regardless of citizenship. Yon Kawakita said, "We got our orders to evacuate and, of course, the [Italian] family next door, they were kind of worried they'd have to go." That family stayed, though. At the time, Kawakita said, it never crossed his mind to ask, "Hey, how come they're not going?!" although he wondered why he, an American citizen, was being removed.[27]

---

[24] Daniels, Taylor, and Kitano, *From Relocation to Redress*, 82; and Sandra C. Taylor, *Jewel of the Desert: Japanese American Internment at Topaz* (Berkeley: University of California Press, 1993), 46.

[25] Taylor, *Jewel of the Desert*, 50-51. The Tolan Committee, headed by U.S. Congressman John H. Tolan, began a series of hearings along the West Coast to investigate "national defense migration," but extended its charge to include the forced eviction of those deemed "enemy aliens."

[26] T. Matsueda, interview by yamada.

[27] Y. Kawakita, interview by yamada, March 2, 1998.

The military and the U.S. government still had no plan where the Japanese would go. War Relocation Authority (WRA) Director Milton Eisenhower, on April 7, met with the governors or representatives of the Western states to ascertain whether they would accept the displaced Japanese. Only Colorado Governor Ralph Carr and Utah Attorney General Grover Giles offered to cooperate. The others rejected the idea of a Japanese presence in their states. No California officials attended the meeting.[28]

The Japanese were encouraged at first to leave voluntarily, which meant moving out of the designated military zones along the West Coast and relocating further inland. One hundred thirty-nine San Mateans took advantage of this alternative. Edes (Nakashima) Enomoto spent the war years with her family in Colorado. Although they were not behind barbed wire, she said she was still waiting. "It's a funny thing. You get your brain in gear and say, 'When the time comes, they'll let us go.' We never had hopes and saying, 'Oh, it's going to end'…because after two years go by, you don't have any hopes. You just say, well, when the time comes, the government says, 'Go home,' we'll go home."[29]

Voluntary resettlement was feasible only for those who had the means and ability to do so.

"We couldn't leave unless we had enough money so we wouldn't be a hardship," said Enomoto. At the time of the Pearl Harbor bombing, she had been married for two years and living in Redwood City, where the Enomoto family had a big nursery. Her mother and siblings and also her husband's mother and siblings all decided to move to Denver, where a Buddhist priest opened his home to them. "In Redwood City, [we took] the last train out. They said, 'If you don't get on that train, you don't go'…We didn't have time to get all our possessions. We had to store everything where we could."[30]

Edes (Nakashima) Enomoto's father and her father-in-law Sadakusu Enomoto had been taken away earlier because they were both prominent men in the Japanese community in San Mateo. "We went to visit [my father-in-law] one day. [My husband William] cried. His father got real angry, you know, because he said, 'Men don't cry. Now you just go take my place and get going.'…That's the only time I saw him cry."[31]

Once the Enomotos arrived in Colorado, many members of the family found jobs as gardeners. Edes stayed at home with her two small children and felt she was lucky because the family could afford for her not to work. The people she encountered in Denver were "really nice and…

---

[28] For details of the meeting discussion, *see* Peter Irons, *Justice at War: The Story of the Japanese American Internment Cases* (Berkeley: University of California Press, 1983), 71-72.

[29] General J. L. DeWitt, U.S. Department of War, *Final Report Japanese Evacuation from the West Coast 1942*, Headquarters Western Defense Command and Fourth Army, Office of the Commanding General, Presidio of San Francisco, Calif. (Washington, D.C.: Government Printing Office, 1943), 364; and E. Enomoto, interview by yamada.

[30] E. Enomoto, interview by yamada.

[31] E. Enomoto, interview by yamada.

polite. You know, a streetcar would be coming down the street, and you'd be coming up this way, and the guy sees you. He stops and waits, and says, 'Come on aboard.' And then you go to the grocery stores, and they don't just say, 'Thank you,'" she said. "They say, 'Thank you **kindly**.'"[32]

Nobuo and Notoko Higaki's family, flower growers from Redwood City, also resettled but they went to Idaho. The Higakis had been invited by the parents of the Japanese school teacher's wife in San Mateo County who owned a farm. "We had our own truck since we were in our business, the flower business," remembered son Harumi "Harry" Higaki, "and put our things in the truck and moved...The teacher...was waiting for us when we got to [Twin Falls], so it wasn't a situation where we were going to a place that was totally unfriendly or you didn't know anyone."[33]

The Higakis helped on the family's farm and, since there were so many of them, were hired to work on neighbors' farms as well. They lived upstairs in the large house, "but the dining area was too small to accommodate everyone, so we built our own shack on the side where we had our dining room, where we ate our meals, and then that's where we relaxed. We just went to sleep in the house," said Higaki.[34]

It was an arrangement of trust, for no money ever changed hands; the Higakis lived there "in exchange. There was no oral or written contract or anything, but we never got paid, and we worked on the farm."[35]

Though the Higakis adjusted to a different kind of farm life, the change in food was harder to accept. "They didn't have any Japanese grocery store, but there was a Japanese owner that ran a restaurant...We didn't have any difficulty getting rice," said Higaki, but "in those days, we ate more bread than rice...Cabbage and a lot of potato."[36]

Headlines of newspapers in a newsstand at Fourteenth and Broadway Streets in Oakland. February 27, 1942. *Photograph by Dorothea Lange, National Archives*

---

[32] E. Enomoto, interview by yamada.

[33] H. Higaki, interview by yamada.

[34] H. Higaki, interview by yamada.

[35] H. Higaki, interview by yamada.

[36] H. Higaki, interview by yamada.

Higaki only remembered a single discriminatory incident in Idaho. "We went out to this apple orchard during harvest time to pick apples, and I fell out of the ladder and had a gash, cut my face. It was [a] pretty ugly, pretty good-sized wound. So I went into town to the doctor. The first doctor I went to...to get treatment, and he says, 'Are you a Jap [sic]?' And he said, 'Get the hell out of here!' And so he kicked me out of the office." Other than that, Higaki remembered, "Those people in Idaho were pretty tolerant. Friendly."[37]

The Higakis were luckier than many. Most families did not have the resources or ability to just pick up and move to some unfamiliar destination. They were at the mercy of the government's actions.

In the meantime, a series of Public Proclamations and Civilian Exclusion Orders, including restrictions on travel and contraband, and a curfew had been issued, all addressing the Japanese and American-born Japanese. By March 27, Public Proclamation No. 4 prohibited any further voluntary relocation.

On April 1, April Fool's Day, instructions were posted along the West Coast, officially ordering people of Japanese ancestry to report for removal.

The Wartime Civil Control Administration divided the West Coast into 108 zones, each with about 250 Japanese families. Officials told

I think the hardest thing is losing your freedom—not being able...to pursue your education, leaving your fellow classmates, starting all over, so to speak, in a new environment, to not know what the future's going to be. There are many things that run through your mind at that time as to what's going to become of you. Here you're a citizen of the United States, you've never been to Japan, the only thing you hear about Japan is through your folks, and you're forced to leave!

— YONEO "YON" KAWAKITA[38]

the Japanese to bring only what they could carry, including bedding and linens, clothing, toilet articles, dishware, and other personal effects. No personal items or household goods could be shipped.

And they still did not know where they were going.

---

[37] H. Higaki, interview by yamada.
[38] Y. Kawakita, interview by yamada, March 2, 1998.

The one item I was sorry [we couldn't take] was a big, beautiful doll that was left on top of the piano. The children wanted to take it with them but it was too big, and I told the doll, "Please wait for us and guard all the belongings for us until we come back." The children were very sad, and they cried, but we had to part. I felt so sorry for the children.

We just left the car there and the pets that we had. We just let them loose. We couldn't do anything else. We had a duck, and we had to let it loose. Someone must have had a good duck dinner.

— AYA (MIYAKE) TAKAHASHI
a Japanese schoolteacher in Belmont before the war [39]

They only knew they had but a few weeks to pack, close down businesses, sell or lease their homes, and sell or dispose of household belongings and personal items. Signs advertising goods for sale popped up in the windows of homes and businesses owned by those of Japanese ancestry. Kyoko (Takeshita) Sasano poignantly remembered those bleak days:

We tried to sell all our goods, but people didn't buy them. Lot of the things, if they did buy, we had to sell it for less. And we had just bought a brand new car, a Nash, that was our first possession that we had bought. It was our pride and joy. Our parents had worked so hard for it, but we only had it for just a short time, and we had to sell it and practically give it away. [40]

Nursery owners with greenhouses, entrepreneurs with stores, farmers with crops and equipment—all had to be ready to leave on their appointed day. Pescadero farmer Kaoru Yoshifuji sold some farm equipment and a new tractor for fifteen hundred dollars and ended up giving away his four horses and two dogs. Other families, dismayed by the tight timeline and the situation over which they had no control, resorted to deliberately breaking and dumping household possessions rather than be exploited by the many bargain hunters who came to prey on the Japanese at this time. [41]

---

[39] Aya (Miyake) Takahashi, interview by Yasuko "Ann" (Ishida) Ito, San Mateo, Calif., November 15, 1994.
[40] K. Sasano, interview by Ito.
[41] K. Yoshifuji, interview by Ito.

For Tatsuye (Hamasaki) Haraguchi, then twenty-five years old, the prospect of incarceration was somewhat of a relief since no one would hire her husband as a gardener. She now no longer had to worry about how to feed her family.[42]

Fearing economic reprisals by the government, the California Chrysanthemum Growers Association had replaced Issei members of its board of directors with American-born Nisei. With the forced evacuation looming, the association office was in turmoil. The board hired J. Elmer Morrish, Vice President of the First National Bank of Redwood City, as its agent to represent the association and oversee its affairs. Morrish helped both members and non-members with their affairs during this forced evacuation period and throughout the war.[43]

San Mateo families were ordered to register at the Masonic Temple Building on Ellsworth Street on either Monday, May 4, or Tuesday, May 5. There, families received forms, a family identification number, and individual tags for every family member and every piece of luggage.

The next weeks, recalled Hamae (Tanizawa) Miyachi, then age thirty-eight and married with four children, were spent getting ready. "I had to stitch the bags to put in our belongings...I made

My sister comes home with a tag with a number on it, with the instructions that we have to go to put all of these tags on our luggage, what we could carry, when we go to the assembly center. And the only time that you go by numbers, other than your social security number, is when you go into the service or go to prison... To think that you're in that particular category without being in the service, the armed forces, I think it's quite traumatic...I think it's demeaning.

— YONEO "YON" KAWAKITA
a teenager when he was evacuated from San Mateo County[44]

all their bags and put in all our dishes and spoons and other utensils. I remember we had to bring a shallow metal pan...Oh my, it was so depressing. I felt like it was worse than being a beggar."[45]

---

[42] Tatsuye (Hamasaki) Haraguchi, interview by Yasuko "Ann" (Ishida) Ito, San Mateo, Calif., March 3, 1994.

[43] During the war years, Morrish performed many services at no cost. Among other things, he collected rents, inspected properties, corresponded with those incarcerated, signed numerous letters of recommendation for those who wanted to go into work release programs outside camp, negotiated sales of automobiles and other assets, and arranged shipments of personal possessions. James K. Mori, "J. Elmer Morrish," Exhibit for the "History of Japanese Americans in San Mateo County," February 2001-June 2001, San Mateo County History Museum, Redwood City, Calif., February 16, 2001.

[44] Y. Kawakita, interview by yamada, March 2, 1998.

[45] Hamae (Tanizawa) Miyachi, interview by gayle k. yamada and Yasuko "Ann" (Ishida) Ito, Mountain View, Calif., June 12, 1997.

Shigeharu "Shig" Takahashi (*on right*) shown in front of the Masonic Temple, waiting for the bus to Tanforan. May 9, 1942. *Photograph by Dave Neptune, courtesy of San Mateo Chapter, Japanese American Citizens League*

When the order came to be evicted, the Sato home became a staging area for those of Japanese ancestry along the coast to prepare to leave. Their home, on land they leased, was the white house on the right. Behind the house was French Men's Creek. *Circa 1940.*[46] *Courtesy of Yoshiko "Yoshi" [Sato] Mizono*

When word came they would be evicted, Yoshi (Sato) Mizono, who was living in Half Moon Bay at the time, remembered, "Our house became the center where they came to do vaccinations, immunizations...The doctors came from San Mateo and San Francisco." She also recalled that getting ready to relocate was trying. "A girl from class, her mother had a dress shop at home. She was my Sunday school teacher, and I went to her house to go buy some clothes, and [the mother] was there and I saw her, but she wouldn't answer the door."[47]

On May 7, 1942, in the *San Mateo Times*, the following message from the San Mateo County chapter of the Japanese American Citizens League was published:

A MESSAGE OF THANKS AND GRATITUDE...
TO THE CITIZENS OF SAN MATEO COUNTY

Shortly after December 7th, the Japanese residents of San Mateo County wholeheartedly expressed their willingness to aid in whatever war effort the United States called upon them to do. Their desire came as a natural result of living the American way of life and as a violent protest against anything that would try to destroy it.

Today as evacuation orders affect Japanese aliens and American Citizen Japanese, the sorrow at the thought of leaving their homes is eased by the knowledge that by cooperation and

[46] Yoshiko "Yoshi" (Sato) Mizono, letter to gayle k. yamada, April 27, 2002.
[47] Y. Mizono, interview by yamada, March 25, 1998.

sacrifice, they are aiding the United States war efforts.

They look forward to participating in the Foods for Victory program at the various resettlement areas. They hope that later they will materially add something to the flow of war supplies that is now bombarding the Axis aggressors. They are proud to continue sending their sons into the armed forces of the United States as a patriotic and privileged right.

The departing Japanese and American Citizen Japanese sincerely feel that these statements are in some way a measure of their gratitude for the friendship given them by the people of San Mateo County.

— *San Mateo County Japanese-American [sic] Citizens League* [48]

Yon Kawakita, then a high school senior, remembered leaving San Mateo High School for the last time. "After we turned in all our books and everything, we were walking to my car, and I saw these guys up there waving goodbye. It's a sad feeling. I don't know who they were, but they were up in the windows on the upper floor waving goodbye." The memory of the departure remains vividly painful even after all these years. [49]

Executive Order 9066 affected 891 people in San Mateo County, 133 of them American citizens under the age of twelve. By military decree, the county was to be cleared of all people of Japanese

ancestry by noon, Saturday, May 9, 1942. Formal eviction was scheduled for the preceding day.

On eviction day, the Japanese immigrants and their American-born children from San Mateo County gathered at the Masonic Temple, dressed in their Sunday best and bringing only what they could carry. Yoshi (Sato) Mizono who was there from the coastal town of Half Moon Bay, remembered, "Kind ladies from the San Mateo Congregational Church were at the Masonic Hall helping and serving us coffee and cookies." Parents told their children to take a good look around–it might be a long time before they saw home again. Then they silently began to board the buses. [50]

Fifteen-year old Jim Hiroshi Nakano remembered how heart-wrenching it was for him and his thirteen-year old brother Kei to leave their dog Topsy behind. "I remember the bus picked us up… We had a pet dog that we had to leave behind, and we just cried to see the dog by itself." Kei added, "It was really sad to see our poor dog looking so lost and not knowing what to do." [51]

Although it was a bus trip of only a few miles, the road to the Tanforan Assembly Center where they were destined symbolized a long journey from home and freedom to an alien environment and incarceration.

It would be three years before they were allowed to return home.

---

[48] *San Mateo* (Calif.) *Times*, May 7, 1942, 3.

[49] Y. Kawakita, interview by yamada, March 2, 1998.

[50] Yoshiko "Yoshi" (Sato) Mizono, letter to gayle k. yamada, May 18, 2000. The Congregational Church women were aided by Quakers from Santa Clara County. *San Mateo* (Calif.) *Times*, May 8, 1942, 4.

[51] J. Nakano, interview by Ito; and Kei Nakano, telephone conversation with Yasuko "Ann" (Ishida) Ito, December 5, 2001.

Exterior of Tanforan Assembly Center in San Mateo County from outside the fence. June 16, 1942.
Photograph by Dorothea Lange, National Archives[1]

---

[1] Early in April 1942, Lange began photographing the eviction and incarceration of those of Japanese ancestry for the WRA. She was assigned to cover Northern California. "What I photographed was the procedure, the process of processing," she said. "Everything [the Japanese and Japanese Americans] could possibly do for themselves, they did, asking the minimum, making practically no demands." She remembered the war years as one of her most intense times as a photographer. Milton Meltzer, *Dorothea Lange: A Photographer's Life* (New York: Farrar Straus Giroux, 1978), 240-241.

New York Times critic A.D. Coleman wrote about Lange, "She was precisely the right photographer for the job...She functioned in effect as our national eye of conscience in the internment camps. Her constant concerns–the survival of human dignity under impossible conditions, the confrontation of the system by the individual, and the helpless innocence of children–were perfectly suited to the subject." Lange was opposed to Executive Order 9066, and she had a few disagreements with military authorities. Fellow photographer Ansel Adams said she had "advanced political liberalism." That she sympathized with the plight of those of Japanese descent is well known. A.D. Coleman, *New York Times*, September 24, 1972, as quoted in Meltzer, *Dorothea Lange*, 242; and Karin Becker Ohrn, *Dorothea Lange and the Documentary Tradition* (Baton Rouge: Louisiana State University Press, 1980), 146.

CHAPTER 6

TANFORAN RACE TRACK:
THE FIRST STOP

First of S.M. County Japanese
Taken to Concentration Camp Today

— ARTICLE HEADLINE IN THE
SAN MATEO [CALIF.] *TIMES*
AND DAILY NEWS LEADER
San Mateo, Calif., May 8, 1942

They came by the busload, thousands of them. Family after family of people of Japanese ancestry, dressed in their best clothes, arrived at what had been the Tanforan Racetrack in San Bruno, California. Designated the Tanforan Assembly Center in April 1942, it became the temporary home of 7,816 people of Japanese descent, many of them American citizens. Most of its population came from San Francisco, the East Bay, and the Peninsula—including 891 from San Mateo County.

From the day President Franklin D. Roosevelt signed Executive Order 9066 on February 19, which essentially permitted the U.S. Army to remove some 110,000 people of Japanese ancestry from the West Coast, there was not enough time to build facilities needed to incarcerate them. As a temporary measure, the Wartime Civil Control Administration (WCCA)—a civilian branch of the army—set up fifteen assembly and detention centers, twelve of them in California.[2]

Four factors determined site selection: (1) adaptable pre-existing facilities suitable for shelter and community services; (2) immediate availability of power, light, and water; (3) access to road and rail services; and (4) space within the enclosure for recreation and other activities. Based on these criteria, the WCCA expropriated primarily racetracks and fairgrounds.[3]

---

[2] WRA figures show more than 110,000 people were forcibly evacuated from the West Coast and about 120,000 people were detained in designated government "relocation centers." War Relocation Authority Publication, May 1943, Council of Churches, Seattle, Box 15, Manuscripts and University Archives, University of Washington Libraries. Also, DeWitt, *Final Report*, VIII.

[3] DeWitt, *Final Report*, 151.

"There was freedom right outside of this fencing. Right in front. We could see all the people and their freedom...Home was so close, you see, and we didn't know how long we'd be here." —Maya Nagata Aikawa, incarcerated at Tanforan at age fifteen.[4] Unpublished pencil sketch, "The Other Side of the Fence," by Siberius Saito, who was held at Tanforan. 1942. *Courtesy of Kaoru "Ruth" Saito*

---

[4] Siberius Saito was born on a ship in the early 1900s as his mother was traveling to the United States from Japan. Before the war, he graduated from the University of California, Berkeley, with a degree in architecture. After the war, he settled in Waterloo, Iowa, where he and a partner had an architectural firm. Kaoru "Ruth" Saito, conversation with Yasuko "Ann" (Ishida) Ito, San Mateo, Calif., April 19, 2001. Maya Nagata Aikawa, interview by Dianne Fukami, Oakland, Calif., February 16, 1995.

The last family to arrive at the Tanforan Assembly Center from San Francisco on April 29, 1942. *Photograph by Dorothea Lange, National Archives*

The government caption to this photograph reads, "Family of Japanese ancestry arrives at assembly center at Tanforan Race Track. Evacuees will be transferred later to War Relocation Authority centers where they will be housed for the duration." April 29, 1942. *Photograph by Dorothea Lange, National Archives*

Japanese and Japanese Americans arrived at Tanforan two days after it opened. Here, they lined up outside the mess hall at Tanforan, in front of newly-built barracks. April 29, 1942. *Photograph by Dorothea Lange, National Archives*

It's a sinful waste of human energy, ability, brains, and productivity to lock up thousands of people and force them to do nothing.

— TOMOYE "TAMI"
(NOZAWA) TAKAHASHI

twenty-seven years old when she was incarcerated in Tanforan[5]

The Tanforan Assembly Center was in the shadow of San Bruno Mountain, just south of San Francisco. 1942. Unpublished pencil sketch by Siberius Saito. *Courtesy of Kaoru "Ruth" Saito*

The U.S. Army claimed that having the assembly centers so "close to home"–the army's own words–yielded several advantages for those who would be held there. First, they could settle last-minute financial and property matters. Second, they faced only minimal travel. And third, they could accustom themselves to group life in a familiar climate.

Tanforan became the second largest assembly center in population, after Santa Anita in Southern California. A shopping center today, Tanforan is located in San Bruno, in San Mateo County, the county immediately south of San Francisco. It is bordered by Noor Avenue on the north, Forest Lane on the south, El Camino Real on the west, and the Southern Pacific railroad on the east.

Buses carrying Japanese and Japanese Americans began rolling into Tanforan in late April 1942. As the buses pulled up to the race-track, barbed wire, watchtowers, and armed guards greeted the passengers. At the entrance, they underwent an induction process that included registering all family members and undergoing searches for contraband items such as weapons and liquor. After the search, each person was subjected to a medical examination. It was a vivid memory more than fifty years later for Yoshio "Yo" Kasai, who came to Tanforan from Oakland:

First thing, I felt like a prisoner.
Because you felt the barbed wire fences,

---

[5] Tomoye "Tami" (Nozawa) Takahashi, interview by gayle k. yamada, San Francisco, Calif., April 15, 2002.

the guard towers, you felt like being in a prison camp. I don't know how it feels like being in a prison camp but watching movies, you think this has gotta be like it. I guess the first thing that they gave us was the number, just like a prison. Next, I think we had our fingers printed. All ten of them... I think we were in that [entrance] area about one hour, an hour-and-a-half, because they pat-searched everybody. And the women were pat-searched, too. I don't know what they expected us to have, maybe guns or bombs, or whatever. They pat-searched us. It's an unusual feeling to have them put hands on you, and it's the first time I had it done to me. I think everyone felt the same way. We were treated like prisoners.[6]

For many, one of the most dehumanizing parts of the experience was still to come: housing assignments. WCCA policy allotted a space of two hundred square feet per couple, in dimensions of ten-by-twenty feet. In practice, however, the general rule of thumb for the assembly centers was that eight-person families were placed in twenty-by-twenty-foot rooms, six people in twelve-by-twenty-foot rooms, and four people in eight-by-twenty-foot rooms. At Tanforan, the newly constructed barracks had larger rooms; the older horse stables were smaller, measuring only nine-

My first impression was, "This is terrible." After we got settled, I just walked away and walked to the grandstand, and I cried, because after being in the Boy Scouts and never having been to Japan, and here I looked over my shoulder, and there is El Camino and airplanes taking off.

— JIM KAJIWARA
*twenty-six years old
when he was incarcerated*[7]

by-twenty feet. These confined spaces served as both sleeping and living areas for the six months people were housed involuntarily at the racetrack and stables.[8]

Families were kept together when possible, and bachelors—first assigned sleeping quarters among the general population—were later separated

---

[6] The federal government lists the dates Tanforan was opened and occupied as April 28, 1942-October 13, 1942. DeWitt, *Final Report*, 227; and Yoshio "Yo" Kasai, interview by Dianne Fukami, San Leandro, Calif., February 1, 1995.

[7] Jim Kajiwara, interview by Yasuko "Ann" (Ishida) Ito, San Francisco, Calif., April 26, 1994.

[8] DeWitt, *Final Report*, 186.

These three older prisoners just registered and are resting before being assigned to living quarters. The large tag worn by the woman on the right indicated special consideration because she was old or infirm. April 29, 1942. *Photograph by Dorothea Lange, National Archives*

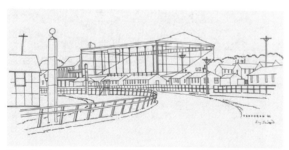

How the barracks in the infield of the racetrack appeared to inmate Siberius Saito, who had been trained as an architect before the war. 1942. Unpublished pencil sketch. *Courtesy of Kaoru "Ruth" Saito*

into the grandstand area where a makeshift dormitory housed hundreds of them, cot to cot. In a diary he kept during his days at Tanforan, then-bachelor Charles Kikuchi wrote:

> The Grandstand is almost filled with single men and it probably is the most interesting place in camp. There are about 500 men in there and when they all take their shoes off, the odor that greets you is terrific. What a stench! They don't have any fresh air circulating around and the old clothes and closeness of body smells doesn't help out any.[9]

Eventually, Tanforan had 180 buildings, twenty-six of them converted horse stalls. The living quarters were divided into "blocks," each consisting of six hundred to eight hundred people. Each block had its own restroom facilities, washroom and, when possible, mess hall.[10]

Although some barracks had been hastily built in the center of the track, by the time prisoners began arriving, construction was still underway. For this reason, many families had to live in converted horse stalls: half had housed the horse and the other half, the tack and fodder. Tomoye "Tami" (Nozawa) Takahashi, who lived at Tanforan with her husband, father, sister, and sister-in-law,

---

[9] Charles Kikuchi, *The Kikuchi Diary*, ed. John Modell (Urbana: University of Illinois Press, 1993), 64. Kikuchi was recruited by the Japanese American Evacuation and Resettlement Study (JERS), a sociology project at the University of California, Berkeley, that studied the implications of confinement on the Japanese and Japanese American community. In his observations, he also reported gambling in the grandstand, as well as allegations of solicitations by Japanese prostitutes. Kikuchi's published diary is an abridged version of the one he kept for JERS. John Modell, an academician interested in ethnic communities, edited the document for publication. Official records put the bachelor grandstand population close to six hundred.
[10] Taylor, *Jewel of the Desert*, 65.

Male prisoners, shown here digging a drainage tank in front of horse stalls, handled maintenance work for eight dollars per month for a forty-eight hour week. June 15, 1942. *Photograph by Dorothea Lange, National Archives*

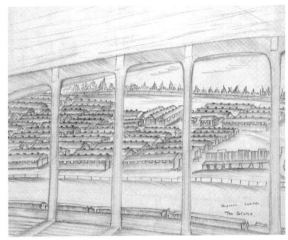

The view from the Grandstand as prisoner Tadashi Sakuma saw it. 1942. Unpublished pencil sketch. *Courtesy of Tadashi Sakuma*[12]

recalled, "Where one pedigreed horse was stalled, five adults...were assigned there." Kimiye Ota, a young mother then who said she was one of the last people forced to evacuate San Mateo, said that, in her case, "The pail for feeding the horses was in the stall with the horse's name. The name on the container was Ginger." Although the stalls had been whitewashed prior to the arrival of their new human occupants, cleaning had been minimal. Hay, horsehair, and dung were embedded in the newly whitewashed walls.[11]

Maya Nagata Aikawa, who went to Tanforan with her sister and widowed mother, remembered how her mother instructed both

Life at Tanforan Assembly Center was designed by the government to accustom the so-called "residents" to life behind barbed wire. 1942. Unpublished pencil sketch by Siberius Saito. *Courtesy of Kaoru "Ruth" Saito*

---

[11] T. Takahashi, interview by yamada; and K. Ota, interview by Ito.

[12] Sakuma was born in San Mateo on December 28, 1918 and went to Japan as a youngster, returning to the United States in 1938. He finished his education first at Turnbull School, then San Mateo High School. Sakuma was drafted into the U.S. Army just before Pearl Harbor but was discharged after World War II broke out. Sakuma was twenty-three years old when he was removed to Tanforan. Tadashi Sakuma, conversation with Yasuko "Ann" (Ishida) Ito, San Mateo, Calif., April 21, 2002.

These former horse stalls were now government-mandated "homes" to thousands of people of Japanese ancestry. April 29, 1942. *Photograph by Dorothea Lange, National Archives*

The government caption to this photograph reads, "Barrack home in one of the long lines of converted horse stalls. Each family unit consists of two small rooms–the rear room without outside door or window." June 16, 1942. *Photograph by Gretchen Van Tassel, National Archives*

daughters to sit on their suitcases outside their newly-assigned stable so she could use the disinfectant she had brought with her to "Lysol" the whole room.[13]

The stench of horse manure was overpowering. Over the years, manure had become encrusted on the floor and seeped between the floorboard cracks, collecting underneath the stables. Twenty-three-year old Redwood City native Yoneko (Inouye) Arimoto had a severe reaction. "The manure was coming out from the wood...My eyes would be swollen, and I was allergic to it...I never knew anything like that before, like swollen mouth and swollen eyes when I got up."[14]

Efforts to scrub the floor and walls with warm water and soap only made the smell worse.

Some enterprising people covered the floors with cardboard or pieces of linoleum ripped out of the racetrack's clubhouse in attempts to block out the odor from below. Twenty-two-year old Masako (Hanyu) Iwase who was employed working as a domestic worker when war broke out, remembered her mother collecting eucalyptus leaves to hang on the wall to try to mask the horse and manure odors. Oakland native Yoshio "Yo" Kasai tried to sleep that first night at Tanforan with a bar of Lux soap under his nose. At eleven years of age, Janet Miyata understood what the indignity of it all symbolized. "When I saw the horse stables, it was so grim. I thought, well, by that time, I had gotten the realization that the Japanese people were not looked upon with great favor. Even at

---

[13] M. Aikawa, interview by Fukami.
[14] Y. Arimoto, interview by Ito.

my age, finally it dawned on me, and I remember saying right out loud, 'Well, if you had any doubts as to what they think of us, this is it. This filthy horse stables.'"[15]

Shazie (Yamaguchi) Tabata and her husband Nobu had bought a house the month before Pearl Harbor was attacked. Since larger families were assigned to the barracks, she tried to avoid setting up home in the stables by voluntarily requesting to live with her husband's parents and brother, in addition to her own husband and child.[16]

The barracks, though clean, still had many drawbacks. They were flimsy and, as the unseasoned wood used in their construction shrank, cracks developed and let in the wind and cold air. Plus, the "apartments" had partitions that went up only three-quarters of the way rather than all the way to the ceiling. As a result, there was no privacy; people could hear each other twenty-four hours a day–intimate conversations, domestic quarrels, and crying babies.

Kei Nakano, thirteen years old at the time, recalled his experience with the lack of privacy and his misplaced pajamas. "Someone had blown out the fuse and I couldn't find my pajamas [in the dark]. I said, 'Where is my pajamas?' Well, [my aunt] had put them in the pillow, stuffed it in

Tadashi Sakuma sketched "Our Sweet Home" at Tanforan, depicting the interior of his horse stall. September 25, 1942. Unpublished pencil sketch. *Courtesy of Tadashi Sakuma*

---

[15] M. Iwase, interview by Ito; Y. Kasai, interview by Fukami; and Janet Miyata, interview by Yasuko "Ann" (Ishida) Ito, San Mateo, Calif., May 12, 1995. Miyata's father was Japanese and her mother was Caucasian. Mrs. Miyata was not forced to go to Tanforan since she was Caucasian, but her husband and *hapa* daughters had no choice. So Mr. and Mrs. Miyata and their four girls chose to go to Tanforan as a family. The term *"hapa"* derives from the Hawaiian phrase *"hapa haole,"* which literally means "half foreigner." Once considered derogatory, it has become a simple and acceptable way to describe a person of partial Asian or Pacific Islander ancestry. Hapa Issues Forum website, www.hapaissuesforum.org.
[16] S. Tabata, interview by Fukami.

there. I couldn't find them. Next morning every-body in the whole barracks knew that I couldn't find my pajamas. They asked, 'Did you find your pajamas?'"[17]

Those now forced to stay at Tanforan for an uncertain length of time set out to make their living quarters as comfortable as they could. General DeWitt's final report on the removal of Japanese from the West Coast indicated that each "apart-ment" was furnished with army steel cots, blankets, pillows, and mattresses. In fact, Tanforan prisoners received cots and little else. For mattresses, they were given canvas bags of ticking and told to go to the hay pile to fill them up. Yon Kawakita, who was eighteen when he went to Tanforan, remem-bered, "We used to shove [the hay] in and take them back. And then, after the first night, you had to take it back and get some more because it got so patted down." Many people still remember how the hay poked out of the ticking, jabbed them and made noise with every movement. For those with allergies, this signaled the beginning of runny noses and watery eyes that lasted for months.[18]

The prisoners were shocked by their new living quarters. The earliest arrivals found that the communal washrooms, laundry rooms, and latrines had not yet been completed, and that the grandstand had the only functioning toilets. People who lived farther away had to allow time both for the walk and the wait in line.

"If we lined up, we could claim bags with ties on them. And we were directed to go to heaps of straw to fill these bags with straw. That was to be used as a mattress, but the straw blew away because Tanforan is located in a wind tunnel."
—Tomoye "Tami" (Nozawa) Takahashi shared a horse stall with four other adults in her family at Tanforan. 1942.[19] *National Archives*

Those who arrived at Tanforan during the rainy days of April had to tromp through ankle-deep mud. Most people had not brought boots and thus had difficulty walking through the suck-ing mud. Drainage was poor; the odor of sewage and manure constantly filled the air. Everything was dirty. Yoshio "Yo" Kasai said that among his family members, his mother was affected the most. "My mother just sat down and cried. She just cried her heart out. She really felt like she was

[17] Kei Nakano, interview by Yasuko "Ann" (Ishida) Ito, San Mateo, Calif., March 7, 1996.
[18] DeWitt, *Final Report*, 1886; and Y. Kawakita, interview by yamada, March 2, 1998.
[19] T. Takahashi, interview by yamada.

being treated like a criminal. Japanese people are very proud people, and they are not used to this kind of treatment. I think her heart was really upset. We were all upset, but mostly my mother, because she was a lady, a real lady. She just didn't feel like she belonged in a place like that."[20]

To add to the dehumanizing experience, in the beginning, all meals for the thousands of people were served in one big mess hall on the ground floor of the grandstand. People had to bring their own eating utensils and stand in line with more than seventy-eight hundred other people also waiting to get their food, cafeteria-style. Shazie (Yamaguchi) Tabata, a young mother when she was evicted, still has not forgotten what it was like. "Standing in line for food. That was tragic for me, most tragic. Holding out your plate to be filled, and they actually threw it at us, you know. We didn't like that," she said. "I think that was the hardest part."[21]

The diary of seventeen-year old Isabel Miyata from San Francisco provides insight to life behind barbed wire. Her entry on May 3, 1942 reads, "The only thing I'm complaining about is the meals—not the food—but the system. Everyone goes early to stand in line—if you don't, you don't get a table or your share of the food. So the meals get earlier every day and you get hungry before you go to bed."[22]

Many, however, **did** complain about the food. Prisoners themselves handled preparation, but many did not have the experience to cook for the masses. In his memoirs, George Fukui, a cook's helper, wrote, "My first job was to learn to cook huge quantities of rice in twenty-gallon galvanized circular wash tubs with makeshift wooden lids. It's amazing that we could cook rice just as we did at home in large quantities in those makeshift pots." In the beginning, the kitchens ran out of food before everyone could be fed. The daily food allowance was fifty cents a day per person, but the Tanforan Assembly Center administration spent

Standing in line waiting for their shift to eat, prisoners had to bring their dishes and eating utensils in bags to protect them from the dust. After they ate, they individually washed their dishes since dishwashing facilities in the mess halls proved inadequate. Many people preferred the second eating shift because second helpings sometimes were available. The groups were rotated every week. Eventually eighteen mess halls were established at Tanforan. *Photograph by Dorothea Lange, National Archives*

[20] Y. Kasai, interview by Fukami.
[21] S. Tabata, interview by Fukami.
[22] Isabel Miyata, unpublished diary entry, Tanforan, Calif., May 3, 1942.

an average of only thirty-seven cents per person. The basic army rations reflected no sensitivity to the dietary preferences of the elderly Japanese. People who lived there remembered being fed tripe, liver, beans, sauerkraut, canned luncheon meat, and canned sausages.[23]

Kei Nakano, who was living at Horgan Ranch in Redwood City before he was removed to Tanforan, cannot forget his first assembly center meal. "We lined up at the Grand Mess Hall over there, and we had the JELL-O, the hardest JELL-O you can ever have, and the Vienna sausage and some other stuff we couldn't eat. I remember the JELL-O. We could throw it on the floor, and it would bounce back and make faces at you. It was the worst thing."[24]

JELL-O was also a key memory for Tomoko Kashiwagi whose father Shiro was once a partner in the Hata Merchant Tailor Shop in San Mateo:

> I remember going to meals. We had to bring our own dish, so we had rice and meat and vegetables and JELL-O all in one dish. We had to eat the JELL-O first, then we washed our own dishes in the soap water and go to the next sink and rinse it and dry it with your own towel, and take it home. And we come back for lunch and did the same routine over again.[25]

Those who worked in the mess halls did not escape the trauma of the meals either, as then nineteen-year old Sachi Kajiwara remembered, "My brother was made a mess hall manager, and he would come back in the middle of the day and lie down to sleep, and he would be cussing out loud because there's not enough meat again today. We ended up eating a lot of beans and a lot of apple butter, and to this day, I can't eat it."[26]

The meal routine, along with other contributing factors, affected the solidity of the family unit. In the past, families had eaten meals together at the kitchen or dining room table. Many parents initially insisted their families continue this tradition. Kei and Jim Hiroshi Nakano's parents were in this group. "There were eight of us. We actually had a table, and we all sat with our family," said Kei Nakano. "The thought at that time was to try and keep the family unit intact as much as possible and try to simulate a family environment as much as possible." Some mothers went as far as waiting in line and bringing meals back to eat in their rooms back at the barracks. Tanforan's mess hall meals, though, did little to encourage family togetherness. As time went on, many parents found it easier just to allow their children to eat with friends.[27]

---

[23] George M. Fukui, unpublished memoir, June 4, 1997, 8; and DeWitt, *Final Report*, 186.

[24] K. Nakano, interview by Ito.

[25] Tomoko Kashiwagi, interview by Yasuko "Ann" (Ishida) Ito, San Mateo, Calif., October 14, 1993.

[26] Sachi Kajiwara, interview by Dianne Fukami, San Lorenzo, Calif., February 2, 1995. In addition, there were unconfirmed reports that Caucasian administrators stole the better rations and gave the prisoners the leftovers. Rumors claimed horse-meat was also being served.

[27] K. Nakano, interview by Ito.

The food situation improved weeks later after the first food manager was replaced. Later, other mess halls in different parts of Tanforan opened up and, in defiance of the rules, two of them served meals family style instead of cafeteria style.

Cases of mass diarrhea often broke out, forcing residents to use the latrines night and day. Chizu Togasaki, who was one of the five nurses at Tanforan, remembered one incident in which flurries of latrine activity through the night caused guards to suspect that some sort of conspiracy was underway. An investigation later revealed the night activity stemmed from severe stomach problems.[28]

In her diary on May 21, 1942, teenager Isabel Miyata wrote, "Yesterday about 50 cases of food poisoning turned up–really serious–from some old ham they served. Poor cooks were so frightened, but you can't blame them. After all, they only serve what's given to them. Besides, it was very hot yesterday, and there was a shortage of ice."[29]

An upset stomach put Kei Nakano in an extremely embarrassing situation. "I remember the time I had diarrhea…The only thing that was open was the 'colored gents' stall [an old stall used by African Americans who worked at the former horseracing track]. So, I sat in there, and lo and behold, the wind came and blew the door wide open, and I was sitting right smack on that

One night, when I got diarrhea, I was afraid to go out to use the toilet because there was a military police right above me. If he saw me going out there in my bathrobe, he probably would think I was trying to escape. So what I did was the best thing I could do. I found this coffee can and used it. I covered it with a newspaper and stuck it under my cot, but my younger brother started hollering because it smelled so bad. My mother was after him, saying, "How can she help it if she is sick?"…I got up and put it outside and had to get up early in the morning to get rid of it before people started going to the mess hall and see me carrying this thing. There were so many humiliating things such as that.

– TSUYAKO "SOX" (KATAOKA) KITASHIMA
twenty-two when she was imprisoned in Tanforan with her widowed mother, sister, and brother[30]

[28] Chizu Togasaki, interview by Dianne Fukami, Walnut Creek, Calif., February 2, 1995.
[29] I. Miyata, diary entry, May 21, 1942.
[30] Tsuyako "Sox" (Kataoka) Kitashima, interview by Yasuko "Ann" (Ishida) Ito, San Francisco, Calif., April 6, 1994.

throne and all the people were going to the mess hall," said Nakano.[31]

Personal hygiene took place in military-style latrines with communal sinks, showers, and half-walls to separate the door-less toilets. For the culturally modest Japanese, it was the ultimate offense.

"The toilets that the blacks used which were near the horse stalls where the blacks tended the horses were the ones that we had to use. So there were no toilet seats. There were planks of wood, I would say maybe the lumber was one by twelve or one by fourteen or however standard planks of wood come in a lumber yard. And they would be maybe twelve feet long. And have round holes maybe every three feet. That was the ladies' facility...there were no stalls. There were no walls for privacy."
—Tomoye "Tami" (Nozawa) Takahashi who was incarcerated at Tanforan from her home in San Francisco.[32] June 16, 1942.
Photograph by Dorothea Lange, National Archives

Tsuyako "Sox" (Kataoka) Kitashima recalled the gratitude felt for one man who sacrificed his long underwear so the women could cover at least their faces with it while they went about their business sitting on the toilets. Many older Japanese, accustomed to baths instead of showers, found innovative ways of converting barrels and other items into bathtubs.[33]

Hot water was often at a premium because of the sheer demand and the unreliability of the boilers that heated the water. Many took to showering and bathing late at night when there was less demand for hot water and more privacy. New parents often ran into each other in the laundry room in the wee hours of the morning as they took care of family washing needs. Mitsuye (Yamashita) Hirotsuka, the mother of three children, had to take extra steps to do her laundry. "Our laundry didn't have any hot water, so I had to walk clear over to the other side [of Tanforan] by crawling under the racetrack fencing. I went to launder every morning at four o'clock and would meet up with Dave Tatsuno, who was also doing diapers because he had a baby. The two Okada brothers saw me crawling through the fence, so they cut the board so I wouldn't have such a hard time. There was no laundry line, so we had to make our own."[34]

Not everyone was able to make the adjustment so easily, however. On May 13, 1942, the

---

[31] K. Nakano, interview by Ito.

[32] T. Takahashi, interview by yamada.

[33] T. Kitashima, interview by Ito.

[34] Mitsuye (Yamashita) Hirotsuka, interview by Yasuko "Ann" (Ishida) Ito, Redwood City, Calif., November 1, 1994.

San Francisco News reported that twenty-one-year old Clarence Sadamune had escaped from Tanforan, then had attempted suicide. In his unpublished autobiography, Yoshio "Yo" Kasai detailed the event:

> I can never forget an incident that happened when we were first herded into the Tanforan racetrack. Clarence Sadamune, who was half Japanese and half Portuguese, rebelled as soon as he got to camp. His associations were mostly with Caucasians and he did not feel comfortable in an all-Japanese environment. Both of his brothers, who were good friends of mine, were in the military services, and he also wanted desperately to join the armed forces. He did not look at all Japanese so he could easily pass as a Caucasian. In his determination to leave the camp, he felt that he could easily fool the guards when he said he was not Japanese.
>
> We were allowed visitors at a certain hour every day and each visitor was required to obtain a pass to enter and to leave the grounds. He was stopped at the gate and was asked for his pass. Clarence told the guard that he had lost his pass and since he did not look Japanese, the guard believed him and allowed him to leave. He boarded a bus in San Bruno and headed for San Francisco to volunteer for the armed forces. He went first to the air force recruiting office, then to the naval recruiting office, then to the marine recruiting office and last, to the army recruiting office. He was rejected at each one of the four branches of the services when he told them he was half Japanese. He was so disillusioned that he went to the nearby drug store, bought some poison and returned to the Army recruiting office. He went into the restroom, drank the poison, and as the poison began to take effect, he was barely able to stagger out to the recruiting desk and to tell them what he had done. They called for an ambulance immediately and rushed him to the hospital, where they pumped his stomach out. He was sent back to camp, escorted by the military police and met at the gate by his father and sister.[35]

Kasai also wrote that Sadamune, accompanied by his father and sister, was immediately sent to a camp in Arizona for being a troublemaker.

Tadashi Sakuma's rendition of the laundry facilities at Tanforan. September 25, 1942. Unpublished pencil sketch. *Courtesy of Tadashi Sakuma*

[35] Weglyn, *Years of Infamy*, 292; and Yoshio "Yo" Kasai, unpublished memoir, San Leandro, Calif., 1994.

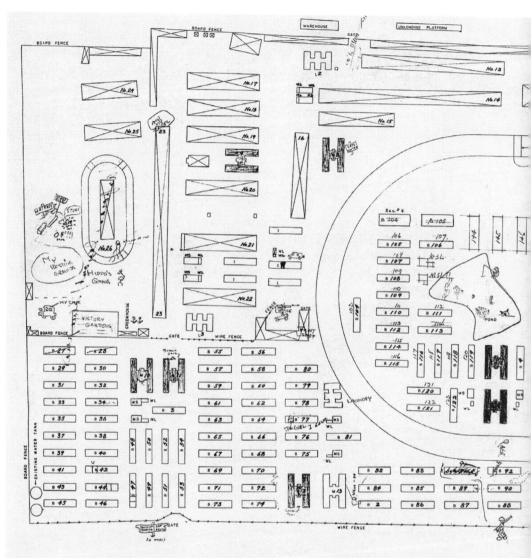

Map of Tanforan Assembly Center by District Regional Engineer Office, San Francisco and Vicinity. *Courtesy of Daisy (Uyeda) Satoda*

84

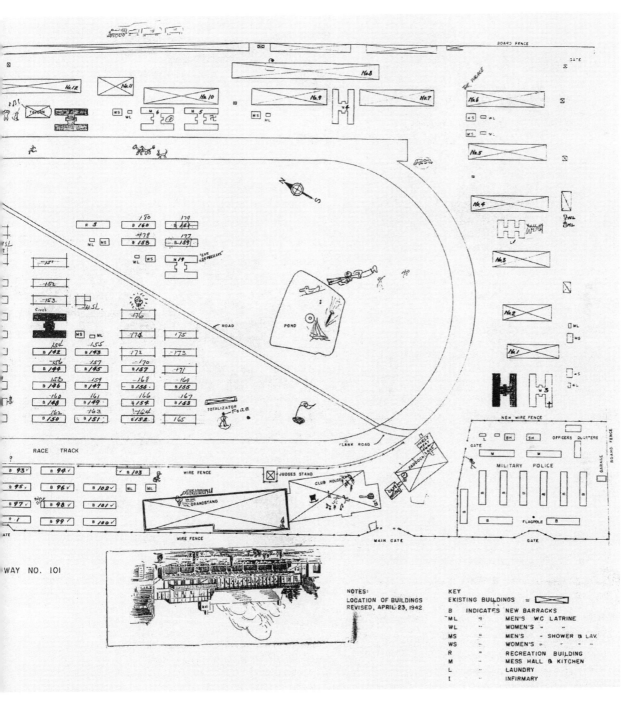

NOTES:
LOCATION OF BUILDINGS
REVISED, APRIL 23, 1942

KEY
EXISTING BUILDINGS =
B   INDICATES NEW BARRACKS
ML   "   MEN'S WC LATRINE
WL   "   WOMEN'S   "
MS   "   MEN'S   " SHOWER & LAV.
WS   "   WOMEN'S "   "
R   "   RECREATION BUILDING
M   "   MESS HALL & KITCHEN
L   "   LAUNDRY
I   "   INFIRMARY

In an attempt to make living quarters more habitable, this elderly man used scrap lumber to make the bench seen in the foreground. April 29, 1942. *Photograph by Dorothea Lange, National Archives*

In dealing with their status as prisoners, most of those in Tanforan adopted the attitude of "*shikataganai*," an often-used expression meaning, "it can't be helped." It embodied the Japanese cultural trait of making the best of a bad situation. They were resourceful in finding ways to make their rooms more habitable. No woodpile was safe; assembly center carpenters who left their work in the evening returned in the morning to find their materials depleted. People used the lumber to make shelves, tables and chairs.

To cook and provide heat, some people brought electric hot plates into their barracks. Unfortunately, this practice often overloaded the already-stressed electrical circuits, and blown fuses kept recurring.

As the new barracks in the infield were completed, inmates began to give the roads familiar names such as "Alameda Avenue," "Berkeley Way," and "San Francisco Avenue." Not knowing how long they would be at Tanforan, people also set to work beautifying their small spaces and landscaping; organizing recreational programs and sports teams; starting classes for children and adults; and setting up a library, dental clinic, and medical clinic.

Slowly, Tanforan was becoming "home."

The medical clinic was a barrack with no running water and with cots lined up along the walls. Even essentials, such as urinals or bedpans, were missing, and the only medications available had been brought in by Japanese American doctors incarcerated in Tanforan. Dr. Norton Benner, a San Mateo physician, recalled, "They were tossed into camp, and I remember my dad [Dr. Alan Benner] coming home and saying, 'Gee whiz, they didn't even give them any medical stuff to take. They didn't even give them pencils and papers to write down their records of the people they were taking care of!' So my dad took pencils, and my mother took up pens and papers and whatever else they needed in Tanforan."[36]

Childbirth took place in the clinic, with laboring women receiving little comfort and no privacy. The first baby born at Tanforan was seven-and-a-half pound Judy Naruo, born to Michio Naruo, arriving Monday, May 11, 1942. Later, due to red tape, a premature infant died before he

[36] Norton Benner, M.D., interview by Yasuko "Ann" (Ishida) Ito, San Mateo, Calif., July 24, 1996.

Baseball was a favorite pastime, so a backstop was built at Tanforan and a field groomed. Unpublished pencil sketch by Tadashi Sakuma. *Courtesy of Tadashi Sakuma*

Youths played basketball at one of eight recreation areas at Tanforan. June 16, 1942. *Photograph by Dorothea Lange, National Archives*

could be transferred to the nearby county hospital. San Mateo resident Tatsuye (Hamasaki) Haraguchi, a *kibei* who had returned to the United States in 1933, blamed the conditions at Tanforan for her difficult labor and minimal post-partum care:

> My son was born in Tanforan and had a very difficult delivery. When the baby was born, the doctor said the baby did not need a 2 a.m. feeding, and so the baby cried, and I cried with the baby. The whole barrack suffered. Everyone could not sleep. Even to this day, people recall how he suffered. The baby developed a hernia from crying so much for lack of milk for the two o'clock feeding. I didn't have enough milk for the baby, because I had diarrhea because of too much greasy food. The doctor did not relent, and we had a miserable time. This is one experience I cannot forget.[37]

For the Tanforan library, all books and supplies were donated, and prisoners made the bookshelves from scrap lumber. June 16, 1942. *Photograph by Dorothea Lange, National Archives*

Nineteen-year old Toshio Furusho's mother Natsuye had given birth in April 1942, just before the family was forced from their home in Centerville, which is now a district in Fremont. After

---

[37] *Tanforan Totalizer,* May 14, 1942; Taylor, *Jewel of the Desert,* 81; and T. Haraguchi, interview by Ito.

The Tanforan medical clinic lacked adequate supplies and was understaffed. June 16, 1942. *Photograph by Dorothea Lange, National Archives*

"The Hospital Group," depicted by prisoner Siberius Saito. 1942. Unpublished pencil sketch. *Courtesy of Kaoru "Ruth" Saito*

several days, Mrs. Furusho became ill and was transferred to the San Mateo County General Hospital where she died. Hers was the first funeral at Tanforan. The Furushos wanted to bury her in Centerville and had to obtain a permit and use a military escort to leave Tanforan. Friends pitched in to help the Furushos care for the infant girl, Sachiye.[38]

Just days after arriving at Tanforan, San Francisco native Fred Hoshiyama shared his own observations about the care at the medical center in a letter he wrote to his uncle Lincoln Kanai:

> It seems that the medical center is definitely understaffed when they have to get untrained personnel to handle vaccination, typhoid shots and etc. They are using Dr. [Shozo] Fujita, Dr. [Carl] Hirota, Dr. [Tim] Yamasaki, Dr. [Tokuji] Hedani, etc., all not physicians, but dentists, optometrists and amateur girl nurses to administer medical aid. Don't let this get out, but lots of complaints have reached my ears about the deplorable condition at the medical centers. It's not the fault of the personnel because they are definitely understaffed and under-equipped. Only one registered nurse to handle 3,000 people and with more people coming by Saturday, it's going to take all of us 15 hours to help.[39]

During the nearly six months that Tanforan operated as an assembly center, sixty-four babies were born and twenty-two people died.[40]

Despite the lack of privacy and the oppressive setting, romance did bloom and marriages followed. Newlyweds received special permission

---

[38] Toshio Furusho, interview by Yasuko "Ann" (Ishida) Ito, San Mateo, Calif., February 4, 1995.
[39] Fred Hoshiyama, letter to Lincoln Kanai, May 1942, Hoover Institution, Stanford University, Palo Alto, Calif.
[40] DeWitt, *Final Report*, 202.

Artist Chiura Obata captured Natsuye Furusho's funeral. She was forty-six years old when she died. 1942. *Courtesy of Kimi Kodani Hill*

and escorts to leave the compound and obtain marriage licenses, but they had to return to Tanforan as quickly as possible. Wedding celebrations were usually low-key affairs with very few refreshments and fellow inmate guests unable to give the kind of lavish gifts they might have in the past. Honeymoons took place in stables, surrounded by the odor of horse manure and with the knowledge that family members were just on the other side of the partition.

The Japanese American people realized that so much idle time among the prisoners could become a problem, so they organized social activities. Between meals, Tanforan's mess halls eventually served as recreation halls where people came to watch movies, dance, and do arts and crafts.

East Bay resident Sachi Kajiwara, who became a recreation hall worker, recalled how the young girls in her care decorated the hall for a July 4 dance. "My seven- to ten-year old girls cut strips of newspaper and used pieces of crayons we got in camp to make paper chains and we had red, white, and blue paper chains all round in the room in the rec hall. It was very ironic that we were celebrating the Independence Day when we were behind the barbed wire fences."[41]

---

[41] S. Kajiwara, interview by Fukami.

We decided to get married in Tanforan. We didn't know what's coming tomorrow, so we thought we might as well get married. My parents thought the same way.

We got into this panel truck, and they pushed us in there to go get the license in Redwood City or someplace. There was a [Tanforan official who was the] driver, and they took us to the place to get our license. We couldn't see out, and we went and signed some papers. I thought it was very unfair, and I thought, here I am, an American citizen and I'm pushed into this panel truck to go get my license. That sure is not fair.

There was nothing to get prepared for our wedding. I told my hakujin *[Caucasian] friend Mary Lou that I was going to get married and could she do anything about it. She said, "I could get you a gown." And that she did. We were the same height and same type, so what she got, it fit me perfectly. And then I had a very good Japanese friend, and they had a nursery, and they had rented their place out, and she told them that her good friend was getting married and would they send some flowers in from the [family's] nursery. So I had flowers and my wedding gown.*

Then my dad got Reverend Gill from Berkeley, and he came out to officiate. It was not bad—I had my reverend, wedding gown, my groom, and flowers. A girl played the piano. I think she played the Wedding March. *We couldn't have any festivities afterwards. We did have our honeymoon [trip]—around the racetrack twice. We were in a car. I guess it took about ten minutes.*

We went to another stable on our wedding night. It was a smelly one. My sister-in-law thought she would be real helpful, and she took this bucket of hot water and mopped the floor, but right underneath was all this horse manure and that steamed it up, and then it was really smelly. You overlook all these things when you are in love and it's your wedding night. It was almost funny. We laugh about it.

— SHIZU "SUGAR" (MITSUYOSHI) HIRABAYASHI
who turned twenty-four just before her incarceration [42]

---

[42] Shizu "Sugar" (Mitsuyoshi) Hirabayashi, interview by Dianne Fukami, San Jose, Calif., February 6, 1995.

George Fukui, a student at the University of California, Davis in 1941, located the drums, bugles, and flags from San Francisco Boy Scout Troop 12, a Japanese American troop that had been based in three San Francisco Japanese American Christian churches, and had them brought into Tanforan. "We were able to gather about twenty boys all eager to start up the unit, which had numbered about one hundred just before evacuation. When we started off with our drum 'roll off' and brought in our bugles, cymbals, and bells into the introduction of *Semper Fidelis*, all our Mess 10 associates who knew nothing of our musical experience watched in awe, wide-eyed, and listened intently and broke out with a booming applause as we completed the piece."[43]

A service held on May 24 included a flag-raising ceremony, complete with the Pledge of Allegiance, national anthem, invocation, greetings, and a presentation about the history of the flag. Six thousand people attended, and they closed the program by singing *God Bless America*. The event symbolized the patriotism they felt: they were, at their core, Americans.[44]

Over the Labor Day holidays, Tanforan held celebrations. Activities included sports tournaments; dancing; garden and greenhouse displays; and exhibitions of needlecraft, painting, and drawing. In his final report, General John DeWitt stated,

Mess halls served as multi-purpose rooms. April 16, 1942. *Photograph by Dorothea Lange, National Archives*

"The festival was topped with a coronation costume ball when the queen chosen by the evacuees received the acclaim of beauty and personality."[45]

Organized religion offered another activity for Tanforan inmates. Government policy regarding religious worship during incarceration permitted Japanese prisoners "to promote religious services within the various centers and to request such Caucasian assistance for coordination of religious activities as might be necessary." The government prohibited practice of the Shinto religion, however, because officials linked it to emperor worship, and also forbade the use of the Japanese language during services "except where the use of English prevented the congregation from comprehending the service."[46]

---

[43] Fukui, unpublished memoir, 8. Fukui worked for the Japanese American Evacuation and Resettlement Study (JERS), which was formed to study the sociological ramifications of the Japanese/Japanese American community in confinement.

[44] Fred Hoshiyama, "Recreation," May 26, 1942, Japanese American Evacuation and Resettlement Study (JERS), Bancroft Library, University of California, Berkeley, Berkeley, Calif., as cited in Taylor, *Jewel of the Desert*, 301.

[45] DeWitt, *Final Report*, 211.

[46] DeWitt, *Final Report*, 211-212.

Inmate Siberius Saito sketched Barrack #10, a laundry, the Buddhist Church, and the art school. 1942. Unpublished pencil sketch. *Courtesy of Kaoru "Ruth" Saito*

Religious devotion was no shield against incarceration, so a number of ministers were imprisoned in Tanforan along with members of their congregations. On April 9, 1942, Buddhists gathered in a mess hall to hold their first service behind barbed wire, conducted by Bishop Ryotai Matsukage, the titular head of the church. Protestant ministers at the assembly center included the Reverends Taro Goto, Isao Tanaka, John Yamashita, Masamoto Nishimura, Eiji Kawamorita, Howard Toriumi, Joseph Tsukamoto, Norio Ozaki, Jiryu Fujii, Eihi Suyehiro, Shigeo Shimada; and seminary students George Aki and Sakae Hayakawa. At Tanforan, these men formed the Ministerial Association, which organized joint

worship services in Japanese and English, Bible study groups, and prayer meetings. Tanforan's Sunday religious schedule included Protestant, Catholic, Buddhist, and Seventh Day Adventist services.[47]

Originally there was no provision for education in the assembly centers since these sites were meant to be temporary and most of the inmates arrived so close to the end of the school year. Because there were so few activities for the young people who comprised nearly half of Tanforan's population of approximately seventy-eight hundred, they had a lot of idle time on their hands. School seemed a good solution. At first, school was a haphazard arrangement. Students met by grade in various areas of the grandstand. Without books or supplies and only a few credentialed teachers, classes were mostly in lecture format. Those who were college educated and wanted to teach ran the program. The tenuous nature of the incarceration at Tanforan did not help with student motivation. Older students, in particular, did not see the purpose in studying, completing assignments, or taking tests when their futures were so uncertain.

Sixteen-year old Frances Kimura Morioka considered it a waste of time. "If they wanted to call it school, they can call it that, but it really wasn't a school. We just went. You didn't learn anything. Nobody knew how long we were going

[47] April 9, 1942 may be an incorrect date cited in this passage because Tanforan did not open until late April. *San Mateo Buddhist Temple: 70th and 75th Anniversaries* (Fresno, Calif.: Self-published by the San Mateo Buddhist Temple, *circa* 1986), unnumbered 24; and Lester E. Suzuki, *Ministry in the Assembly and Relocation Centers of World War II* (Berkeley, Calif.: Yardbird Pub. Co.,1979), 60-63.

Children lined up outside a nursery school at Tanforan. June 16, 1942. *Photograph by Dorothea Lange, National Archives*

This nursery school at Tanforan was taught by Japanese American student teachers, who themselves were taught by Japanese American Mills College graduates. June 16, 1942. *Photograph by Dorothea Lange, National Archives*

to be there, and there was no way of getting a diploma. I don't remember having any books in Tanforan. I don't remember any structured study. All I remember is that we were supposed to go to school, so we went. We sat at these tables, and I don't remember doing anything."[48]

San Mateo High School senior Yon Kawakita, forced to leave San Mateo High School just one month before graduating, had a different experience. His teachers came to Tanforan to visit him and their other students and gave them assign-

ments to prepare for final exams, which they later administered. Kawakita remembered the teachers returned a few weeks later to hold a graduation exercise. "It was quite fancy. I think there were about six of us, and I was a member of the school band, so the school band teacher Eugene Brose was there with a small group of band members, and they played *Pomp and Circumstance* and gave us a diploma. And it was quite nice."[49]

Younger children seemed to enjoy the organization and stability that the school day

[48] Morioka was *hapa*, or racially mixed. When the war broke out, the FBI picked up her Japanese father. The government initially did not have a policy about Caucasian parents and *hapa* children. In the case of the Kimura family, mother and children ended up in Tanforan. Frances Kimura Morioka, interview by Yasuko "Ann" (Ishida) Ito, San Mateo, Calif., May 12, 1995. For a discussion about *hapa* children and their parents, *see* footnote 15 of this chapter and also Taylor, *Jewel of the Desert*, 85.

[49] Y. Kawakita, interview by yamada, March 2, 1998.

Obata captured the bleakness of Tanforan in this *sumi-e* painting, "Finding New Dwellings," Tanforan. April 30, 1942. *Courtesy of Kimi Kodani Hill*

Chiura Obata, an associate professor of art at the University of California, Berkeley, before being evicted, helped establish an art school at Tanforan. This morning art class learns free-hand brush strokes. June 16, 1942. *Photograph by Dorothea Lange, National Archives*

offered. Janet Miyata, then age eleven, remembered having report cards and doing spelling and arithmetic.[50]

Some graduates of Mills College in Oakland, including sisters Keiko and author Yoshiko Uchida, began a nursery school in a shack they cleaned.[51]

Even adults took advantage of their leisure time to take in some educational classes. For many

Issei, imprisonment at Tanforan was the first time they did not have to work from sunup to sundown to eke out a living. Many of the older people used this time to improve their English, study American history, and participate in arts and crafts activities.

Tanforan Assembly Center became well known for the quality of its art classes, which were taught by a prestigious faculty of artists, among them University of California, Berkeley, art professor Chiura Obata; Matsusaburo "George" Hibi and his wife Hisako, both painters who had been living in Hayward, California, when they were forced into Tanforan; and Miné Okubo, who preserved her incarceration experiences via text

[50] J. Miyata, interview by Ito.

[51] Yoshiko Uchida wrote several books about her wartime experiences, including *Desert Exile* and *Journey to Topaz*.

94

and illustrations in her book, *Citizen 13660*. Out of the despair and imprisonment they experienced during World War II, they still managed to see beauty and create art.[52]

Those with green thumbs used their talents to plant victory gardens and to landscape the area surrounding a lake created by prisoners. Author Miné Okubo wrote, "On August 2, North Lake was formally opened. It had been transformed from a mere wet spot in the Tanforan scenery into a miniature aquatic park, complete with bridge, promenade, and islands. The lake was a great joy to the residents and presented new material for the artists. In the morning sunlight and at sunset it added a great beauty to the bleak barracks."[53]

One of the more pleasant memories shared by nearly everyone at Tanforan is of shows presented at the grandstand, where ready-made seating made it an ideal location to stage ceremonies and shows. Many recalled the musical performances, especially that of a young Goro Suzuki, who later came to be known as actor Jack Soo in the musical *Flower Drum Song* and the television show *Barney Miller*. A favorite was the song "Tanforan," with new lyrics set to the old tune, "Tangerine:"

One bright day Mother went out with a sketch book and sat near the barbed wire fence and started to sketch the hills of South San Francisco. The colors were already changing from the green to the yellow ochre. When she came to Tanforan in May the hills were all green. She was busily moving the color pencils and crayons on the paper. An internal security officer came and took away that sketch without a word. She was terrified and afraid to ask him, "Why couldn't I sketch that scene?" at that time.

— HISAKO HIBI
referring to herself as "Mother" in the third person[54]

---

[52] Matsusaburo "George" Hibi, an immigrant from Japan, donated about fifty of his paintings to the Japanese American community. Hisako Hibi painted at least seventy works between 1942 and 1945 while she was incarcerated at Tanforan and Topaz.

[53] Miné Okubo, *Citizen 13660* (New York: Columbia University Press, 1946), 99.

[54] Hisako Hibi, unpublished children's story, San Francisco, Calif., *circa* 1950-1980s. Artist Hisako Hibi, in 1950, began writing a children's story about her family's incarceration experience. This excerpt from the unpublished manuscript was given to Dianne Fukami by Hibi's daughter Ibuki (Hibi) Lee.

Yoshiye Fujita was married to Tad Fujita, a community leader at Tanforan and later at the Central Utah Relocation Center, commonly known as Topaz. She is shown here working in a vegetable garden in front of her barrack. June 16, 1942. *Photograph by Dorothea Lange, National Archives*

Tanforan Lake, captured by Tadashi Sakuma on September 25, 1942. Unpublished pencil sketch. *Courtesy of Tadashi Sakuma*

TANFORAN

Tanforan,
It is all they say
In a horse's stall
On mattresses of hay

Tanforan
Could I only wipe
From my memory
The soggy taste of tripe
There I am
Back in Tanforan
Nineteen forty-two
Forget it if you can

In my nostrils
Still is a smell
And it sure in hell ain't Chanel
It's horse manure at
Tanforan!

— *Lyricist unknown*[55]

Those of dating age attended dances held at various recreation halls throughout Tanforan, and danced to the music of the 1930s and the big band sounds of the 1940s. Some young men, such as Yon Kawakita, acquired instruments during their time at Tanforan and formed a band that provided live music at dances. A popular–and ironic–favorite tune was, *Don't Fence Me In*. More one-on-one social interaction was difficult, however, as Yoshio "Yo" Kasai recalled. "There was no privacy, and if you wanted to go visit a young girl,

---

[55] *Tanforan*, lyricist unknown, Tanforan (San Bruno), Calif., *circa* 1942. Lyrics given to Dianne Fukami by Sadie Tajima, who was incarcerated at Tanforan.

you had to do the visiting during the day. If you want any privacy, when the mother and the father and everybody else is out of the house, you had to go sneaking over there. It was not easy to go visiting and have any kind of semblance of privacy."[56]

Another shared Tanforan memory was the "Blue Ghost of Hollywood Bowl." According to teenager Yon Kawakita, the "ghost,"–or *hinotama*, the "soul of a dead person"–appeared on moonlit nights after it rained. Moisture seeped under the stable floor and wet the horse manure underneath, causing steam to rise. As the moon reflected on the steam coming through a knot hole in the wall, the reflection appeared like a *hinotama*.[57]

Although the Japanese and Japanese Americans worked hard to make incarcerated life as bearable and as normal as possible, they had constant reminders of their status. Jim Hiroshi Nakano, a clean-up crew member, said, "We used to walk along the fence and clean the place, and I'll never forget the feeling we had. The fence was right alongside the El Camino Real. The cars and buses are going back and forth and a fifteen-foot fence…We are in the inside, and the other people are on the outside. That's when you really felt like prisoners. Because the guards were patrolling, walking back and forth, and as soon as we get close to the fence and put our fingers on the fence to look outside, they say, 'Get back, get back.'"[58]

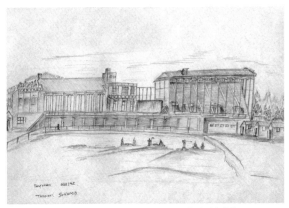

The Grandstand as it appeared to inmate Tadashi Sakuma. 1942. Unpublished pencil sketch. *Courtesy of Tadashi Sakuma*

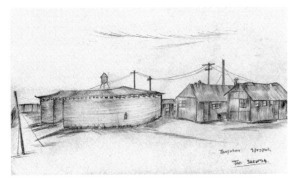

The name "Hollywood Bowl" came from the shape of the land, which is slightly concave like the Hollywood Bowl in Southern California. People who lived at Tanforan called the Hollywood Bowl *"maru no uchi,"* which means "roundhouse." September 23, 1942. Unpublished pencil sketch by Tadashi Sakuma. *Courtesy of Tadashi Sakuma*[59]

Outsiders granted permission to visit Tanforan were treated much like those at a prison. After they registered, guards searched them before allowing them to go to a special meeting room at

[56] Y. Kasai, interview by Fukami.

[57] Y. Kawakita, electronic correspondence to yamada, December 4, 1999.

[58] J. Nakano, interview by Ito.

[59] Tadashi Sakuma, conversation with Yasuko "Ann" (Ishida) Ito, San Mateo, Calif., April 3, 2002.

Guard towers were ever present. 1942. Unpublished pencil sketch by Siberius Saito.
Courtesy of Kaoru "Ruth" Saito

the grandstand to chat across tables with inmates. Armed guards patrolled the area the whole time.

Those incarcerated could only shop for clothing and domestic goods via mail order catalogues or through friends. They often asked people from the outside to bring this or that item during their next visit. Martha Imai was in Berkeley with her husband Yuji while he awaited transfer to teach Japanese at the U.S. Navy's language school in Boulder, Colorado. She remembered visiting friends and family in Tanforan and bringing them requested items. Sears and Montgomery Ward mail order catalogues

became very popular. Masako (Hanyu) Iwase, Redwood City-born, remembered depending on those catalogues, "but we couldn't find anything we want[ed]. They brought the catalogue, and they had so many pages they had marked. But, when the time came, they didn't have all the things we ordered, so anybody who ordered a certain kind of dress, we all had the same kind of uniform."[60]

Twelve-year old Amy (Tamaki) Doi, who had lived in San Francisco since she was six, was convinced that the stores used the camps as a dumping ground for leftover stock. "We got nothing

---

[60] The U.S. Navy had a Japanese language school at the University of Colorado at Boulder to train non-Japanese naval and marine corps officers during the war. The instructors were Issei and Nisei. Yuji Imai was hired as an instructor. The U.S. Army was the only service that accepted Japanese Americans. Carole Slesnick, electronic correspondence to gayle k. yamada, July 20, 2002.

we ordered," she said, "just whatever they wanted to send."[61]

In the world outside Tanforan, anti-Japanese propaganda was rampant. Politicians called for the removal of Japanese Americans and their families away from the West Coast, yet few inland states wanted them to come live within their borders. Newsreels in movie theaters, magazines, and newspapers portrayed all Japanese as the enemy, and some specifically targeted the prisoners. For those who condemned the treatment and the incarceration of the Japanese Americans, the military provided propaganda photographs and film that showed the people in the assembly centers happy and well treated.

Minoru Tamura, who had moved to San Mateo from San Francisco, was angered by the military crews who came to Tanforan to take such pictures and movies. "I remember one time I was passing near the grandstand, and I saw the U.S. Signal Corps coming in, and they were taking propaganda pictures of the little kids. They must have given candies so the kids were smiling. They were taking movies. This is for their propaganda. This really got to me, though. Showing everything is rosy, they're taking care of us. This is not right."[62]

The prisoners quickly began to find out how vulnerable they still were outside of Tanforan's barbed wire fence. Dave Tatsuno, whose

My younger sister and I would go to the fence… It was right on El Camino, and I would hang on the fence. I remember especially a very warm day, hanging on the fence, looking out. Everybody is free but our families. Of course, in those days, people traveled on weekends… I could see them over the fence and I remember saying, "Why can't we go out?" [The guard] laughed and said, "No, you have to stay in. You're enemies." I remember going to my mother when she was sitting with friends up the stairs in the reception area where visitors came and said, "Are we prisoners? Are we prisoners?" My mother just put her arm on me and she said, "Yes, we are." That was the first time I realized that we were really prisoners. It was a jail. Then my younger sister and I were talking, and I said, "What did we do?" She said, "We didn't do anything." I said, "Why are we here?"

— MAYA NAGATA AIKAWA
incarcerated in Tanforan at age fifteen[63]

---

[61] Amy (Tamaki) Doi, in an interview, San Mateo, Calif., February 22, 1994.

[62] Minoru Tamura, interview by Yasuko "Ann" (Ishida) Ito, San Mateo, Calif., September 16, 1993.

[63] M. Aikawa, interview by Fukami.

family owned the Nichi Bei Bussan store in San Francisco, was able to secure a pass to leave Tanforan under escort and check on his property and the house he had rented out to a Caucasian family. His unannounced visit resulted in a surprise to both his renters and himself. They had broken into locked storage rooms and had helped themselves to Tatsuno family possessions that had been put away for safekeeping. Sachi Kajiwara's parents, both storeowners, found themselves being sued by the building owner when their imprisonment forced them to break their lease.[64]

Counterbalancing those experiences were stories of many people who guarded and preserved the property and possessions of their Japanese friends during the years of incarceration. At Horgan Ranch in Redwood City, members of the flower-growing Mori and Nakano families remembered fondly how well formerly employed Filipino workers took good care of their homes during their absence.[65]

At Tanforan, military police handled external security. They patrolled the perimeter and monitored the entrances and exits. Caucasian civilians—many of them deputized to handle lawbreakers—took charge of internal security. They performed constant patrols, twice-daily roll calls, and inspections for contraband articles—which included Japanese language Bibles, flashlights, short-wave radios, alcohol; and potential weapons, such as screwdrivers, knives, scissors, chisels, and saws.

Some resourceful prisoners occasionally got around the inspection. Masako (Hanyu) Iwase, then twenty-two, explained one incident: "We had a knife that my mother had brought in...I remember the couple next door had two kids so we bundled the kid with the knife inside, and I went for a walk with my cousin," said Iwase. "She took the girl, I took the boy and went for a walk." Kei Nakano confessed that he and his family hid contraband sugar under a loose floorboard during inspection.[66]

The government caption to this photo reads, "Many of the evacuees suffer from lack of their accustomed activity. The attitude of the man shown in this photograph is typical of the residents in assembly centers, and because there is not much to do and not enough work available, they mill around, they visit, they stroll, and they linger to while away the hours." June 16, 1942. *Photograph by Dorothea Lange,* National Archives

---

[64] Dave Tatsuno, interview by Dianne Fukami, San Jose, Calif., February 5, 1995; S. Kajiwara, interview by Fukami.

[65] J. Nakano, interview by Ito; and K. Nakano, interview by Ito.

[66] M. Iwase, interview by Ito; and K. Nakano, interview by Ito.

A father and son in front of their home in the barracks whittled small wooden animals for the children. June 16, 1942. *Photograph by Dorothea Lange, National Archives*

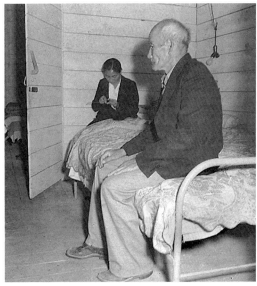

Life behind barbed wire disrupted traditional family life. This elderly man, Mr. Kondo, shared two small rooms with his two sons, his married daughter (seen here sitting behind him) and her husband. Before he was evicted, he was a farmer in Centerville in Alameda County. June 16, 1942. *Photograph by Dorothea Lange, National Archives*

Morale became a big problem for the prisoners, especially among the men who, prior to incarceration at Tanforan, had been breadwinners and heads of their households; many of them were near the high point of their lives and careers. While many of the women continued to care for the children and domestic matters, the men found themselves idle and purposeless. At any given time, one could find people playing traditional Japanese strategy games such as *go* or *shogi*.

The existence of the family unit was at risk. In addition to mess hall-style group meals, the lack of structure and difficulty in adapting to a new lifestyle during the first few weeks of Tanforan incarceration contributed to reduced parental involvement in their children's lives. Since there was no need for concern regarding traffic and other safety issues, youngsters spent all day playing with each other, exploring their new environment with little adult or parental supervision.

For many adults, work became the saving grace. Every adult was given the opportunity to work, and the survival of Tanforan depended upon the labor of the cooks, dishwashers, latrine cleaners, doctors, nurses, and teachers. Initially, people worked on a voluntary basis, but soon they began to get paid for their work. Pay ranged from eight dollars a month for unskilled laborers, such as dishwashers, cook's helpers, or junior clerks;

to twelve dollars for skilled positions including accountants, cooks, nurses, and senior clerks; to sixteen dollars a month for some professional workers, such as physicians, engineers, and teachers. Only thirty percent of all assembly center inmates had jobs, yet they worked an average of 47.7 hours per month for every adult in the assembly centers.[67]

Tanforan began to resemble a small city.

The WCCA ran all the assembly centers. Organized so that decisions would be made at the top, WCCA leadership was largely composed of Caucasian men, many of whom had no sympathy for the incarcerated people of Japanese ancestry. As time behind barbed wire grew longer, the Tanforan prisoners began to organize themselves and to facilitate resolution of their own grievances via an initially WCCA-approved self-governing body. Block managers, representing the people who lived in each of the forty-five blocks, were appointed by the WCCA administration to serve as liaisons. They formed a council, elected officers, and met every morning to discuss problems to bring before the administration.[68]

Elections for council members were an ironic exercise in democracy and self-governance being practiced in a government prison center holding American citizens who had committed no crime.

Just as importantly, though, perceived power was shifting in the community. The FBI was still holding many of the Issei community leaders

In a general election for five members of the Tanforan Assembly Center Advisory Council, Tanforan voters lined up to cast their ballots for council members from their precinct. U.S. naturalization laws prevented Issei from voting in national and local elections though they had voted for people to represent them in organizations such as churches. June 16, 1942. *Photograph by Dorothea Lange, National Archives*

in Department of Justice internment camps so they had not yet been reunited with their families. Thus, for the most part, the mantle of leadership fell to the second generation, or Nisei.

Among the Nisei at Tanforan, various political factions existed. Some felt hostility toward the Issei, whom they blamed for the incarceration. Then there was the Japanese American Citizens

---

[67] DeWitt, *Final Report*, 205.

[68] *See* Taylor, *Jewel of the Desert*, 73. Similar governing systems were set up at other assembly centers.

League (JACL), which some people considered suspect because the group encouraged voluntary evacuation and full cooperation. Members of the Communist Party, opposed to Japan's militarism, allied themselves with the JACL. The Young Democrats were considered radical for their anti-fascist stance against Japan but were also seen as anti-*kibei* and anti-Issei; they believed all Issei were pro-Japan. Ironically, their leader was a *kibei*: Ernie Iiyama, who was from Berkeley and did not like Japan's militarism. With support from the *kibei*, that is, Nisei educated in Japan, he won a Tanforan Council seat in a hotly contested election.[69]

The reality of self-governance behind barbed wire was short-lived. At the end of May 1942, a WCCA memo ended any real power council members might have had when it mandated that they serve strictly in an advisory capacity and offer opinions on fairly innocuous topics, such as recreation, sanitation, and discipline.[70]

One of the points of contention between the imposed Tanforan administration and the council was the *Tanforan Totalizer*, a newspaper, that the inmates wrote and edited. The Japanese Americans intended it to be a real newspaper that provided a forum for the prisoners to discuss issues. Administration officials, however, wanted it to be a house organ for the government, so they censored it from time to time. Tomoye "Tami" (Nozawa) Takahashi, whose husband Henri helped

We all talked about the food, and we complained. And then we gather our notes together and bring it to the administration that Japanese do not eat cheese, and they are not used to liver, or brains, or tongue. Then they tell us, "This is war, and meat is rationed," and we cannot have meat. The cooks would get together and improvise something more edible…In other words, we complained about our living situation, especially those that lived in the horse stalls complained about the odor, mice running around. Here again, we managed. We had to; there was no choice.

— TAD FUJITA
Tanforan block manager[71]

---

[69] The term *"kibei"* refers to someone born in America who was sent to Japan for formal schooling. Taylor, *Jewel of the Desert*, 75-76.

[70] Taylor, *Jewel of the Desert*, 79.

[71] Tad Fujita, interview by Dianne Fukami, Berkeley, Calif., February 1, 1995.

THE TANFORAN TOTALIZER

Vol. I. No. 1   Tanforan Assembly Center, Calif.   May 15, 1942

ASSEMBLY CENTER HEAD GREETS RESIDENTS

EDITORIAL...

The Tanforan Totalizer is intended to be this center's paper in every way. Its interests are those of all the residents here. It is not the organ of any self-seeking group and it will not play any politics. It will seek to promote a democratic and cooperative spirit within the community as the basis of all action whether individual or collective.

That the paper may be truly representative of the whole community, it will be open to every sort of suggestion from its readers for improving it from issue to issue. All those interested in the venture are invited to take active part in the publication.

The present temporary staff has taken the initiative in starting the paper in the belief that the common good would be served thereby. Final adjustments within the staff will be based on ability and willingness to do the work.

p.o.'s daily tote hits 6000

Handling about 6000 pieces of mail—3000 going out and an equal number coming in—the Tanforan postoffice is today one of the busiest places in the center.

Of the outgoing mail, about 1000 are postcards. But the most hectic activity of the postoffice is in selling and cashing money orders.

Postmaster Gill Juckert reports that his office sells more money orders daily than the town of San Bruno, even though hours for handling them are limited to the morning.

The postmaster advises those who have not yet done so to notify the home town postoffice of changes in address, otherwise mail may be delayed two days.

According to Frank Iwanaga, in the lost letter department, over 1000 letters a day are received by the office because barrack and apartment numbers are lacking.

Although it may be provided later, no special delivery service has yet been established. Regular deliveries occur twice a day. Letters leave camp (Cont'd on P. 3)

(Cont'd on P. 3)

MEDICAL CENTER

EMERGENCY!

If you slice a nice gob of yourself or something akin, the report's to be dashed to the Medical Center (main hospital) where an ambulance and a sedan are on 24-hour duty for cases warranting use.

HAVE YOU BEEN SHOT?

Typhoid shots and vaccinations for smallpox are being given during May at the Center on Mondays and Wednesdays, 9-11 a.m. All residents still unshot are to report.

THE CENTER

The Medical Center (see map on page 4) at present has five buildings, with 1 as the general clinic; 2 as the main hospital; 5 as the dental and special baby clinic. Dr. Hajime Uyeyama and his staff are in charge. Dr. Carl Hirota and Miss Mame Mori, RN, head, respectively, the dental and nursing staffs. Clinic schedules have been posted throughout our City.

COOPERATION STRESSED

Wm. R. Lawson, Tanforan Assembly Center Manager, today greeted residents here in a statement made to this paper as follows:

"May I take this opportunity of extending my greetings to all the residents of Tanforan Assembly Center and to congratulate them on the first issue of their newspaper. This paper can play a most important part in the community life of this Center and I wish it every success.

"I would like to impress upon every resident the importance of accepting his full share of responsibility in the operation of the Center...There is a big job to be done and everyone must do his or her part.

"It will be the policy of the management to make this community as self-governing as possible. The success of this policy and the happiness and welfare of everyone will depend on the cooperation of all concerned.

"Only such rules and regulations will be made by the management as are necessary for the health, welfare and best interests of all concerned. Strict compliance with these regulations is essential."

MRS. NARUO SETS PACE WITH JUDY...

The newest Tanforan arrival is 7½ lb. Judy Naruo, born to Mrs. Michio Naruo last Monday at 8:50 p.m., Dr. Kazuo Togasaki attending.

Mother and infant are both reported doing well in the center hospital.

The proud parents reside in B. 110, A.3 and are from San Leandro.

The *Tanforan Totalizer* began publishing soon after the inmates arrived. May 15, 1942.

start up the *Tanforan Totalizer*, recalled it was mimeographed legal-size sheets that were distributed one newspaper to a unit. "The only things that we could print were births and deaths, reports of illnesses, meetings of church groups and hobby groups and new rules and regulations, results of elections, like we would elect a leader for one section of the shacks. Just things of that sort."[72]

In his book, *The Kikuchi Diary*, Charles Kikuchi frequently mentioned his work on the newspaper and reported that the censor would not allow references to people being idle or information on how people in Tanforan could acquire copies of the *Tolan Reports*, which were prepared by the Congressional committee that investigated the exclusion of Japanese on the West Coast. Even after all these years, dog-eared copies of *Totalizers* show that it documented events that happened at the assembly center–not only those of which the administration approved reporting but also those that gave a feel for the times.[73]

One event concerning a Tanforan prisoner took on historical importance decades later: the case of Fred Korematsu, who was arrested for evading forced evacuation. An interesting entry in Kikuchi's diary, dated Friday, June 19, 1942, concerns a visit to Hi Korematsu's room to discuss his brother Fred:

Fred Korematsu wanted the group's opinion on whether he should plead guilty to [evasion of] evacuation orders. He is here on $1000 bail furnished by the ACLU and has until Monday to make up his mind...He has a clean record and [ACLU lawyer Ernest] Besig wanted him for a test case to determine the constitutionality of the evacuation...We agreed that the discussion could not be ours since Fred would be the only one to suffer in case he lost. But we told him that we would all back him as most of us by this time believed that the pressure groups would go ahead with their program regardless of whether we kept quiet or put up a fight. Since evacuation, we believed, the liberal groups had come more to the fore and this would be the time to test the principle since we did not think evacuation was purely a military necessity, but partly on a racial basis.

...Fred has the "guts" to fight the thing. I don't believe that the group would suffer by it. In fact, we have everything to gain. We are not prisoners of war and our civil rights have been taken away without due process of law. Fred has not made his mind up yet, but he is thankful that many Nisei believe as he does in regard to this situation.[74]

---

[72] T. Takahashi, interview by yamada. A "totalizer" at a racetrack is a board that shows race results.

[73] Kikuchi, *The Kikuchi Diary*, 131-132. *See also* 111-112,160-161,168. Kikuchi was hired by the JERS project to report his observations about life behind barbed wire. He is best known through the publication of his diary, which he kept during his Tanforan and Topaz incarcerations.

[74] Kikuchi, *The Kikuchi Diary*, 136-138.

As I write this we are waiting for the train and are seated on dad's good old trunk number 437. This morning we sent 7 crates, etc. by baggage. This is going to be very messy looking since I am writing on my red bag. I feel so sorry for Elsie and Janet May—they cried over Mickey [our cat] coming all the way here. It really was so hard to leave her behind. But we must be brave as we were when we had to leave Brightly and Tippy. We [sisters Elsie and Janet May and I] just came into the laundry room to wait. Mom and Lillian have stayed outside to get the sun. We had a swell breakfast this morning and our lunch consisted of sandwiches and cookies. It's past 1 o'clock now. We came early because dad said it would be better. We have quite a long wait ahead of us. It's so warm now...We also had a long ride around Tanforan with dad. I'll never forget this sky this morning—it was the most beautiful sight I have seen for a long time. I want to look around now for a little while.

— ISABEL MIYATA
seventeen when she went to Tanforan[75]

In the Korematsu case, the U.S. Supreme Court in 1944 ruled that the evacuation orders did not violate the Constitution.[76]

Some people had other reasons for leaving Tanforan. On June 6, fifteen Tanforan inmates–part of a contingent of fifty-four Japanese from the various assembly centers–were escorted out to be repatriated to Japan at their request. Records show there were four men, six women, one boy, and four girls; none came from San Mateo. They traveled to New York City, where they boarded the *S. S. Gripsholm*, which would take them on the long journey to Japan.[77]

In late summer 1942, news began circulating of plans to move the Tanforan prisoners to permanent confinement camps. The official closing of Tanforan that fall was preceded by two camp-wide inspections, one conducted by WCCA authorities looking for contraband and the other conducted by the U.S. Army with an armed guard posted at each section during the search. Finally, those incarcerated at Tanforan received word to pack up and prepare to move out. There was still no word about their destination, but inmates nevertheless hurriedly packed and crated their possessions for wherever their next stop would be.

The first people left Tanforan on September 9, 1942, via train to the Central Utah Relocation

---

[75] I. Miyata, diary entry, October 13, 1942.

[76] The *Korematsu* decision was vacated in 1983 by Judge Marilyn Hall Patel, U.S. District Court, Northern District of California, on a *coram nobis* petition, which revealed that the original Supreme Court ruling had been based on lies by government officials. This effectively undermined the factual basis for the eviction and incarceration.

[77] DeWitt, *Final Report*, 308, 319. Though "repatriate" has become the commonly-used term in this situation, it is not totally accurate because it implies a prior connection or loyalty to another place. Many Japanese Americans who had never even been to Japan went there only because their parents did.

Tanforan is recognized today for the role it played in the incarceration of those of Japanese ancestry during World War II. *Photograph by Yoneo "Yon" Kawakita, courtesy of Yoneo "Yon" Kawakita*

Center, commonly called, "Topaz." These first prisoners helped prepare the camp for the arrival of the others. Word trickled back to the others in Tanforan about what to expect of Topaz life, including dust storms, scorpions, and lizards. Tanforan gradually emptied as its prisoners were sent in waves to Topaz.

The last people left Tanforan Assembly Center on October 13, 1942—169 days after the first prisoners had arrived. "Leaving Tanforan on the train as we approached San Mateo, we weren't allowed to pull that curtain," remembered Michiko Mukai, a San Mateo native who was six when the war broke out. "But we peeked, and we saw our house, and it was so good to see our house. It wasn't our house, because we rented it, but still it was home to us."[78]

Kei Nakano, who grew up in Redwood City, echoed the memory of leaving the lush Bay area. "It was quite a trip going to Topaz, especially when the train stopped in Redwood City, and they came around and told us to pull the shades. We knew exactly where it was. It was the end of town. Even if I was [only] thirteen, my heart said, 'Here we are.'"[79]

---

[78] M. Mukai, interview by Ito.
[79] K. Nakano, interview by Ito.

TOPAZ:
A HOME "FOR THE DURATION"

I didn't think about the future.
Only the present. I didn't have any future.

—KAORU YOSHIFUJI
then twenty-eight years old[1]

You're still kind of apprehensive about what the future's going to hold for you...When you get on that train, you know, you've got to keep your shades drawn and you've got armed guards standing over you, you know, on each end of the cars, and what gives? What's going to happen? You're completely bewildered as to what the future's going to be.

— YON KAWAKITA
then eighteen years old[2]

They said, "Here you are. Welcome to your new home." We looked around and there were no homes... We were assigned to a tar-papered barrack.

— JIM HIROSHI NAKANO
then fifteen years old[3]

Although the train ride from Tanforan to Topaz took only a little over two days, the psychological distance was a quantum leap. George Fukui, a student at the University of California, Davis before he was incarcerated, captured the journey in his memoirs:

The train ride to Topaz was dismal, to say the least. The railroad cars were old and dusty. It seemed like they had not been cleaned in ten or more years. Again, we had to carry all our belongings and board the train and find our seats. Once we got going, it seemed like we had to stop for all other trains–getting the last priority. So it was a very long journey from Tanforan, across the Bay, and then slowly moved up toward Sacramento and to Lake Tahoe and Donner Pass. I remember the

---

[1] Kaoru Yoshifuji, interview by gayle k. yamada, San Mateo, Calif., February 11, 1998.
[2] Y. Kawakita, interview by yamada, March 2, 1998.
[3] J. Nakano, interview by Ito.

"Every freedom I had been fighting for was violated in my own backyard." — Roger Walker, a firefighter in Topaz when it closed, fought in the Pacific Theater during World War II.[4] *Photograph by Kameo Kido, courtesy of Yasuko "Ann" (Ishida) Ito*

A welcome sign over the mess hall door greeted prisoners. *National Archives*

first get-up-and-stretch stop was in Winnemuca, Nevada, in the godforsaken desert. Before we could get off the train for air, the military guards had to get off and position themselves along the railroad tracks to prevent us from escaping. We were allowed about 15 minutes and [then] back on the train headed for Salt Lake City and then on to Delta, Utah. We arrived in Delta about 3 p.m. the following day. Herded off the train and onto buses to be driven to Topaz. As the bus pulled out of the railroad station and headed west, it seemed like we were leaving civilization and headed for the mountains with no houses or sign of life in view.

About thirty minutes on the dusty roads we saw a military camp-like unit with barbed wire fences all around. Then as the bus pulled into the gates, we realized that we had reached Topaz. As we got off the bus, the soft silt-like dust was about a foot deep, just like flour.[5]

The place that 722 San Mateans of Japanese ancestry would call home for the next three years was a combination of public domain land, tracts that had reverted to Millard County for non-payment of taxes, and several privately-owned lots. The name came from nearby Topaz Mountain, where semi-precious stones could be found. Ironically, the Central Utah Relocation Center became known as the "Jewel of the Desert."[6]

Those who lived there simply called it "Topaz."

---

[4] Jane Beckwith, "Forty Years Later: Delta High School Students Look at Topaz," *Japanese Americans: From Relocation to Redress*, edited by Roger Daniels, Sandra C. Taylor, and Harry H. L. Kitano (Seattle: University of Washington Press, 1991), 100.
[5] Fukui, unpublished memoir, 8-9.
[6] Niiya, *An A-to-Z Reference*, 331.

Like the nine other concentration camps, Topaz was chosen because it had access to water and electricity and offered agricultural possibilities. Moreover, it was accessible by railroad and, like the others, was isolated and away from populated areas. Yoshi (Sato) Mizono of Half Moon Bay recalled life in the middle of nowhere. "Since my sister had a baby, we were one of the last contingents to leave Tanforan and thus were separated from those we knew who had arrived in Topaz earlier. When we got to Topaz, it was so desolate. I was never so depressed in my whole life."[7]

Topaz, the Gem of the Desert
(*Sung to the tune of* Columbia, Gem of the Ocean)

Oh, Topaz, the gem of the desert
The home of the Bay region Jappies [sic].
Our bare barren desert
   will be blooming,
And in time it will be a place to see.
But our city still is an infant,
Diarrhea rampant everywhere.
Deadly scorpions, rattlesnakes,
   and coyotes,
Crawl in bed with us every night.
Every night, every night snakes in bed.
Every night, every night
   makes me scared.
But with all this lousy conditions,
We hope you'll like it here,
   we think it's swell.
Like Hell!

— LYRICIST UNKNOWN[8]

---

[7] Ten concentration camps were hastily constructed in desolate areas in states west of the Mississippi River for the 120,000 people of Japanese ancestry who were incarcerated. In the order in which they were opened, the relocation centers' names, locations and opening dates were Manzanar (Manzanar, Calif. Manzanar opened as an assembly center on March 22, 1942 and came under War Relocation Authority jurisdiction June 1, 1942), Colorado River (Poston, Ariz., May 8, 1942), Tule Lake (Newell Lake, Calif., May 27, 1942), Gila River (Rivers, Ariz., July 20, 1942), Minidoka (Hunt, Idaho, August 10, 1942), Heart Mountain (Heart Mountain, Wyo., August 12, 1942), Granada (Amache, Colo., August 27, 1942), Central Utah (Topaz, Utah, September 11, 1942); Rohwer (McGehee, Ark., September 18, 1942), and Jerome (Denson, Ark., October 6, 1942). Niiya, *An A-to-Z Reference*, 146, 150, 160, 193, 233, 285, 297, 332, 336; Jeffrey F. Burton, Mary M. Farrell, Florence B. Lord, and Richard W. Lord, *Confinement and Ethnicity: An Overview of World War II Japanese American Relocation Sites* (Washington, D.C.: Western Archeological and Conservation Center, National Park Service, U.S. Department of the Interior, 2000); and Arrington, *Price of Prejudice*, 17; and Y. Mizono, interview by yamada; also Yoshiko "Yoshi" (Sato) Mizono, letter to gayle k. yamada, November 18, 1999.

[8] *Topaz, the Gem of the Desert*, lyricist unknown, *circa* 1943-1945, Topaz, Utah. Song sheet given to Dianne Fukami by Sadie Tajima, a former Topaz prisoner.

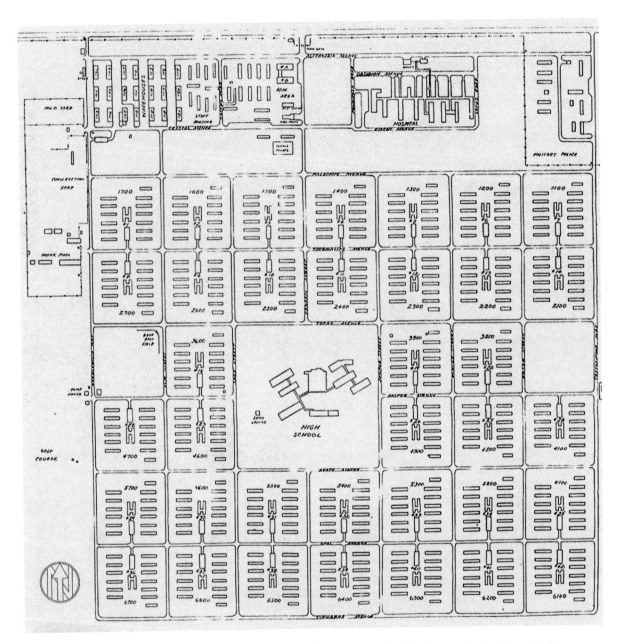

The official map of "Topaz," the Central Utah Relocation Center, created by the Design Unit. September 7, 1943.
Courtesy of Tomoko Kashiwagi

While the entire project covered 19,800 acres, the "city"–designed to house 9,000 persons–was a mile square, and was divided into areas for evacuee residents, administrative personnel, and military police. The evacuee area consisted of forty-two checkerboard blocks, of which thirty-four were living quarters or residential blocks. Each block was uniformly constructed to house and service 250 to 300 persons, and had twelve single-story resident barracks buildings, a central mess or dining hall, a recreation hall, a combination washroom-toilet/ laundry building, outdoor clotheslines, and an office for the block manager. Each barrack was divided into six single rooms, ranging from 16 by 20 feet to 20 by 25 feet in size. Each room was "home for the duration" for a family with several children or for four or five unrelated individuals.

— *Leonard J. Arrington,*
The Price of Prejudice[9]

Topaz was in the desert, sixteen miles from the nearest town of Delta (population 1,500), and 140 miles southwest of Salt Lake City, in an arid, barren valley 4,600 feet above sea level, surrounded by mountains. The weather was as cold as 30 degrees below freezing in the winter and as hot as 106 degrees in the summer; temperatures varied

TOPAZ STATISTICS [10]

CONSTRUCTION DATES
Between July 1942 and January 1943

AREA COVERED
19,800 acres

COST
$3,929,000

NUMBER OF PEOPLE
ON THE PROJECT
More than 800

COST OF ADDITIONAL
STRUCTURES
About $1 million

PEAK POPULATION
8,130

OPENED
September 11, 1942

CLOSED
October 31, 1945

---

[9] Leonard J. Arrington, *The Price of Prejudice*, (Delta, Utah: The Topaz Museum, 1997), 23.
[10] Arrington, *Price of Prejudice*, 17, 23.

as much as 50 degrees in one day. Rainfall averaged seven to eight inches a year and, after a rain, the non-absorbent soil bred mosquitoes. Windstorms constantly swirled clouds of dust.[11]

The soil was so alkaline it seemed suitable only for saltgrass, a native perennial grass on which salt crystals form, and a wiry, gray ground-cover shrub called greasewood. Because of the soil, heat, and winds, only the hardiest of vegetation could survive. The government initially landscaped the camp with seventy-five large trees, seventy-five hundred smaller ones—mostly Siberian elms, Utah junipers, Russian olives, and black locusts—and ten thousand cuttings of tamarind trees, willows, and black currants. Most, however, died. Artist and writer Miné Okubo recalled, "Hardy trees and shrubs were brought from the distant mountains and transplanted throughout the camp. It was doubtful that anything would grow in this alkaline soil, but to our surprise, in the following spring, green began to appear in the trees and the shrubs, especially on those planted near the washrooms."[12]

Tanforan had been temporary; Topaz was permanent. It was not much better, though. The 214 prisoners who were among the first workers to arrive were carpenters, ditch diggers, and other laborers to complete construction and take on

Topaz, the "Jewel of the Desert." Kameo Kido, who took this photograph, was an inmate at Topaz. March 1944. *Photograph by Kameo Kido, courtesy of Yasuko "Ann" (Ishida) Ito*

transportation duties. They readied the camp for the rest of the inmates who began arriving by train at the railhead town of Delta five days later, on September 16, 1942, and who were bused to Topaz where an improvised band greeted them. In all, sixteen trainloads each carried about five hundred people to the camp. The last one arrived on October 15, a month after the process of removal to this "permanent" home had begun.[13]

So it was to this newly and hastily-created city, this "Jewel of the Desert," that these people were forced to come. Its first "residents" were 7,676 Californians who had been incarcerated at the Tanforan Assembly Center, 577 from the

---

[11] Arrington, *Price of Prejudice*, 20-22; also Yoshiko Uchida, *Desert Exile: The Uprooting of a Japanese-American Family* (Seattle, Wash.: University of Washington Press, 1982), 110.

[12] Arrington, *Price of Prejudice*, 21-25 contains an excellent description of the Central Utah Relocation Center. This description is drawn largely from it and also from the Japanese American Curriculum Project, *Japanese American Journey: The Story of a People* (San Mateo, Calif.: JACP, 1985), 11-13; and Okubo, *Citizen 13660*, 149.

[13] Suzuki, *Ministry in the Assembly and Relocation Centers*, 170, as cited in Taylor, *Jewel of the Desert*, 89.

114

Dillon S. Myer, WRA Director, on a February visit to Topaz. The sign in the photograph was made by the Design Unit. *National Archives*

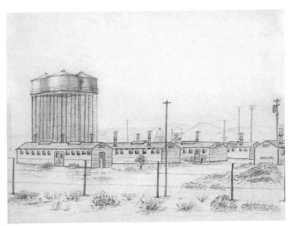

The barracks all looked the same. Unpublished pencil sketch by Tadashi Sakuma. *Courtesy of Tadashi Sakuma*

Santa Anita Assembly Center in Southern California, and five more from the Fresno Assembly Center.[14]

Topaz arrivals received an instruction sheet of what Yoshiko Uchida, who later wrote about her war experiences, recalled as a lesson in euphemisms. It included "a paragraph about words. 'You are now in Topaz, Utah,' it read. 'Here we say Dining Hall and not Mess Hall; Safety Council, not Internal Police; Residents, not Evacuees; and last but not least, Mental Climate, not Morale.'"[15]

So hastily was Topaz built that when the first detainees began arriving on September 11, 1942, only about two-thirds was completed. The barracks were crowded and, as work crews raced to finish the housing, single rooms often held

Winter in Topaz. January 1944. *Photograph by Kameo Kido, courtesy of Yasuko "Ann" (Ishida) Ito*

two families or as many as eight bachelors. Before all the ceilings and inside walls were finished, people had little besides towels to protect their faces from the constantly blowing dust and falling rain while they worked and slept.

---

[14] Arrington, *Price of Prejudice*, 45.
[15] Uchida, *Desert Exile*, 109.

From left: Photographer Tony Sato's wife, Fusako, and his mother, Masaji Sato, posed for a photograph in front of their "home" in Topaz. 1945.[16] *Photograph by Tokuye "Tony" Sato, courtesy of Fusako Sato*

"The sheeting had cracks at least a quarter of an inch between each board...No insulation whatsoever," said Roger Walker, a former serviceman who worked at Topaz during its final year. "There were bare bulbs, eight to every hundred and twenty feet, and that's all the wiring was. Just one wire down the length and a switch over by the door...It is really difficult to see how they survived."[17] *National Archives*

"When we got to Topaz," Redwood City native Yoneko (Inouye) Arimoto recalled, "there was a sandstorm there. I couldn't believe why everyone had white hair. It was all sand." The strong winds and dust made such an impression on Hamae (Tanizawa) Miyachi that when she was interviewed at the age of ninety-four, she still remembered, "The sand fell from our roof and all our blankets, and everything turned white with sand. I couldn't even cry if I wanted to." Yon Kawakita called it, "Terrible. I mean, it was out in the middle of an alkaline desert. And any time it wasn't dusty or the wind didn't blow was when it

was wet, either snow or rain. They tried to cultivate between the barracks to keep the dust down, but when that wind came up, you had to wear a bandana or something over your mouth to keep the dust out."[18]

For many San Mateans, the first snow in October was a new experience. "I had never seen snow before," remembered Mitsuye (Yamashita) Hirotsuka. She was the mother of three children

---

[16] Tokuye "Tony" Sato, incarcerated at Topaz, left to resettle in Staten Island, New York, where he worked as a welder. Fusako Sakata, whom he met in Topaz, left camp with her family to resettle on a relative's farm in Colorado. Sato took these photographs when he and Fusako returned to Topaz to visit the Sato family in 1945, after they had married and were expecting their first child.

[17] Roger Walker, interview by Wendy Walker, Delta, Utah, January 1983 (for Jane Beckwith's high school class) as cited in Taylor, *Jewel of the Desert*, 93-94.

[18] Y. Arimoto, interview by Ito; H. Miyachi, interview by yamada and Ito; and Y. Kawakita, interview by yamada, March 2, 1998.

Artist Chiura Obata depicted
the trying conditions at Topaz
in this watercolor entitled,
"Dust Storm." March 13, 1943.
Courtesy of Kimi Kodani Hill

Living at Topaz was a constant
struggle with the elements.
Painter Matsusaburo "George" Hibi
titled this oil painting of Topaz,
"Looking at East." March 4, 1945.
Courtesy of Ibuki (Hibi) Lee

117

whose husband was later taken to the Department of Justice Internment Camp in Bismarck, North Dakota. "One night I wanted to go to the bathroom, and when I opened the door, I didn't

This was some of the first snow many of the Californians who were incarcerated here saw. November 1942. *Photograph by Kameo Kido, courtesy of Yasuko "Ann" (Ishida) Ito*

Prisoners tried to make their living quarters as homey as they could. *Circa* 1942-1945. *Unpublished pencil sketch by Tadashi Sakuma, courtesy of Tadashi Sakuma*

know it was snow. So I had to wake my husband, and he said that was snow. I wanted to go to the bathroom but my slippers sank into the ground, and it was hard to walk." Yoneko (Inouye) Arimoto, twenty-three years old, once became disoriented in the snow and went to the wrong barrack. With the snow came the cold, and it was extremely cold. "My father would come back from the shower and his towel would be straight up," recalled Kazuye (Honda) Mori who, along with her husband Torao, raised chrysanthemums at Horgan Ranch before the war. "Just frozen in not even three or four minutes."[19]

In addition to the daunting climate, living arrangements also constituted a major difficulty in what turned out to be three years of incarceration. The tarpaper barracks were not insulated, and the walls had cracks between the boards. Green lumber had been used to construct the barracks and when the wood dried, it shrank, creating the cracks. Wind blew through the cracks and with it came dust.

The housing was crude and hastily built, but at least these were barracks built for **them**, not for horses as the stalls at Tanforan had been. Although there were no stables at Topaz, the barrack walls were thin and, within each family's room, no built-in partitions sectioned off areas for individual members. The government provided black pot-bellied coal stoves, canvas army cots, mattresses, and two army blankets per person.

---

[19] Kawaguchi, *Living with Flowers*, 53; M. Hirotsuka, interview by Ito; Y. Arimoto, interview by Ito; and Kazuye (Honda) Mori, interview by Yasuko "Ann" (Ishida) Ito, Redwood City, Calif., April 4, 1996.

Hisako Hibi captured her five-year old daughter, Ibuki, in 1944 at Topaz, in this oil painting entitled, "Windy." She wrote on the back, "As though a little girl had been blown off by a force, 'My daughter' and wind in the cold stillness." *Courtesy Ibuki (Hibi) Lee*

People had no choice but to make their own tables, chairs, and other furniture from whatever scrap lumber they managed to find.

Rooms had no plumbing or running water. Latrines, showers, and baths were centralized in an H-shaped building in each block. "When you went into the shower in the bathroom," said prisoner Yon Kawakita, "you had to be careful where you stepped because you would see scorpions walking around...In the summertime, we had mosquitoes, but the worst thing, I think, was the scorpions."[20]

The water supply for Topaz, stored in four elevated redwood tanks, came from three drilled

This pot-bellied stove provided heat and prisoners used it as a heating plate as well. Florence Nagamoto with her son, Thomas, and daughter, Charlotte. 1945. *Photograph by Tokuye "Tony" Sato, courtesy of Fusako Sato*

[20] Y. Kawakita, interview by yamada, March 2, 1998.

Chiura Obata saw the water tower at Topaz through an artist's eyes. "Sunset, Water Tower." March 10, 1943. *Courtesy of Kimi Kodani Hill*

Doctors, nurses, and hospital staff were Japanese and Japanese Americans who lived at Topaz. 1945. *Photograph by Tokuye "Tony" Sato, courtesy of Fusako Sato*

wells, capable of supplying 1.3 million gallons per day. The water's alkalinity rendered it almost undrinkable.[21]

Meals, once cherished family times, were no longer shared with only family members. As at Tanforan, breakfast, lunch, and dinner were served in central dining halls. Young children ate with their mothers, but older children often ate with their friends, and the men sat at separate tables.

Life with the father as head of the family continued to disintegrate. Kawakita recalled his family situation, which represented many families' circumstances:

> I'm sure my dad felt... he lost a little bit of control of the family. You've got to remember that before he went to camp, he was the breadwinner. He and my

mother, they were the ones that put the food on the table. Then we get to camp, and they're not responsible; we go on our merry way. We eat whenever we care to, and then we don't depend on them for clothing or food or whatever. It's a feeling that they can't tell us what to do... Many of those younger people felt as if I can live my own life now; I don't have to rely on my folks.[22]

Topaz was a self-contained city, the fifth largest in Utah, costing about $5 million annually to operate. It had its own schools, newspaper, hospital, post office, library, churches, fire station, gymnasium, community auditorium, and shops, including a canteen, shoe repair, and barber shop. Prisoners established a fifteen-acre community

[21] Arrington, *Price of Prejudice*, 24.
[22] Y. Kawakita, interview by yamada, March 2, 1998.

120

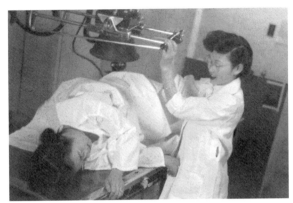

In this photograph, inmate Tokuye "Tony" Sato documented what a medical procedure at Topaz was like. 1945. *Photograph by Tokuye "Tony" Sato, courtesy of Fusako Sato*

Topaz was a city with its "residents" all of Japanese descent. Among other things, it had its own barber shop. March 29, 1945. *Photograph by Francis Stewart, National Archives*

garden. They also created a small cemetery that was never used.[23]

The camp's administrative area contained maintenance and construction sheds, military police headquarters, and barracks. About half of the two hundred Caucasians staffing Topaz lived nearby and the rest lived and ate in a segregated area of the camp. They received civil service wages for their work. They did not have to live under the restrictions imposed on the Japanese— they came and left as they pleased.

That, of course, pointed to the most notable difference between Topaz and any other American city: lack of freedom. High barbed wire fences ringed the perimeter. Tall guard towers equipped

Prisoners worked side by side with their non-Japanese co-workers. 1945. *Photograph by Tokyue "Tony" Sato, courtesy of Fusako Sato*

---

[23] Figures on the number of deaths vary. According to Arrington, there were 139 deaths; the bodies were sent to Salt Lake City where they were cremated and the ashes returned and held for burial in the San Francisco area after the war. Taylor cites two figures: 156 on a list that Alice Kasai of the Salt Lake City Chapter of the Japanese American Citizens League obtained from the Nickle Mortuary in Delta, Utah, that includes stillbirths and several other deaths; and 131 with no citation of source. Arrington, *Price of Prejudice*, 45; and Taylor, *Jewel of the Desert*, 223, 321.

Twenty-seven-year old Shig Takahashi's father was one of the first to die in Topaz.

"It was tough because I was at work…I found out he had a stroke. And he asked for help but, at that time, nobody was home…And he wrote a note, and you can see how he wrote. When he started to write it was very legible, and by the time he ended, it was just plain lines…Most of our friends were interned there anyway, and they all came and attended the funeral, and it was very nice. It wasn't, you know, wasn't just the family. We had a lot of friends there. So after that I went and told my mother [who was hospitalized and couldn't attend the funeral] it was nice. Everything was white from snow. And then they took, you know, my father out to have him cremated because my mother wanted to bring him home to San Mateo. So she kept the ashes in her room until we reached San Mateo." [24]

with searchlights stood at each corner and in the middle of each side. At the entrance was the guardhouse, where all visitors and every prisoner leaving or entering Topaz had to check in. Between 85 and 150 armed guards, supervised by up to five officers, policed the camp day and night.

Though Topaz inmates had no idea how long they would be there, they made every effort to live "normal" lives. Despite communal eating situations and public lavatory facilities, they tried to make life behind barbed wire as close to mainstream America as they could.

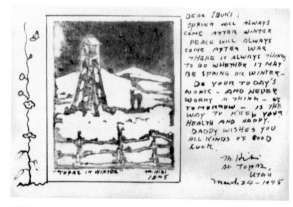

While in Tanforan and Topaz, artist Matsusaburo "George" Hibi kept a journal to share with his five-year old daughter Ibuki. Next to this sketch of a guard tower, he wrote, "Dear Ibuki, Spring will always come after winter. Peace will always come after war. There is always things to do whether it may be spring or winter. Do your today's work–and never worry a thing–or tomorrow–is the way to keep your health and [be] happy. Daddy wishes you all kinds of good luck." March 24, 1945. Unpublished sketch by Matsusaburo "George" Hibi. *Courtesy of Ibuki (Hibi) Lee*

---

[24] S. Takahashi, interview by yamada.

People sought to make these one-room "apartments" look and feel like a home. They made partitions from sheets and blankets, fashioned wall decorations and ornaments from shells, and carved vases from indigenous wood they found. Yon Kawakita remembered his own father making furniture from orange crates and others using sagebrush and other available vegetation to make decorative artifacts. Kaoru Yoshifuji of Pescadero said, "We didn't have any problems getting lumber or wood, so I made a lot of things. I made a guitar (laughs)...I made a chair, not much of a chair, but I made a chair."[25]

Privacy continued to be a problem. In a humorous vein, San Mateo native Tomoko Kashiwagi remembered how everyone in her barrack listened day after day to an aspiring saxophonist stumble at the same place in the song, *Sleepy Lagoon*. There was a communal sense of relief the day the musician finally mastered that portion and was able to make it past his former stumbling point.[26]

It was difficult for families to live in such close quarters. "Our family was totally broken up," recalled Janet "Inako" (Hirano) Matsuoka, a young child in Topaz. "I know there were a lot of sacrifices they made...My mom wanted us to be able to eat together without having to wait in line.

Artist Matsusaburo "George" Hibi expressed his feelings about living in Topaz in this painting. Karin M. Higa, curator at the Japanese American National Museum, wrote, "The perspective used in the painting is not one of documentation but of the imagination. Hibi uses his art to psychologically remove himself from the confines of camp. The coyotes...symbolize the cruelty and terror of the world as well as symbolizing a free entity to be envied." *Courtesy of Ibuki (Hibi) Lee*[27]

So she would go in there and get in line...I learned very early that if my father was mad at me, all I had to do was run to the women's room. I knew he was not permitted to go in there. He would shout, 'Inako, come out now! I'm your dad!'"[28]

[25] Y. Kawakita, interview by yamada, March 2, 1998; and K. Yoshifuji, interview by yamada.

[26] T. Kashiwagi, interview by Fukami.

[27] Karin M. Higa, "Japanese American Art from the Internment Camps," *Japanese and Japanese American Painters in the United States–a Half Century of Hope and Suffering 1896-1945* (companion book for traveling exhibit co-organized by the Japanese American National Museum, Los Angeles, Calif., October 25, 1995-January 28, 1996), 136.

[28] Janet "Inako" (Hirano) Matsuoka, interview by Dianne Fukami, Oakland, Calif., February 17, 1995.

Parents tried to make life for their children as normal as possible. Here Hiroshi and Florence Nagamoto play with their children—Charles on his tricycle, Charlotte with her father, and Thomas in his mother's arms. 1945. *Photograph by Tokuye "Tony" Sato, courtesy of Fusako Sato*

As inmates were able to get access to cameras, they took family snapshots like this one of *(from left)* Hiroshi Ito's stepfather Iwao Takahama; Ito, who was on leave from Camp Hale, Colorado; his mother Kaya Takahama; his sister Tomiko Kido; and her husband Kameo Kido, who owned the camera. August 1943. *Courtesy of Yasuko "Ann" (Ishida) Ito*

Although the prisoners had lived in racetrack facilities for several months, the Topaz bathroom facilities were still a shock to many. Some of the toilets had neither seats nor doors, and the modest Japanese found them unacceptable–but what could they do? "No privacy," remembered Shizu "Shazie" (Yamaguchi) Tabata, then twenty-eight years old. "No privacy. It was hard."[29]

The original plan had four showers for the men and four bathtubs for the women in each block's bathroom, but some had not been built by the time the Japanese arrived. The men could not continue the custom of the *ofuro*, or "bath," in which bathers soap and rinse themselves outside the tub before entering the tub to soak in very hot water. Author and artist Miné Okubo recalled that in her block, "The women's showers were provided with four tiny bathtubs. Later the desperate old men repartitioned the walls so that one of the tubs was on their side of the shower room."[30]

Three times a day the inmates were fed their meals. "We just walked into the mess hall–we called it a mess hall –and each family had their own table, and the food was there on the table," recalls Shizu "Shazie" (Yamaguchi) Tabata. Unlike Tanforan, however, she said, "You didn't have to stand in line and get the food." Cooking facilities were limited; except for the lone light bulb wired in the ceiling, individual rooms had neither electrical outlets nor gas.[31]

[29] S. Tabata, interview by Fukami.
[30] Okubo, *Citizen 13660*, 180.
[31] S. Tabata, interview by Fukami.

Nearly everyone complained about the food. Though adequate, it was nothing like that to which the Japanese were accustomed. "There wasn't that much meat, and whatever meat there was, it was usually mutton," recalled Yon Kawakita. "I couldn't stand the smell of mutton, the way they cooked it...stewed...you know, the smell of mutton if it's improperly cooked, without any proper seasoning to kill that real distinct mutton flavor." A typical meal might consist of rice, bread, and macaroni, or stewed meat and rice, or often, as in Tanforan, animal parts considered inedible in the Japanese culture–tripe and organ meats, such as liver and heart.[32]

Had camp administrators considered the roles of men and women in traditional Japanese culture, they would have realized that women did

Cooks tried to prepare more interesting fare, such as these apple turnovers being made for an evening meal. *Photograph by Tom Parker, National Archives*

Despite the WRA's euphemism of "dining hall," inmates continued to call eating facilities "mess halls." 1945. *Photograph by Tokuye "Tony" Sato, courtesy of Fusako Sato*

By early 1943, the tofu factory that the prisoners established produced some fifteen hundred pounds of tofu a week. *National Archives*

---

[32] Y. Kawakita, interview by yamada, March 2, 1998.

the cooking and may have been better suited as meal planners and head cooks. Instead, women were relegated to cooking assistants.

Eventually, Topaz administration officials set up farming projects outside the confines of the Topaz barbed wire so inmates could grow a variety of fresh vegetables to supplement their diets. Prisoners also made their own Japanese food–including *tofu*–and helped raise chicken, hogs, and cattle for consumption. Twenty-year old George Fukui found a job at a cattle ranch about three miles away from Topaz. He was assigned a horse, saddle, and tack and taught to mend barbed wire fences and posts, "unbloat" cattle, as well as brand, de-horn, castrate, and take them to slaughter, where they would be used as food at Topaz.[33]

The government food allotment was forty-five cents a day per person, five cents less than the fifty cents allowed for U.S. soldiers. The WRA estimated it spent an average of about forty cents per person. That amount reportedly decreased to only thirty-one cents because the prisoners provided some food that they themselves grew, raised, and made.[34]

As people grew accustomed to the rules and practices at Topaz, some families began to bring their meals back to their rooms to eat. More commonly, described Yon Kawakita, "They used to, with the potbelly stove, periodically warm up hot

This prisoner was responsible for the care of the baby pigs. The government caption to this photograph says, "This specialized care is largely responsible for the fact that the death rate among the livestock here is far less than the national average." March 16, 1943. *Photograph by Francis Stewart, National Archives*

water, have tea or whatever, and then make us some kind of leftover food from the mess hall... A lot of families did that."[35]

Regardless of how long the incarceration might last, the nearly two thousand children there had to be educated. Instruction begun at Tanforan continued at Topaz. If begun right away, the school year would fulfill Utah's nine-month requirement. Prisoners set up three nursery schools and two elementary schools as well as a combined junior-senior high school for the teenagers. "Schools"

[33] U.S. Office for Emergency Management, War Relocation Authority, Topaz files, February 4, 1943, Record Group 210, National Archives; Okubo, *Citizen 13660*, 196; and Fukui, unpublished memoir, 11-12.

[34] DeWitt, *Final Report*, 186; War Relocation Authority Publication, May 1943, University Archives, 4; and Taylor, *Jewel of the Desert*, 96.

[35] Y. Kawakita, interview by yamada, March 2, 1998.

Construction beginning at the new high school in Topaz. July 8, 1943. *Photograph by R. Bankson, National Archives*

Students at Mountain View Elementary School at Topaz. *National Archives*

initially meant just a room, as writer Yoshiko Uchida recalled. "We were shocked to discover, however, that all the school barracks were absolutely bare. There were no stoves, no table or chairs, no light bulbs, no supplies, no equipment of any kind. Nothing."[36]

Despite the lack of preparation for students, teacher Eleanor Gerard Sekarak considered herself fortunate because the parents of her former students in Oakland, where she had taught prior to teaching at Topaz, who were non-Japanese American, were "supportive, liberal-minded parents not overly concerned with public opinion. They not only encouraged me but later sent to Topaz cartons of pencils, paper, chalk, crayons, tacks, and other things necessary for a classroom but in short supply in our early days."[37]

Children attended classes in schools established at Topaz. *Photograph by Francis Stewart, National Archives*

Teachers, especially Caucasian ones, were few. Because Japanese Americans had not been permitted to teach in California prior to arriving at Tanforan, credentialed teachers were not among

---

[36] Uchida, *Desert Exile*, 117.
[37] Eleanor Gerard Sekerak, "A Teacher at Topaz," from Daniels, Taylor, and Kitano, *From Relocation to Redress*, 38. Sekerak's previous classes at Technical High School in Oakland included some Nisei students.

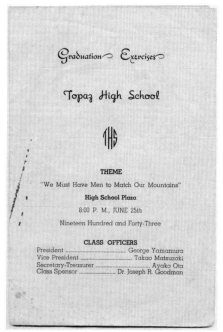

Graduation Exercises

Topaz High School

THEME
"We Must Have Men to Match Our Mountains"

High School Plaza
8:00 P. M., JUNE 25th

Nineteen Hundred and Forty-Three

CLASS OFFICERS
President .... George Yamamura
Vice President .... Takao Matsuzaki
Secretary-Treasurer .... Ayako Ota
Class Sponsor .... Dr. Joseph R. Goodman

This program is from the first graduation at Topaz in 1943. *Courtesy of Yoneo "Yon" Kawakita*

The Class of 1945 was the only class that went through its entire high school years in Topaz. *National Archives*

the "resident" population, nor could they get credentialed while in camp. Japanese Americans— many with college educations—could, and did, teach in camp, however. In the beginning, all twenty-six pre-school teachers and the two supervisors, twenty-eight of the thirty-five elementary school teachers, and twenty-five out of the forty high school teachers were Nisei:[38]

> School organization [in Topaz] was an improvement over Tanforan. The curriculum followed the requirements of the state of Utah and the school was staffed by Caucasian teachers and by teachers selected from among the evacuees; the latter received only standard camp wages.
>
> — *Miné Okubo, who recorded her experiences at Topaz in* Citizen 13660 [39]

Despite the hardships, such as a lack of proper teaching materials and school supplies for children, school did keep them busy and gave some structure to their lives. But students reacted differently to this educational opportunity. Kei Nakano, who was then thirteen years old, maintained that it was largely a waste of time, that he and his fellow students were not motivated, and that he was ill-prepared for high school when he returned to San Mateo after the war. But his brother Jim, older by two years, attended Topaz High School during the same time and said he

---

[38] U.S. Office for Emergency Management, War Relocation Authority, "Education in Topaz," Topaz files, January 1, 1944, Record Group 210, National Archives.
[39] Okubo, *Citizen 13660*, 166.

had motivation to hit the books: he wanted to leave Topaz and attend college.[40]

Adults as well as children took classes that included basic English, sewing, auto mechanics, carpentry, painting, *bonsai*, music, jewelry making, and Americanization. Other people spent their time making rock gardens and flower arrangements.

For those who liked to read, the library at Topaz was considered one of the best of any of the ten camps. Gifts from friends, California schools, and public libraries started the library with five thousand books. Additional books and magazines increased the Topaz Public Library's holdings to seven thousand. A nickel rented a current bestseller. The Salt Lake County Library lent selected titles, and the college libraries at the University of California, Berkeley, and the University of Utah provided interlibrary loans.

Other forms of recreation were available as well. Favorable response to a concert of classical recordings prompted the library to institute weekly concerts, complete with mimeographed program notes. Sports played an important part of life at Topaz. As they had at Tanforan, the inmates quickly organized school and recreational teams in football, basketball, and baseball. Organizations such as the Boy Scouts, Girl Scouts, 4-H, YMCA, and YWCA also flourished. Dances were held weekly, and talent shows entertained the community.[41]

Photography class at Topaz. *National Archives*

Sewing class teachers making a service flag. April 24, 1943. *Photograph by Russell Bankson, National Archives*

Unpublished pencil sketch by Tadashi Sakuma shows the Topaz Public Library. *Courtesy of Tadashi Sakuma*

---

[40] K. Nakano, interview by Ito; J. Nakano, interview by Ito.

[41] Y. Kawakita, interview by yamada, March 2, 1998.

Lack of equipment did not stop these young men from playing football. October 19, 1942. *Photograph by Tom Parker, National Archives*

Yon Kawakita recalled, "My mother used to go to a class where they made ornaments from all these various unique things out of seashells, because that alkaline desert way back, there must have been some water in that area and there were a lot of seashells [from the old Sevier Lake bed]. And the Topaz mountains, where it obviously got the name of Topaz, the topaz was found up in the hills, and they made all of these intricate ornaments and jewelry."[42] *Photograph by gayle k. yamada, courtesy of gayle k. yamada*

Life appeared almost normal for these young people enjoying beverages in Topaz. *From left:* Tony Sato's younger sister, Ruby; Kim Ihara; Tony's wife, Fusako; Tony Sato; and Yuki Tsuchihashi. 1945. *Courtesy of Fusako Sato*

Youth excursions to a camp outside of Topaz were also available. One trip to Antelope Springs, which was known for its natural springs, still stood out in the memory of Kyoko (Takeshita) Sasano who had moved to San Mateo as a child. "We went to Antelope Springs for one week. I remember going with a church group or young people's group...My brother went as a counselor for a week. I remember sewing a dress just for that."[43]

As time wore on, rules relaxed somewhat, and that affected recreational activities. Block shopping was instituted, allowing people to get passes to shop for their block in Delta. Student football and basketball teams played games around the state, and a girls' team from Wasatch Academy, about seventy-five miles to the east in the town of Mt. Pleasant, even spent a weekend at Topaz as guests.[44]

---

[42] Y. Kawakita, interview by yamada, March 2, 1998.

[43] K. Sasano, interview by Ito.

[44] U.S. Office for Emergency Management, War Relocation Authority, Topaz files, March 25, 1944, Record Group 210, National Archives.

130

Golf was another sport duffers took up on a makeshift tee. The government caption notes the golfer here is a former California tournament runner-up. October 19, 1942. *Photograph by Tom Parker, National Archives*

Despite being locked up, life was not grim all the time. America's favorite pastime brought pleasure to players and spectators alike. 1945. *Photograph by Tokuye "Tony" Sato, courtesy of Fusako Sato*

Despite the increasing freedom and the drives for scrap metal, clothing, and blood donations to help in the war effort, there were ever-present reminders that those who lived in Topaz were, indeed, still prisoners. Sei (Kashiwagi) Sakuma, who was incarcerated with her sister Tomoko and their widowed father, had no choice but to order her wedding ring from the mail order catalogue. Weddings still had to take place behind barbed wire.[45]

Henry Yamashiro watched Tad Horita, both members of the Topaz fire department, play horseshoes. March 12, 1943. *Photograph by Francis Stewart, National Archives*

Many prisoners took solace in their religion. Protestant denominations and Buddhism were prevalent, each with about forty percent of the camp population. The other twenty percent was a mixture of Catholic, Seventh Day Adventist, various other religious groups, and non-believers. Attending Bible class once a week intensified the devotion of Yoshi (Sato) Mizono of Half Moon Bay. "I got baptized at Topaz. I wasn't sure if I'd been baptized as an infant…So I asked my sister if

Photographer Tokuye "Tony" Sato captured a prisoner at play. 1945. *Photograph by Tokuye "Tony" Sato, courtesy of Fusako Sato*

[45] Sei (Kashiwagi) Sakuma, interview by Yasuko "Ann" (Ishida) Ito, San Mateo, Calif, October 14, 1993.

they knew if I had been baptized, and they didn't know, and my father couldn't remember, so no record. Easter morning [1943]…we were on a platform for, you know, a sunrise service, and six or

Talents were displayed at banquets, including this one held to induct a new Community Council. Here, Anne Kaku is accompanied by Hajime Mizuta on the *shakuhachi*, or "Japanese bamboo flute." March 10, 1945. *National Archives*

twelve–I don't remember how many of us–were baptized then."[46]

Protestants worshiped together at an interdenominational service led by various ministers who rotated preaching duties. Buddhists met on Sundays as well and, like the Christians, conducted services in English and Japanese. Topaz became the headquarters of the Buddhist Churches of America, presided over by Bishop Ryotai Matsukage.[47]

The WRA required all incarceration centers to publish an official newspaper to disseminate administration policies. At first the camp's official mimeographed newspaper, the *Topaz Times* came out thrice weekly, then daily. It carried news of camp activities, as well as statistics on births and arrivals from other camps, camp sports scores, and the comics.

Although edited by inmate Henri Takahashi and written by fellow prisoners, the *Topaz Times*

The Boy Scouts' drum and bugle corps played at community events such as the dedication of the hospital. October 17, 1942. *Photograph by Tom Parker, National Archives*

Youngsters were allowed to go on excursions to a nearby camp for recreation. *Photograph by R. A. Bankson, National Archives*

---

[46] Y. Mizono, interview by yamada.

[47] The title of the Buddhist Mission of North America, of which the San Mateo Buddhist Temple was a member, was officially changed at Topaz to the Buddhist Churches of America on April 6, 1944. Buddhist Churches, *75 Year History*, 65.

A Wedding at Topaz

Kyoko Hoshiga Mukai, who had attended Mills College in Oakland before her incarceration, remembers Topaz as the place where she, like 135 other brides, got married. Her fiancé Cromwell had left Topaz five days after he arrived as part of the student relocation program, then found a pharmaceutical research job in Detroit. When they decided to marry, Cromwell Mukai returned to Topaz a few days before the wedding, which took place on October 26, 1944. Kyoko Mukai remembered:

> *It was a regular wedding, believe it or not, in the church, and then we sat at a reception in one of the barracks. And people were just really wonderful. They saved their coupons and one was a baker outside camp, and they saved and got coupons from other people, sugar coupons, and they made a cake with all that, you know, bridal cake with frosting on it. And it really was a luxury, wasn't it? And we invited all of our guests...*

> *I sent [for fabric] by mail and then made my own dress. And a friend of mine lent me her veil and the tiara was made of shells. It was all handcrafted in Topaz...*

> *My father and his workers went looking for some pine branches. They had to go miles and miles out of there. He had the freedom to use that truck [they used for raising pigs], though...and got all of these beautiful, firm branches, which we would never have found inside Topaz. And they put that up for the wedding.*

Personal cameras were still banned, but a professional photographer was allowed to take pictures. A fourteen-year old girl was her attendant, and the best man, a friend from Berkeley. Kyoko Mukai recalled how they spent their wedding night:

> *...in the barracks, the one they gave us just for the two of us. We didn't have to go back to our families (laughs)...People had been leaving all along, so an empty apartment was no problem at all.*

The newlyweds left for Detroit two days later. Kyoko Mukai said she will never forget:

> *...one thing, though, it was very poignant. You know, they all wanted to give a wedding present but, under the circumstances, what can one do? So they each gave us two dollars, you know, just like we would give a much bigger amount. But can you imagine, in that circumstance, to do that? And I remember writing the thank-you letter in Detroit for that, a letter to each person...It was so wonderful... Unless you've been in camp, you don't appreciate that and...saving the sugar coupons and all that.*

> *It turned out really above what it would have been outside. The ministers were there, and I had a friend who was interested in music and in singing, and she sang for me...My father took me down the aisle. It was just like an outside wedding–we had rather drab surroundings, that's about it.[48]*

---

[48] Kyoko Hoshiga Mukai, telephone interview by gayle k. yamada, May 27, 1998.

Love bloomed, no matter what the circumstances were. Kyoko Hoshiga Mukai's only has a few photographs from her wedding. They were taken by an official photographer, an Issei from Oakland, California who was the only photographer authorized to take pictures. October 26, 1944. *Courtesy of Kyoko Hoshiga Mukai*

The staff of the *Topaz Times* prepared the last issue, which was dated August 31, 1945. *National Archives*

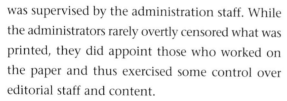

The staff assembling the newspaper's final issue. August 1945. *National Archives*

was supervised by the administration staff. While the administrators rarely overtly censored what was printed, they did appoint those who worked on the paper and thus exercised some control over editorial staff and content.

Almost from the beginning, prisoners did seasonal agricultural labor outside Topaz. They filled an agricultural labor shortage in Utah by doing such work as harvesting sugar beets and potatoes. In his memoirs, San Francisco native George Fukui, a student at the University of California, Davis before the war, wrote about answering the call for sugar beet harvesters in the nearby town of Delta. He and twelve other men from Mess 10 in Topaz received work permits and ended up at a sugar beet farm for two months, housed in an old abandoned farmhouse with just an outhouse and a pump for water. He recalled

getting paid about five hundred dollars for two months of work. Some workers, like Pescadero farmer Kaoru Yoshifuji, were gone from Topaz for the entire harvest season. "We stay there half a year, picking potato, sugar beets, all kinds of jobs…I feel freedom outside." He sent boxes of produce back to his family in Topaz, but laughed as he remembered how "by the time they get to camp, half of them are gone."[49]

---

[49] Fukui, unpublished memoir, 10-11; and K. Yoshifuji, interview by yamada.

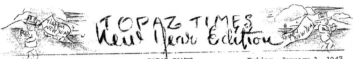

New Year Edition   TOPAZ TIMES   Friday, January 1, 1943

MESSAGE

By Charles F. Ernst
Project Director

With most people December 31 serves the dual purpose of dismissing the old year and welcoming in the new. It is not always clear which of these two events we celebrate. There is no doubt but what most of us face this new year of 1943 with courage and hope and, above all, determination to do what we can to make it count in our lives.

For there is hope in the very fact that we can, as individuals, and more particularly as part of a great national community, do something to influence the course of events in this coming year.

And so as we wish each other a Happy New Year, let us accept the responsibility of helping each other with faith and determination and hard work, knowing that our services will produce results beneficial to all mankind.

In that spirit I wish all residents of Topaz a truly "Happy New Year."

HISTORY OF UTAH PART II...

By W. Richard Nelson

I. The part played by the Mormons in the opening of the American Frontier:

Harsh frontier intolerance, which was severe and destructive, resulted in merciless persecutions and finally in the expulsion of the Saints from the State of Missouri.

A new haven where temporary peace and tranquillity were obtained was in Illinois. There the prophet Joseph Smith put into effect ideas which he had long before conceived in the building of the city of Nauvoo. It was patterned after the plan of the "City of Zion," and became a model American city in orderliness, discipline and beauty.

Once again frontier intolerance broke out in full fury. The beloved prophet was murdered and his followers were forced to seek safety in a more hospitable land.

Under the direction of Brigham Young, the Saints looked toward the great West, located more than a thousand miles from any other American frontier, as a place in which to establish their homes.

But even in the desolate, barren wastes of the Great Basin the Mormons did not remain free from conflict and persecution. There the federal government took a hand in the conflict, causing many of the devout church members to seek refuge outside the bounds of the United States, as all of the frontiers in this country were now occupied. Thus at the close of the nineteenth century, faithful Saints settled new frontier districts in Canada and Mexico.

II. The American Frontier.

What is meant when one speaks of the American frontier? What conditions prevailed there during the early part of the nineteenth century which contributed to the rise, growth, and perpetuation of the restored Gospel of Jesus Christ? Why did the Mormons move westward from one frontier to another until the last American frontier was occupied by white men?

These and many other vital questions can be answered only partially in this brief history. However, through the perusal of the entire course of Mormon history, much light will be thrown upon the foregoing interrogation. We shall follow the heroic Saints—true frontiersmen—in their noble effort in helping to open several American frontiers to land settlement, and in their remarkable achievements in establishing a commonwealth in the Far West.

A SKETCH By Toshio Mori

On October 9 two men were watching laborers put up fence posts around the city of Topaz. The two men were late arrivals from Tanforan taking an afternoon walk. They stood for a long time without comment. Then the shorter one spoke, "It looks bad. Fences around us once again. Just like the days at Tanforan."

He shook his head and nudged his friend. The latter did not speak. He watched the men with the posts and then slowly turned to his friend.

"What's wrong with it, friend?" he slowly asked.

The shorter one shook his head again. "Everything. I want to feel free. What are the fences for? We won't run away."

"Look here, friend," the other one quietly replied. "There are two ways of looking at it. It might limit your travels but it also protects you. Don't you think it is meant for protection too? For example, suppose we start a poultry farm. Coyotes roam nearby and the animals need protection. You can never tell when a fence comes in handy."

The short man was silent this time. He did not look at his friend. He watched the men working on the fence.

"Fences are natural in life," his friend continued. "We all have fences—within and without. A fence is a symbol of our limited capabilities. And another thing, friend. We have our own fences within ourselves which hinder understanding and cooperation."

This time the short one chuckled and patted his friend's shoulders. "Very true. I never thought of a fence that way. Maybe I can break that fence down from within, eh? That's a thought."

The two men continued their walk. They hailed the workers. The men grinned at them, thinking of their sad roles and unaware of the message of a fence.

New Year's edition of the *Topaz Times*, dated Friday, January 1, 1943. *Courtesy of Kimi Kodani Hill*

135

A meeting of the Topaz Community Council. March 11, 1943. *Photograph by Francis Stewart, National Archives*

Even within the confines of Topaz, jobs were plentiful. "This friend of mine told me, 'You're young. Why don't you get a job as a truck driver,'" remembered Yon Kawakita, who was eighteen years old then. "I was thinking of working in the mess hall again. I believe I worked there for a short time in the mess hall, but as soon as I heard about this truck driver job, I applied at the motor pool and was able to get one."[50]

Topaz relied on incarcerated labor for several reasons. First, on a purely practical level, staffing was needed. The work also kept those in camp busy and helped them "maintain their connections with the American scene" and gave the Japanese a way "to prove, by constructive deeds, that they were loyal Americans." The prisoners were paid for their work, at a rate not to exceed the minimum rate of pay for an American army private. In 1942,

this was twenty-one dollars a month. When the private's pay was raised to fifty dollars a month, however, people in Topaz saw no increase in their pay.[51]

The highest rate of pay in Topaz was nineteen dollars a month for professional workers such as doctors, certified teachers, and fire captains. Skilled laborers earned sixteen dollars a month; and unskilled workers twelve dollars a month–a far cry from the $250 a month sugar beet workers like George Fukui were paid on the outside. Those in civilian jobs, including camp administration, earned between $150 and $250 a month.[52]

Within limits, those who lived in Topaz managed the camp. Each block of 250 to 300 people had an administration-appointed manager who listened to complaints, conveyed official announcements from the administration, and insured maintenance of the block's facilities. Block managers earned sixteen dollars a month.

Representatives from each block formed the Community Council, which determined policy and procedures for the prisoners. Inmates who were at least eighteen years of age elected representatives to six-month terms. They could be re-elected. At first, those who wished to serve had to be American citizens older than twenty-one. This requirement recognized Nisei citizenship. In the spring of 1943, Issei were allowed to serve on the council as more and more Nisei left camp.

For political and economic reasons, the government encouraged inmates to leave Topaz

---

[50] Y. Kawakita, interview by yamada, March 2, 1998.

[51] Arrington, *Price of Prejudice*, 33.

[52] Arrington, *Price of Prejudice*, 33-34.

as long as they left the West Coast and relocated to the interior states. Economically, many non-Japanese had benefited when the Japanese were evicted from their land, homes, and businesses, and they did not want the Japanese to return. Plus, with the United States at the height of World War II, much of the West Coast populace still held onto anti-Japanese sentiment and perceptions that people of Japanese ancestry would help the Japanese military in its attacks against the United States. Thus, the government encouraged the Nisei to pursue work opportunities or college educations away from the West Coast, and some college-age prisoners began to leave as soon as they arrived.[53]

Helped by the National Japanese Student Relocation Council, which had been formed in Philadelphia earlier that year by the American Friends Service Committee—also known as Quakers—and college educators, the first contingent of students left Delta, Utah on October 7, 1942. They boarded trains headed for the University of Nebraska, Union College in New York, Huron College in South Dakota, and the University of Utah.[54]

Jim Hiroshi Nakano ended up leaving Topaz early to attend the University of Connecticut.

Among the first people to leave Topaz under the student relocation program were George Hirose (*left*) and Ben Masaoka. *National Archives*

Twenty-one-year old Yoshi (Sato) Mizono left Topaz in 1943 to attend nursing school in Pennsylvania. She said, "The Quakers, through the National American Friends Service Committee, were the best thing to all students! Invaluable assistance!"[55]

As time passed, more and more high school graduates were able to leave to attend universities. By the end of 1944, West Coast schools as well as ones in the Midwest and on the East Coast, were accepting the Japanese American students.

The number of people living in Topaz was dwindling. The WRA had begun emphasizing its resettlement program as early as October 1942. Those who wished to leave the camps had to fill out the proper forms and subject themselves to

---

[53] The words, "relocation" and "resettlement" have been used in a variety of contexts, which causes confusion. Initially, "relocation" was used to refer to "voluntary relocation" when those of Japanese ancestry were allowed to move off the West Coast *before* Executive Order 9066 was issued. However, *after* EO 9066, the word "relocation" was used for the mass involuntary removal and eviction of Japanese and Japanese Americans from the West Coast to imprisonment camps. The official WRA terminology for students leaving camp to attend college was "relocation." "Resettlement" was a term used for people who left camp during the war years and, loosely, a term used by the inmates themselves when referring to starting their lives over after the war.

[54] Taylor, *Jewel of the Desert*, 113.

[55] J. Nakano, interview by Ito; and Y. Mizono, letter to yamada, November 18, 1999.

FBI security checks. Then they received "permanent leave" status, twenty-five dollars for expenses and a train ticket to their destination. To expedite the process, the WRA began a two-pronged propaganda campaign. First, it showed newsreels and photos to the civilian public to convince it that Japanese Americans were loyal and trustworthy as neighbors and employees. Second, within the camps, inmates saw films and photographs depicting how welcoming and attractive life beyond the barbed wire could be for them.

The prospect of freedom and getting a job encouraged many able-bodied young people to leave the camps and begin new lives away from the West Coast. Kazuo Haraguchi left Topaz and went to Denver, looking for a house for his family. After a three-month search, he found a basement flat and sent for his wife and baby. He worked a split shift as a fry cook. Rent was eight dollars a week, and his wages were eighteen dollars for a sixty-hour work week, but it was a lot better than the sixteen dollars a month he earned in Topaz.[56]

Many who remained in the camp were those who could not easily find jobs or housing on the outside: the elderly and families with children.

In the midst of focusing on their future and education and otherwise normalizing their lives behind barbed wire, those of Japanese ancestry were confronted by a situation that all too starkly reminded them that things were far from normal for them. In a 1943 joint operation, the War Department and the WRA decided to circulate a questionnaire to all prisoners seventeen years of age and older designed to determine loyalty. The "disloyal," along with their families, would be segregated at the detention center at Tule Lake, while the "loyal" would be cleared for relocation outside the West Coast exclusion zone or for enlistment into the army. Within the Japanese American community this questionnaire resulted in a huge controversy and created deep rifts that lasted decades after the camps were closed.[57]

Two questions turned out to be crucial. Question 27 asked if one was willing to serve in the U.S. armed forces on combat duty, and Question 28 asked if one was willing to forswear allegiance to the Japanese emperor and swear allegiance to the United States.[58]

The questions offended many and brought much strife and misunderstanding. Some Nisei

---

[56] Kazuo Haraguchi, interview by Yasuko "Ann" (Ishida) Ito, San Mateo, Calif., March 3, 1994.

[57] The army was the only branch of military service that Nisei could join. The "loyal" were eligible for the U.S. Army's Military Intelligence Service and later for the 442nd Regimental Combat Team, an all-Nisei combat unit that would fight in Europe, and the 100th Infantry Battalion (Separate) which began in Hawai`i. The 100th Infantry Battalion (Separate) was so named because it was segregated from other units and was not assigned to a parent unit. gayle k. yamada, *Uncommon Courage: Patriotism and Civil Liberties*, television documentary, 2001; Thomas V. Mukai, telephone conversation with gayle k. yamada, 2002; also Weglyn, *Years of Infamy*, 136.

[58] Question 27 on the form stated, "Are you willing to serve in the armed forces of the United States on combat duty, wherever ordered?" Question 28 asked, "Will you swear unqualified allegiance to the United States of America and faithfully defend the United States from any and all attack by foreign or domestic forces, and foreswear any form of allegiance to the Japanese Emperor or any other foreign government, power, or organization?"

did not want to serve in the armed forces while the U.S. government violated their constitutional rights. Answering "yes" on Question 28 implied that the Nisei, most of whom considered themselves loyal American citizens, once had an allegiance to Japan; and for the Issei, who were not allowed to become citizens by American law, a "yes" left them stateless.

Bitter arguments within families broke out as fathers fought with sons and brothers against brothers in determining how to fill out the questionnaire. Their answers would determine if the family could be released early, if they would stay in Topaz, or if they would be sent to Tule Lake. Yoshi (Sato) Mizono recalled her older brother Ham responding "no-no" to both questions. "He told the FBI agent...'I'm putting no-no, because you look up in the dictionary and see what allegiance means. Allegiance means...swearing allegiance to a country that's going to protect you'... He told the FBI agent this, and the man said, 'I wish you'd change your mind, we need guys like you on our side.'"[59]

The questionnaire divided the people at Topaz. Originally, about seventy-eight percent (5,634 people) said "yes" to Question 27 and twenty-two percent (790 people) said no, qualified their answer, or did not respond to the question. Later, more than thirty percent changed their answers. Nearly fifteen hundred people were sent to Tule Lake, among them San Mateans

Mitsuye Endo won her case in the U.S. Supreme Court. It essentially allowed Japanese Americans to be set free from incarceration camps. Here she leaves Topaz for Chicago. *National Archives*

Kenzo Higashi and his wife Etsuko. That "no-no" response began a four-year journey that took him to Tule Lake with Etsuko, then separately to Department of Justice internment camps in Bismarck, North Dakota, and Santa Fe, New Mexico. He was finally reunited with her in Crystal City, Texas. They were not able to return home to San Mateo until 1947, two years after their fellow inmates.[60]

On December 18, 1944, in a lawsuit brought by Topaz prisoner Mitsuye Endo, the U.S. Supreme Court ruled that Congress had exceeded its

---

[59] Y. Mizono, interview by yamada. Generally, if the father, or head of household, answered yes-yes to the two questions, the family stayed in Topaz.

[60] The Higashi case is rare as most prisoners did not experience such a long delay. K. Higashi, interview by Ito.

The amazing spirit of these people! They were not going to be defeated...In Tanforan, to start with, and Topaz, it was really the spirit of the people...and I think that's remarkable.

— KYOKO HOSHIGA MUKAI
a former Topaz inmate [61]

May 14, 1945, bound for Chicago. Despite the WRA's efforts to resettle people, as of the middle of August 1945, Topaz still had thirty-four hundred people living there.[63]

As WRA Director Dillon Myer prepared to shut the incarceration camps, facilities and activities began to wind down at Topaz. Adult education and vocational training programs ended in midsummer. On October 1, with the population at two thousand, the dining halls began to close.[64]

With one month left to prepare for transition to civilian life, many people were afraid to leave the certainty of the life they had known for the past three years. Where would they live? How could they find jobs? What kind of prejudice would they face? How could they start all over again with limited resources?

On October 26, 1945, the last special train pulled out of Delta. Five days later, Topaz officially closed, with the director locking the gate behind the final busload of the now-freed prisoners. With one dark chapter ending for these people of Japanese ancestry, a new chapter was beginning. But once again, San Mateans faced a future of uncertainty.

authority in detaining a loyal American like Endo, and the ruling applied to others in a situation similar to Endo, or other Americans also incarcerated.[62]

The WRA shortly thereafter announced that it would begin releasing all people from the concentration camps and that, within the year, it would close all the camps. The first train left on

---

[61] K. Mukai, interview by yamada. Mukai speaks in the third person because she left Topaz after her 1944 marriage in the camp.

[62] Though class action lawsuits did not exist in the 1940s, Endo's legal challenge to her detention was brought as a *writ of habeas corpus* which essentially acted as a challenge to the detention of all Japanese Americans. It questioned the power of the U.S. Congress to imprison a loyal American citizen and claimed the incarceration order was unconstitutionally applied to Japanese Americans in violation of the equal protection clause of the Fourteenth Amendment. The U.S. Supreme Court did not address the question of constitutionality but did rule that Congress had exceeded its authority. Dale Minami, electronic correspondence to Diane Yen-Mei Wong, December 10, 2001, and March 30, 2003. Minami, a San Francisco attorney, was lead counsel for Fred Korematsu in the Nisei man's 1983 legal fight to clear his name after he had been convicted of violating World War II exclusion orders.

[63] Director's report to Dillon S. Myer, September 5, 1945, Japanese American Evacuation and Resettlement Study (JERS), Bancroft Library, University of California, Berkeley, Berkeley, Calif., as cited in Taylor, *Jewel of the Desert*, 219.

[64] Taylor, *Jewel of the Desert*, 220.

CHAPTER 8

STARTING OVER:
THE EARLY POST-WAR YEARS

As we came through Vallejo and I saw the fog,
it sure reminded me of the coast side.
Something that I felt really good about inside—
coming back to the coast after four years.

— SAM SATO
former Half Moon Bay resident[1]

In a way, even now, I think, "Gee, when am I going to start my regular life?" Because we come back, and I figure, well, I'm going to start whatever career I'm going to go into and all that. But each year, ten years later, twenty years, "Gee, it's about time I'm going to start my life." And here I'm eighty years old, and I still never got the point where I could pursue my career. It just seemed like with the war, it just went away.

— SHIG TAKAHASHI
San Mateo resident[2]

I came back with my sisters and my mother and grandma by train. We came back to Oakland. We took a ferry and that was the most glorious sight I ever had seen–going across on that ferry and seeing the bridge and everything else. It was cold, but I just stood there and said, "This is heaven."

— KEI NAKANO
former Redwood City resident[3]

The day they had longed for had arrived. Finally, after three years, they were free to return home. But what did freedom mean to those of Japanese ancestry in San Mateo? Feelings of excitement filled some, but many felt anger and trepidation as well.

Yoneji Takaha's Issei mother, who had come to Topaz from Half Moon Bay, was one of those

---

[1] Seishi "Sam" Sato, interview by Dianne Fukami, San Francisco, Calif., March 8, 1996.
[2] Shigeharu "Shig" Takahashi, interview by Dianne Fukami, San Mateo, Calif., February 13, 1999.
[3] K. Nakano, interview by Ito.

The first train left Topaz on August 13, 1945, bound for San Francisco. *National Archives*

They waited for an early morning train to the San Francisco Bay area. 1945. *National Archives*

who refused to leave. "She said, 'You took us, my son and my daughter,'" remembered Takaha, "'and you threw us in this camp for no reason at all except that we're Japanese! And they're American citizens, and you put us here. Now you take us out. I ain't gonna go.'"[4]

Others, like Maya Nagata Aikawa, age eighteen when she left Topaz, feared what the outside would bring:

It took an awful long time to not be afraid. When we first came out of camp, we relocated to Los Angeles, and I stayed at the hostel. I stayed inside the hostel for two solid weeks without leaving. I was so afraid of being called a Jap [*sic*]. If they called me a Jap [*sic*], I don't know what I would have done. I think I would have just stayed indoors the rest of my life. That's the kind of thing that this did to us.[5]

---

[4] Yoneji Takaha, interview by Dianne Fukami, San Mateo, Calif., March 18, 1996.
[5] M. Aikawa, interview by Fukami.

The government caption reads, "First Japanese-American [sic] family leaves Central Utah Relocation Center for California. Mrs. Saku Moriwaki, 33, formerly of Berkeley, and her two-year old daughter, Suga Ann, are bid goodbye at the gate by a Caucasian staff member and her sister, Mrs. [sic] Suga Baba. Mrs. Moriwaki has accepted a position in the home of Mrs. R.A. Isenberg (2175 Cowper Street), Palo Alto. Her husband, Pfc. Yoshiaki Moriwaki, former Berkeley insurance broker, is fighting the Nazis." January 3, 1945.[6] *Photograph by Charles E. Mace, National Archives*

The fear of racism and violence was not unfounded. In other parts of California, some people of Japanese ancestry encountered prejudice and threats of bodily harm. In San Mateo, however, there were no reports of violence.

Those who had left Topaz early and resettled away from the West Coast encountered a different kind of racism. Sakai "Sox" Suyeyasu and his wife Rose (Nakagawa) left Topaz after one year to join their family in Boulder, Colorado. Topaz

officials advised them to use a "Chinese name." Rose also remembered how difficult it was to find a doctor when she became pregnant. "Doctors would not see me since I was Japanese. I had a very difficult first-time pregnancy and had to go to Denver to try to find a doctor who would see me. We finally found one who was kind. However, there were problems with finding a pediatrician. It seems whites were afraid to take care of Japanese at that time."[7]

---

[6] According to family members, Suga Baba was not married until after she left Topaz, so in this photograph she should be identified as "Miss Suga Baba." Haru Baba, conversation with gayle k. yamada, April 7, 2003 and Suga Ann Moriwaki, conversation with gayle k. yamada, April 7, 2003.

[7] Sakai "Sox" and Rose (Nakagawa) Suyeyasu, interview by Yasuko "Ann" (Ishida) Ito, San Mateo, Calif., February 9, 1995.

Shig, Best, and their 19-month old son Jerrold "Jere" Takahashi posing for a War Relocation Authority photographer in front of their home at 108 South Humboldt Street in San Mateo. July 19, 1945. Photograph by Hikaru Iwasaki, National Archives

In California, despite the end of the war, there were still concerted efforts to keep Americans of Japanese descent out of the state. The Native Sons of the Golden West, headquartered in San Francisco, opposed the return of Japanese to the state and even wanted to take away citizenship from the American-born Nisei. Although the pendulum had partially swung the other way and the media was not overwhelmingly opposed to Japanese Americans, some anti-Japanese newspaper articles still appeared. What became clear, however, was that many Japanese had decided not to return to the West Coast. Eviction from their homes and incarceration had resulted in their dispersion and relocation throughout the country. By the time the exclusion orders were

rescinded, 42,600 of the approximately 120,000 prisoners from the West Coast had resettled in nine states outside of California. As late as 1960, only sixty percent of the Japanese American population had returned to its pre-war locations in California.[8]

But many San Mateans were anxious to return home. Kazuye (Honda) Mori, whose family had grown flowers in Redwood City before the war, proudly proclaimed that her husband was among the first people who left Topaz for the West Coast. He left with neighbor Saku Baba Moriwaki, whose departure happened to be well documented in still photographs and film by the U.S. Signal Corps.[9]

Shig Takahashi, thirty-one years old at the time, was also one of the people who left Topaz and returned to San Mateo as soon as the Japanese were allowed back. He began to look for housing for his family so they could move back to the area:

> They wanted some volunteers to come to San Mateo to find out how the feelings were about coming back. Since I was connected with the [Sturge] church and I had friends here that were helpful to us, I said I would volunteer, and my relative Oida said he would accompany me...I gave a sermon at the Congregational Church to the young people. I went to the black church on Mt. Diablo and gave a talk, and

---

[8] Taylor, *Jewel of the Desert*, 266-270, 272. The nine states in which those of Japanese ancestry had settled were Colorado, Idaho, Illinois, Minnesota, Missouri, New Jersey, New York, Ohio, and Utah. Hosokawa, *The Quiet Americans*, 436.
[9] Kazuye (Honda) Mori, interview by Ito.

I went to meet with the Catholic church, and they all said they would welcome us back to San Mateo...I volunteered to come and open the hostel in the Sturge [Memorial] Cottage...The government gave us cots and everything we needed for the sleeping quarters, so we had beds for about ten to twelve, put in a phone and put in an ad in the *San Mateo Times* for work– gardening, or any type of work...[10]

Jubei and Hamae (Tanizawa) Miyachi's family was among those who relied on the Sturge (Memorial Cottage) hostel. Hamae (Tanizawa) Miyachi, who had lived in San Mateo more than twenty years before Pearl Harbor, said her husband left Topaz first to look for housing while she stayed in camp. "After he found a house, he told

Frank Murai, recently arrived from Heart Mountain Relocation Center, selects a bed in the men's dormitory at Sturge (Memorial Cottage) hostel. July 18, 1945. *Photograph by Hikaru Iwasaki, National Archives*

us to come back. We came back late. Those who had homes to come back to, came back earlier."[11]

The San Mateo Japanese, along with thousands of others who had lived on the West Coast before the war, came home not only from imprisonment camps but also other states to which they had resettled. Jim Hiroshi Nakano's family, former Redwood City residents, had gone to Utah. He recalled his family's trip back to California:

My mother decided to return to California. So we loaded up the pickup truck, and–if you remember *The Grapes of Wrath* by Steinbeck, with tin cans and chairs and the boxes and other things stacked on top of other things–and the pickup truck was loaded so high it hardly even moved. And at that time there was a national speed limit of thirty-five miles, but it didn't bother us because we didn't go much faster than thirty-five miles. But I felt like the Joad family [in *The Grapes of Wrath*] coming into California, but I was very happy and very proud that we could do that so my dad and I drove from Topaz into California. We arrived in California either the end of April or the first of May of 1945, after driving through the desert of Nevada. The following day we drove into California, and it was May already so it was lush with rain, and we were so happy to come into California, and we drove into Redwood City the following day.[12]

---

[10] S. Takahashi, interview by Fukami; S. Takahashi, interview by yamada; and S. Takahashi, telephone conversation with yamada.

[11] H. Miyachi, interview by yamada and Ito.

[12] J. Nakano, interview by Ito.

Those who took the train back to San Mateo had to get off in Oakland, take the ferry to San Francisco, and then wait for the ride to San Mateo by car or Greyhound bus. Isao Nakagawa, in high school at the time, recalled, "We all looked like refugees. I still remember walking down Market Street with our suitcases down to the Greyhound bus, caught the bus, and my Dad picked us up in San Mateo. He only had an old jalopy."[13]

Yasukazu Suzuki, who was in seventh grade, remembered receiving a heartwarming welcome upon his return to the Bay Area. "When we got off the train in Oakland, I will never forget it as long as I live. A *hakujin* (Caucasian) man dressed in a suit…came up to me, shook my hand and said, 'Lots of luck.'"[14]

The Japanese found they were going to need more than luck to find a place to live. Housing was tight, with soldiers coming home after the war and shipyard workers around the Bay Area looking for more permanent homes. And now, more than fifty thousand Japanese were returning to the West Coast.

Some, like Kumiko Ishida, who had left Topaz at age seventeen to find a job in New York, returned to the West Coast and found live-in domestic positions that solved both work and housing problems:

> I came home and by that time, my parents were still living in Hayward. In those days many of the girls were, you know, what you called "school-girls" and lived in homes in Hillsborough, and we did small jobs and were given a little allowance, and we went to school from these homes. So I did that for a few months. Then when my parents and my brothers bought a home, I moved back with them.[15]

For a time, the *nagaya* or "longhouse," which had played such an important role as a gathering place in the community's early days in San Mateo, once again became shelter for people who had no other home. Aya (Miyake) Takahashi, forty-six when she and her family returned to San Mateo, remembered she, "asked Mr. Takahama to allow us to stay in the *nagaya*, and we stayed there for three years. I had never worked before, but I wanted to buy a house so badly that I really worked very hard and saved five thousand dollars by doing housework." It took Takahashi a couple of years, but she did it and they were able to put a down payment on a house. Gardener Kazuo Haraguchi and his wife Tatsuye, who had left Topaz early to go to Denver, also ended up living at the *nagaya* for a while when they finally returned to San Mateo.[16]

Throughout San Mateo County, those of Japanese ancestry opened their homes to others who did not have places to stay. Mariko (Tsuma)

---

[13] Isao Nakagawa, interview by Yasuko "Ann" (Ishida) Ito, San Mateo, Calif., January 13, 1994.

[14] Yasukazu Suzuki, interview by Yasuko "Ann" (Ishida) Ito, San Mateo, Calif., January 13, 1994.

[15] Kumiko Ishida, interview by Dianne Fukami, San Mateo, Calif., March 18, 1996.

[16] A. Takahashi, interview by Ito; and K. Haraguchi, interview by Ito.

Endo, whose husband Toshio had the only Japanese-owned auto repair shop in San Mateo before the war, recalled how her family managed:

> When we returned, we had to empty the rooms because we had one bedroom, and we loaned out another bedroom to another family, Mr. and Mrs. Kobayashi. The Ikedas rented one room and did their cooking in their room. Mr. and Mrs. Yutaka Kobayashi had rented their house so they had to stay with us until their house was vacated.[17]

Often, as in the case of the Torao and Kazuye (Honda) Mori family who grew chrysanthemums at Horgan Ranch in Redwood City, generosity extended beyond the offer of housing. Kazuye (Honda) Mori remembered how she also fed and cooked for those she had taken under her wing. "Once a hundred pounds of rice lasted me for only nine days! Just nine days!" she said.[18]

---

[17] Mariko (Tsuma) Endo, interview by Yasuko "Ann" (Ishida) Ito, San Mateo, Calif., February 24, 1994.

[18] Kazuye (Honda) Mori, interview by Ito. Horgan Ranch was divided into parcels of varying sizes. The largest, fourteen acres, was owned by a Chinese family, the Mee family. Nine Japanese American families owned the other land lots, which ranged in size from four to ten acres. All of the Japanese Americans grew chrysanthemums while the Mees grew carnations and other flowers. The families who owned land were the Adachis (who later married into the Sugimoto family), Kashimas, Kitayamas, Moris, Nakanos, Okamuras, Tsukushis, and Yamadas. "Joseph" Iwasuke Rikimaru's family owned a two-acre plot but he did not grow flowers because he managed the California Chrysanthemum Growers Association. James K. Mori, telephone conversation with gayle k. yamada, March 3, 2002.

[19] S. Takahashi, interview by Fukami.

We had a large garage. Half of that we boarded up and made it into a storage space. In fact, some of our wedding gifts weren't even used because it was so close to our wedding. All the different utensils that we got as our wedding presents, we stored them there and locked it up. They had the other side of the garage that we left open for the people that we rented the house to. They were supposed to be dependable, but while we were gone, they broke into the storage space, and when we came back, there was nothing there. All the wedding gifts that we received, we never got a chance to use them because they were all stolen. And the house that we left brand new, only a year old, we came back and it looked like it was ten or twenty years old. They had punched holes in the walls and, of course, we rented it furnished, all the rugs were— they must have poured water on it, or something. It was awful.

— SHIGEHARU "SHIG" TAKAHASHI
married just weeks before removal to Tanforan[19]

The Yamaguchi family stored all their things at the Chanteloup Laundry. They [the laundry owners] had given them a storeroom where they stored everything. Nob's brother Terry was in the Army, so he came to check and nothing was there. Everything that was stored at the Chanteloup Laundry was moved and stored at the Yamaguchi family house on Second Avenue. They had a garage with [an] upstairs storeroom, and they put everything up there with no door, and anyone could get in there and help themselves and it was not locked up. The house was rented that way. Some things were missing, but most things were there.

— SHIZU "SHAZIE"
(YAMAGUCHI) TABATA

*whose family owned the
Sunrise Cleaners*[20]

Slowly, the Japanese and their families began to come home, not knowing what they would find upon their return. Some could not move back into their homes right away because their homes were still leased out in arrangements made when they were first evicted from the Bay Area and their futures were uncertain. Those who had no homes could stay at Camp Funston or Hunter's Point in San Francisco, in government army surplus barracks that closely resembled the incarceration camps they had just left. Those who did return to their homes often found their houses ransacked and household items and treasures stolen.

Seishi "Sam" Sato didn't know what to expect when he returned to his home in Half Moon Bay:

Fortunately, there was a person by the name of Galen Wolfe, a well-known coast side watercolor artist who agreed to keep our personal belongings in his barn. But when we came back, the story was that his brother tried to burn our personal belongings, but Mr. Wolfe put a shotgun against his brother and told him if he touched his friends' belongings, he would shoot him. So he didn't do anything about it. My sister, when she had her baby boy in Half Moon Bay, she named him Galen, after Mr. Wolfe.[21]

---

[20] S. Tabata, interview by Ito.
[21] S. Sato, interview by Fukami.

Even the *nagaya* was not immune from vandals, who threw out items that had been stored inside. *National Archives*

In addition to racism, violence, and uncertainty, those of Japanese ancestry also ran into restrictive housing covenants that basically allowed property owners and realtors to exclude so-called "undesirables" from certain neighborhoods and areas. In the 1940s and 1950s, these types of covenants were common throughout San Mateo County as well as the rest of the Bay Area. Even as they started their lives over again, many young couples faced discrimination when they tried to buy their first homes in the 1950s. Kazuo

"Kay" Mori was rejected when he tried to buy a new house in a development in Daly City.[22]

Yoshikazu and Virginia (Sakamoto) Ishida ran into a restrictive covenant when they decided they wanted to live in Belmont. Luckily, they found a supportive realtor in Gertrude Anderson, who polled the neighborhood to find out if there was any objection to having an "Oriental" family living in the area. She found one person who objected. So, along with her real estate colleague Montgomery "Tom" Reynolds and under her niece's name, she purchased the house on behalf of the Ishidas. The Ishidas put up the money, but it wasn't until several years later the title could be transferred to their names.

In the meantime, according to the Ishidas, when Redwood City and Belmont realtors found out what Anderson and Reynolds had done, they made work harder for the two by excluding them from the multiple listing service. The realty office had to close its San Mateo office, and the two realtors lost their jobs.[23]

Reynolds, in 1959, helped to integrate the city of San Mateo when he found a house for a local Nisei woman, Florence (Makita) Hongo, and her family in the then-all-white Baywood district. Shortly thereafter, Reynolds' colleagues kicked him off the real estate board, thus ending his career. Hongo said:

---

[22] Kazuo "Kay" Mori, interview by Fukami. He eventually bought a home in San Francisco but believes racism played a part in his inability to buy a new home in the Daly City development.

[23] Later both Anderson and Reynolds became members of the San Mateo chapter of the Japanese American Citizens League. Virginia (Sakamoto) Ishida, interview by Yasuko "Ann" (Ishida) Ito, Belmont, Calif., June 17, 1997; and Yoshikazu Ishida, interview by Yasuko "Ann" (Ishida) Ito, Belmont, Calif., June 17, 1997.

It was written up in all the papers, and the ACLU became involved, and it was a big to-do that this Montgomery Reynolds had succeeded in finding us a home in Baywood…And then the neighborhood, they didn't go up in arms, but there was certain people in the neighborhood that was threatening to cause trouble because of our purchasing the house. But we did move in and eventually lived there for seventeen years, and eventually were good friends with everybody in the neighborhood.[24]

Hirosuke Inouye, who had graduated in 1938 from Stanford University with a degree in biological science, inspected chrysanthemums at the Sequoia Nursery in Redwood City. July 11, 1945. *Photograph by Hikaru Iwasaki, National Archives*

The prevailing philosophy of most Japanese at that time, however, was to "know" where the designated "acceptable" areas were. Kumiko Ishida, younger sister of Yoshikazu Ishida, recalled that this area was near the Bayshore Freeway, from Highway 101, to the railroad tracks, from about Third Avenue to Peninsula Avenue. "It was a very prescribed area in which you could buy homes," she said.[25]

After housing, the next priority was finding work. Former soldiers looking for work made for a tight job market. Those of Japanese ancestry found it even tougher. Tad Fujita, who before the war had earned a business administration degree from the University of California, Berkeley, recalled his first job after he returned to the West Coast. It was at the Simmons mattress factory in the North Beach area of San Francisco where many San Mateo workers found employment:

Two hundred and fifty Nisei were there because there was a huge mattress factory at North Beach and all the men had gone off to war and now that the war ended, production started again, but there were no workers. So that was the first job because word gets around that there is a job there. It was the experience of my lifetime because I had never worked in a factory. [You should have seen] the type of people who worked there, compared to all the educated people the Nisei were. Later on, we worked side by side on the conveyor, people who later became bank managers or doctors, they were all there, working together.[26]

[24] It is interesting to note that fourteen years after World War II, sentiments had not changed since the early post-war years, and discriminatory housing practices still existed in San Mateo County. Florence (Makita) Hongo, interview by Dianne Fukami, San Mateo, Calif., March 18, 1996. Hongo encountered this housing problem when she was married to Andrew Yoshiwara.
[25] K. Ishida, interview by Fukami.
[26] T. Fujita, interview by Fukami.

Kumiko Ishida and her brother Yoshikazu both encountered difficulty in getting jobs because of racism. Yoshikazu was a carpenter and could not work in the county because the San Mateo union chapter would not let him join. He and his friend Chet joined the union in San Jose and then transferred their membership to San Mateo. Kumiko could not obtain a teaching position in San Mateo after finishing college and student teaching:

> [T]he principal at the end had said
> very frankly that I had done very good
> work, but he could not recommend me
> for employment because the district's
> policy was, you know, to hire whites.
> And at San Francisco State [College], at
> the placement bureau–this was in 1952–
> they said also that they had a contract
> with the city of San Mateo, and the
> understanding was that they would
> send them only Caucasian applicants.

Ishida persevered, and, in 1952, she became the first person of color hired as a teacher in the city of San Mateo.[27]

Many nursery owners, such as the Kashima, Nakano, and Mori families of the Horgan Ranch area in Redwood City, were able to resume their former lives and occupations. Good friends had watched over their homes and businesses during the incarceration. Others, including Sakai "Sox"

Suyeyasu's father, were not so lucky. He had been a rose grower before the war and had given a friend power of attorney during his incarceration. That person sold the property in his absence for what Suyeyasu described as, "a song." The Suyeyasu family did not receive any money from the transaction.[28]

Mack Takahashi, his parents, his brother, and two sisters, formerly from Vacaville, California settled in Redwood City after spending the war years in the Gila River Relocation Center in Arizona. He is shown working at the Honda Nursery on Valota Road, and expected to be inducted into the U.S. Army within the next thirty days. July 18, 1945. *Photograph by Hikaru Iwasaki, National Archives*

---

[27] Y. Ishida, interview by Ito; and K. Ishida, interview by Fukami.

[28] S. Suyeyasu, interview by Ito. Before the war, many nurseries were run by Issei men. After the war, those who ran operations tended to be Nisei men, many of them brothers.

Frank Onizuka, who had been incarcerated in Topaz, watering chrysanthemums. July 15, 1945. *Photograph by Hikaru Iwasaki, National Archives*

There were other kinds of struggles as well. Yoneo Kawakita recalled returning as a soldier on furlough to San Mateo to visit his parents before he went overseas to Japan as part of the Occupation army. They were working as a live-in gardener and maid in a Hillsborough home. Kawakita "was told by the lady of the house not to eat their food or stay there. I was in my army uniform, but that meant nothing as far as she was concerned. I'm sure that my parents endured a lot of hardship working for this family because my father hastened the building of their new home on the property that was purchased before the war."[29]

Stella Sato Onizuka returned to San Mateo County with husband Frank. They had lived in Los Angeles before the war but had moved to Half Moon Bay after Pearl Harbor so they could be relocated together with the rest of her family. Starting over again after the war was tough. "After relocation, my husband—who was never a farmer—tried farming, and we had a miserable time for ten years. We struggled in Redwood City. We went into partnership in chrysanthemum growing."[30]

U.S. government photos from this period, including one of Frank Onizuka, belied the misery many Japanese Americans felt during these struggles. The government used the photos to show the public how easily the former inmates adjusted to life outside of imprisonment.

The combined stress of finding housing and work strained the family structure, which was already weakened and changed because of the incarceration. Though Yoneo Kawakita did not return to San Mateo until he was discharged from the army in 1947, he said it was a hardship for family and friends:

> Many returned with no place to stay. They had to stay with family friends who were fortunate to have a home. Families with children had to have the older kids work as school-boys and school-girls since there was not enough room for the whole family. They worked in Caucasian homes and did menial chores in place of room and board. The family structure was not a reality until the whole family was able to come under one roof by renting a house or buying one.[31]

---

[29] Yoneo "Yon" Kawakita, electronic correspondence to gayle k. yamada, May 31, 2000.
[30] Stella (Sato) Onizuka, interview by Yasuko "Ann" (Ishida) Ito, San Rafael, Calif., April 1, 1994.
[31] Y. Kawakita, electronic correspondence to yamada, May 31, 2000.

Shigemi (Saiki) Furusho, who was college age, left Topaz for Redwood City and ended up doing domestic work in Burlingame while her sister Yoshiko worked as a domestic in Hillsborough. Because the rest of the family could not find a place to rent, they ended up living in public housing at Hunter's Point, about eighteen miles north in San Francisco. While her mother remained there, the oldest sister went to Utah and her father found a job as a live-in cook in Atherton. As she put it, "The return to the coast scattered the family." Other families experienced similar break-ups as the young adults, in an effort to ease the financial strain on their elderly Issei parents, left the house earlier than they ordinarily might have.[32]

The World War II experience was a huge setback from which many never fully recovered. Kaoru "Ruth" Saito, age thirty-four at the end of the war, reflected, "Coming back, it wasn't hard for me, but it must have been awful hard for all the older people. It was terribly hard on her [my mother]. It was emotional. She broke down every once in a while. She would break down, not knowing how the future would be."[33]

Many Issei men who had been vigorous and active before World War II were now past their prime and unaccustomed to the tough manual labor they had easily handled before. As for the Nisei career men, most had lost their professional

I felt very bitter because it was the prime time of my life. It was a void in my life. Economically, job-wise or profession-wise, that ten years was a void in my life between thirty and forty. That's when all the Yuppies are making all that big money, and here in my life, it was zero. It affected my future: future investments and productivity years. So that was one thing that I lost: my productivity of ten years. Even before that, we had to get ready. We lost our jobs, we went to camp. Coming out, I moved ten times and no jobs, no money, so I had to borrow to start. I had no money to buy a car, no money to buy a house, so my wife went out to do catering. All that was the aftermath of the wartime experience. Life was not easy.

— TAD FUJITA

a University of California, Berkeley, graduate who was not able to get a corporate job until he was in his forties[34]

---

[32] Shigemi (Saiki) Furusho, interview by Yasuko "Ann" (Ishida) Ito, San Mateo, Calif., February 4, 1995.

[33] Kaoru "Ruth" Saito, interview by Yasuko "Ann" (Ishida) Ito, San Mateo, Calif., January 26, 1996.

[34] T. Fujita, interview by Fukami.

When my parents came back [to the West Coast], they were in their sixties and seventies and come back to nothing. And my brothers are in the service, and their older daughter is in New York, and it must have been terrible. It was terrible...I remember going to visit them in Hayward...the nurseries and hothouses are just stifling and having to work in a place like that and starting all over again.

— KUMIKO ISHIDA
whose parents returned to the Bay Area in 1945. She had left Topaz to work in New York and moved to San Mateo in 1946.[35]

Even those young enough to return to San Mateo to resume their education found the adjustment difficult. Michiko Mukai, nine years old when she returned to San Mateo, remembered:

When we came back, we were two years behind in school, and I had to learn English again, and that was a stigma that stuck with me for a long time. I went back to Lawrence School where my friends that I had were, and I was ashamed that I was two years behind, so I became very withdrawn and very shy because of that experience. That's why it was more difficult for me to try and assimilate. I remember our neighbors passing by, and there were more black families at that time, and they were saying, "The Japs [sic] are here."[37]

The war brought many other changes in San Mateo, some specific to the Japanese American community and some applicable to society at large. The San Mateo to which the Japanese community returned was different from the one they had left in 1942, and yet there was also a sense that things had not changed that much. Yasuko "Ann" (Ishida) Ito reflected:

When we first returned to San Mateo County, the situation was very similar to when the Issei settled here. The biggest difference was they were severely handicapped with the language barrier, and

momentum during their incarceration. Yoneji Takaha, then in his mid-twenties, summed up how many felt. "Most of us, the Nisei, were just at the age where 'now we're going to do it!' when the war came, and we just got slammed into [a] darn concentration camp."[36]

---

[35] K. Ishida, interview by Fukami.
[36] Y. Takaha, interview by Fukami.
[37] M. Mukai, interview by Ito.

they had no choice but to work at menial jobs like domestic work and gardening. When the evacuees came back, they were still restricted and had to settle in what is now called the North Central district of San Mateo.[38]

Nevertheless, the Japanese in San Mateo were no longer as insular as they had been before the war. For some, their experiences–sometimes forced–during the war years broadened their horizons. Many had traveled to other parts of the country and the world during the war, from New York to Japan. It was a choice that had been made for them but, for some, it triggered a desire after the war to live elsewhere. Still others came to San Mateo from different places in California and the United States. The Japanese in San Mateo no longer felt restricted to the enclaves in which they had lived before the war, and that changed the makeup of their community.

There were encouraging signs for Japanese Americans, too. Life had been put on hold for three years, and starting over meant building once again. After the war, a chapel was built adjoining the Sturge Memorial Cottage; prior to that it had served only as a meeting place and community center. It officially became the Sturge Presbyterian Church on July 1, 1951.[39]

The Buddhist Temple also grew. The war had halted plans for construction of a new temple but the board had decided to hold on to the land

The San Mateo Buddhist Church finally held its inaugural ceremony on March 22-23, 1952. Construction was delayed by the start of World War II. *Courtesy of Yoneo "Yon" Kawakita*

in spite of the uncertainties of the war. When Japanese Buddhists returned to San Mateo after the war, the congregation met in various homes. In 1947, the Japanese Language School was rented for services. A year and a half later, a fundraising drive for a temple began. The Buddhist Temple was dedicated in March 1952.[40]

Another positive step was taken in 1948, when Congress passed the Japanese American Claims Act, a token effort to compensate Japanese Americans and their families for economic losses stemming from the forced removal from the West Coast. The act, however, caused mixed reaction. Congress appropriated only $38 million to settle all property losses, a fraction of total claims filed: 26,568 claims totaling $148 million. Moreover, claims were limited to real and personal property, and claimants had to provide documentation of

---

[38] Yasuko "Ann" (Ishida) Ito, electronic correspondence to gayle k. yamada, May 31, 2000.
[39] S. Takahashi, telephone conversation with yamada.
[40] *Buddhist Churches of America*, 331.

I really wanted to go into the service and serve my country. I didn't feel there was any reluctance on my part not to serve. I felt that on the contrary, I should serve, I must serve, or I would like very much to serve in spite of what happened to my family and myself. Well, I'm an American and I have to do my duty to my country if I could, in whatever capacity. I think many Nisei felt this way, and that's why Nisei served with such distinction both in Europe and the Pacific.

— JOHN JUJI HADA

a colonel in the U.S. Army and a veteran of the Korean War[41]

losses. Most of that kind of paperwork had been lost in moves to concentration camps or destroyed when property was vandalized. Furthermore, by the time the act was passed, the Internal Revenue Service had destroyed pre-war income tax records that would have helped to show what kinds of property people owned. The last claims were not settled until 1965, and many of the Issei who had needed it most died without ever seeing a penny.[42]

The Japanese American community won two major victories in 1952. The California Supreme Court ruled that the Alien Land Law violated the equal protection clauses guaranteed in both the state and federal constitutions. That meant that non-citizens could finally own property. Just as importantly, Congress passed the Walter-McCarran Act that, in effect, gave Asian nations an immigration quota—albeit token—and also paved the way for them to become naturalized citizens. Now, for the first time since they arrived in this country decades earlier, Issei immigrants who had spent most of their lifetimes in America could become American citizens. By 1965 some forty-six thousand people of Japanese ancestry had become U.S. citizens.[43]

---

[41] John Juji Hada, interview by Dianne Fukami, San Francisco, Calif., March 14, 1996. Hada served in the U.S. Army; the navy and marines did not accept Japanese Americans.

[42] There is a controversy still over the dollar figure used to estimate losses. In the 1940s, the estimated figure ranged anywhere from $200 million to $400 million. But in 1983, the Commission on Wartime Relocation and Internment of Civilians commissioned an analysis of the losses. It came up with an estimate of between $1.2 billion and $3.1 billion; adjusting for inflation at a 3 percent interest rate, the figures increase to between $2.5 billion to $6.2 billion. Daniels, Taylor, Kitano, *From Relocation to Redress*, 166. Also, Taylor, *Jewel of the Desert*, 229.

[43] Robert A. Wilson and Bill Hosokawa, *East to America: A History of the Japanese in the United States* (New York: William Morrow & Company, 1980), 278-279, 281.

Many believe a major contributing factor in the acceptance of Japanese Americans into mainstream American society was the loyalty and bravery demonstrated by the Nisei soldiers who served during World War II in the 442nd Regimental Combat Team, the 100th Battalion in Europe, and the Military Intelligence Service (MIS) in the Pacific. Many of these soldiers volunteered to serve their country because they felt compelled to prove their loyalty.[44]

The 442nd casualty rate was 300 percent; six hundred Nisei soldiers died, and its men were awarded more than eighteen thousand individual decorations for valor. It is ironic that at the same time these young men were willing to sacrifice their lives to prove their loyalty as Americans, back

I felt we'll show them that we Nisei are just as patriotic as anyone else. And I felt that maybe by doing so, it might make it a little easier for my family in general. And if many of us did that, joined, it might help everybody.

— RUSTY KIMURA
who was incarcerated at Tanforan Assembly Center and Topaz. The U.S. Army recruited him to serve in the Military Intelligence Service.[45]

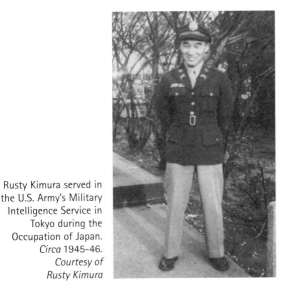

Rusty Kimura served in the U.S. Army's Military Intelligence Service in Tokyo during the Occupation of Japan. *Circa 1945-46. Courtesy of Rusty Kimura*

From left: Rusty Kimura, Salem Yagawa, Ace Fukui, and Grant Ichikawa served in the U.S. Army's Military Intelligence Service at Camp Chalmer in Indooroopilly, Australia. 1944. *Courtesy of Rusty Kimura*

---

[44] yamada, *Uncommon Courage.*
[45] Rusty Kimura, interview by gayle k. yamada, Los Angeles, Calif., February 2, 2000.

You're very careful about going out alone. You're very careful about your surroundings. You're always watchful about the people around you because you don't want to incite that type of behavior, and so you tend to avoid public places. You don't go to restaurants. You know it's just all of those things that you do to kind of protect yourself or try to avoid encountering that kind of situation. But school, you have to go to, so there was no way of avoiding going to school, but we did not socialize... outside of our own ethnic group that year [1945] because of those problems. Yeah, I was never invited to go into a Caucasian home. We just socialized amongst ourselves mainly. So it has nothing to do with our being cliquish. It was a mechanism of self-defense with us, to socialize basically with other Japanese.

— FLORENCE (MAKITA) HONGO
who moved to San Mateo in 1950 as a bride[46]

home in the United States their parents, siblings, wives, and children were imprisoned behind armed guards and barbed wire.[47]

No medals, commendations, or any other kind of compensation, however, could be adequate for the emotional scars inflicted on the more than 120,000 people of Japanese ancestry who were incarcerated during World War II.

Many Nisei remarked how inferior and ashamed they felt after the war; although they had committed no crime, their incarceration made them feel as though they were second-class citizens who had done something wrong.[48]

[46] F. Hongo, interview by Fukami

[47] Hosokawa, *The Quiet Americans*, 410. The Military Intelligence Service received a Presidential Unit Citation in June 2000, more than fifty years after World War II ended, acknowledging its service during the Pacific War. Unlike the 442nd Regimental Combat Team and the 100th Battalion, the MIS had never been recognized as a unit since MIS soldiers often were assigned for temporary duty to various army, navy, and marine units in the Pacific, and to foreign units as well. One of the reasons the MIS mission was considered secret during WWII was the sensitive nature of its assignment, that is, Japanese Americans fighting the Japanese in the Pacific. yamada, *Uncommon Courage*. From San Mateo County, a partial listing of those who served in the U.S. Army during the war includes Kenichi "Ken" Adachi, Sachi Elmer Adachi, Shigeichi "Teiken" Adachi, Edgar Arimoto, N. Roy Fujita, Harry Higaki, Hiroshi "Hip" Honda, Dick Ikeda, R. Joe Ishizaki, Hiroshi Ito, Sat Iwasaki, Hiroji Kariya, Masazo Kariya, Pete Kashima, Kenji Kato, Saichiro "Socky" Kawakita, Yoneo "Yon" Kawakita, Tadashi Masaoka, Shozo Mayeda, James Okamoto, Takeshi Sugimoto, Yoneji Takaha, George Takahashi, Kenge Takahashi, Yoshiya Tanaka, Kenji Yamane, and Takeshi "Doc" Yatabe. Deposited at the San Mateo County History Museum, Museum Archives, Redwood City, Calif. James K. Mori, Electronic correspondence to gayle k. yamada, October 29, 2002.

[48] K. Nakano, interview by Ito.

Others, like Shig Takahashi, felt apprehensive and powerless as a result of the experience. "To me, you've just come back, you're kind of afraid. You can't stand up for yourself and say, 'I should be able to do what everyone else is able to do.' You figure…we just have to take it."[49]

The impact of incarceration and racism was seared into every person, no matter how young or old, and it continues to affect the psyche of Japanese Americans more than fifty years later. The pain may have lessened, but has not gone away. Most of the Issei have passed on, and death gradually is taking the Nisei. Many Japanese Americans in San Mateo and elsewhere–with the help of their Sansei (third-generation) children and Yonsei (fourth-generation) grandchildren–have made it their mission to educate America about what happened to them during World War II. Many Americans have never learned about the forced eviction and incarceration, and still others cannot believe it ever happened.

But it **did** happen, and it can happen again–maybe not to Americans of Japanese ancestry but maybe to some other group of people who become victims of fear and public hysteria.

We all are still at risk. There is still work to do.

What this really means is community empowerment…We have a responsibility to be able to lean down and help somebody else up that ladder. It's important. Because if we don't continue bringing up new community leaders to participate in community activities–including seeking political office–then, to me, we're not doing our job. I think the lesson learned from 1942, in terms of our forced evacuation and internment in camps during World War II, was the fact that we had no entrée to the political element of the day. That's something we've got to make sure never happens again.

— NORMAN MINETA

Secretary of Commerce under President Bill Clinton and Secretary of Transportation under President George W. Bush. He was the first Asian American to become a Cabinet member. A former member of Congress, he co-sponsored national redress legislation, House Resolution 442.[50]

---

[49] S. Takahashi, interview by Fukami.

[50] Norman Y. Mineta, interview by gayle k. yamada, Monterey, Calif., July 1, 2000. HR 442 called for the public apology to all those of Japanese ancestry who had been incarcerated during World War II and a redress payment of $20,000.

While we end our story here, the saga of Japanese Americans goes on. The ensuing years brought a mixture of challenges and opportunities for the Japanese Americans of San Mateo that included discrimination, economic and educational success, and the rise of Japanese Americans as the so-called "model minority," a controversial term.[1]

A new wave of Issei, called *shin*-Issei, immigrated to San Mateo County, bringing with them an infusion of Japanese culture. The first of these waves of *shin*-Issei came in the 1950s as war brides. Subsequent immigrants continued to arrive in the United States during the next decades. Many worked for Japanese corporations located in San Francisco or in the San Jose area (often referred to as Silicon Valley) to the south, but they lived in San Mateo where it was more affordable and had more of a suburban rather than a big city feel. They represented the new Japan, rebuilt after the war, and brought a different feeling to America than the first Issei who had arrived nearly a century before.[2]

At the same time, Japanese Americans in San Mateo began to move away from the ethnic enclaves that had defined their families' existence prior to World War II. The passage of time helped

---

[1] The term, "model minority," refers to Japanese Americans many years after the war because of their success, especially in light of their wartime experiences. The controversy arises because some Asian Americans feel it is a patronizing mainstream stereotype that does not fairly or accurately depict Japanese Americans or Asian Americans. Within the Asian Pacific Islander community, a wide range of reactions to this term exists. Some feel pride because it reflects the accomplishments of their community while others believe it pigeonholes Japanese Americans and precludes society at large from seeing them as three-dimensional individuals with complexities and differences. In recent years, the term has lessened in popularity.

[2] In this case, war brides are Japanese women who met their servicemen husbands in Japan when the United States occupied it, and returned to the U.S. with them. *Shin*-Issei literally means "new first generation."

to change the real and perceived barriers that existed before they were forcibly removed from San Mateo and the rest of the West Coast. Today, they do not feel pressured to live in certain areas because of their race; no longer is there a geographically identifiable "Japanese" area in San Mateo. Japanese grocery stores and restaurants are now scattered throughout the county–as they are around the country–and are evidence of a growing acceptance of things Japanese. A sure sign of American popular culture: sushi bars have become trendy dining establishments.

Like many Japanese Americans throughout the country, Japanese Americans in San Mateo continued their education after the war, eventually fulfilling one of the most important dreams their parents had for them–to become successful professionals. Economically, they continued to integrate into society at large; levels of education and income of Japanese Americans surpass those of the average American.[3]

At the same time, however, racism is not gone. Incidents of Asian-bashing and bigotry, while less frequent and sometimes less overt than sixty years ago, still exist–not always specifically toward Japanese Americans but toward those of Asian ancestry in general. Laws still must exist to guard against racial and ethnic discrimination, and these laws need to be enforced.

With a high percentage of out-marriage, that is, marrying outside of the ethnic group, the face of Japanese Americans is changing. Japanese Americans are a growing part of an increasingly multicultural, multiracial society as evidenced in San Mateo. The Japanese Language School holds classes and school activities at the Buddhist Temple, where an increasingly higher percentage of multiracial students is enrolled. Asian basketball leagues and martial arts classes attract non-Asians as well.

Japanese Americans are adapting, much as their forebears did.

The Civil Rights Movement of the 1960s triggered a parallel Asian American movement in the late 1960s and early 1970s, and propelled many Japanese Americans to take a more activist role in defining their cultural, racial and ethnic identity and in determining where they fit into the larger context of American society. It brought to the forefront efforts to seek redress–a formal apology and monetary payment from the U.S. government for the loss of civil rights when those of Japanese ancestry were evicted from their homes and forced to live behind barbed wire in desolate camps during the war. While redress was a divisive issue nationally among Japanese Americans, those in San Mateo were very cohesive, and the community worked together to raise money

---

[3]According to the 1990 U.S. Census, 34.2% of Japanese Americans by birth over the age of 25 have a bachelor's degree or higher while the figure for the corresponding general American population is 20.3%. The per capita income is $19,373 for Japanese Americans by birth and $14,420 for the corresponding general American population. Bureau of the Census, *1990 Census of Population, Asians and Pacific Islanders in the United States*, CP-3-5 (Washington, D.C., 1990), 1, 71, 81, 141, 151.

for the redress movement. San Mateo played a small but important part of the national effort which slowly gained momentum, acceptance and, finally, approval that culminated in the Civil Rights Act of 1988.[4]

Family, education, and enterprise defined the Japanese who immigrated to America. But who are Japanese Americans now? By what standards and values do they identify themselves? As an ethnic group, who are they becoming? For the most part, today's Japanese Americans have fulfilled an Issei goal of acceptance into American society, and at the same time they have the freedom to openly enjoy and cherish their cultural heritage without fear of discrimination. Thus some are participating in the civic activity to establish a sister city relationship between the city of San Mateo and Toyonaka in Japan; some have formed a Kabuki Club, which promotes classical Japanese theater art.

But while some are comfortable with their ethnic and cultural heritages, others have questions about their ethnic identity and still struggle with what it means to be Japanese American today. Those of mixed heritage also grapple with where they fit into the Japanese American community.

Japanese immigrants were an example of change and adaptation as they started out in a new country. Their children rose like phoenixes from the ashes of World War II, and *their* children struggle with questions of identity and ethnic change. Some of this struggle involves success, be it with family, education, or enterprise. Issues on the darker side of that success have emerged, though–stereotypes and pressures to fit those stereotypes. With these changes, social history is being written by succeeding generations as they build on values their families instilled in them but which are no longer strictly Japanese. Like Americans of other ethnic backgrounds, Japanese Americans have blurred the line between the two cultures.

Preservation and evolution–two aspects of a culture at a crossroads. It is up to future generations to decide what to embrace and what to shed.

---

[4] For the Nisei, "camp" commonly refers to the ten incarceration camps where most of those on the West Coast spent the war years with their families. The term is ironic, for "camp" usually connotes something fun, and that was the image their children first conjured up when they heard their parents had spent the war years in "camp." Nisei, and subsequent generations, continue to use this widely-accepted terminology as they tell their stories and educate other Americans about their experiences and their loss of civil liberties during World War II.

Redress was controversial within the Japanese American community because there were many who wanted to let "sleeping dogs lie" and who were reluctant to bring attention to their incarceration experience.

bento	box lunch
bonsai	the art of growing dwarf trees or shrubs
coram nobis	Latin legal term meaning "the error before us," used as a procedure to re-open or re-argue cases in which errors of fact were knowingly withheld by prosecutors to judges or defendants.
dekaseginin	sojourners, literally, "go-out-to-earn" people
dekasegi-shosei	student-laborers
enryo	to hold back or to show reserve
gaman	to persevere
giri	duty and responsibility
go	Japanese strategy board game
hakujin	Caucasian
hapa	term used to describe someone of partial Asian or Pacific Islander ancestry; *see fuller explanation in Chapter 6, footnote 15, page 77*

hinotama	soul of a dead person
Issei	first-generation Japanese immigrants
judo	Japanese martial art form using principles of yielding or softness (the Way of Yielding)
ken	prefecture in Japan
kendo	Japanese martial art form using bamboo swords to teach fencing (the Way of the Sword)
kenjinkai	social ties based on prefectural ties
kibei	Japanese Americans born in the United States and educated in Japan who return to United States
Kiku Matsuri	Chrysanthemum Festival
kimono	Japanese loose robe or gown tied with a sash, worn as an outer garment by men and women.

kodomo no tame ni	for the sake of the children
maru no uchi	round house
miso	bean curd paste
nagaya	literally means "long house"
nigiri	rice balls
Nihon-gakko	Japanese school
Nihongo-gakko	literally "Japanese language school"
Nihonjinkai	Japanese Association of America
Nippon Gakuen	Japanese school
Nisei	second-generation Japanese Americans; generally, children of first-generation Japanese immigrants
Nishi-honganji	sect of Buddhism
nori	edible seaweed
ofuro	traditional Japanese bath in which users soap and rinse themselves outside of the tub and use the deep tub filled with water for relaxation purposes
on	obligation
onabesan	honorific term for "cooking pot;" here, the name of a play the Blue Jay girls club produced in the 1920s
orei	honorarium
oshogatsu	New Year
Rodo Kumiai	Labor Association
Ryusei	literally means "meteors," and was the name of the San Mateo boys' athletic club begun in the Japanese community in the 1920s
samurai	Japanese feudal warriors

Sansei	person who is third-generation Japanese American or the grandchildren of Issei
school-boy	term used to describe those who went to school by day and earned room, board, and a small wage by doing domestic duties for a household. The term *school-girl* was also used for women in the same capacity.
sensei	honorific term used to connote respect for teachers and doctors
shakuhachi	Japanese bamboo flute
shashin kekkon	literally "photograph marriage," refers to marriages by proxy or "picture brides"; *see fuller explanation in Chapter 1, page 9*
shikataganai	expression that means "it can't be helped"
*shin-*Issei	new first-generation; generally pertains to Japanese immigrants post-World War II
shogi	Japanese game played with tiles
shogun	Japanese military leader
shoyu	soy sauce
tanomoshi	credit association
tofu	soybean cake
writ of habeas corpus	Latin term meaning "you have the body." Used to determine whether an inmate is imprisoned lawfully and whether he/she should be released from custody.
Yonsei	person who is fourth-generation Japanese American or the great-grandchildren of Issei

Aikawa, Maya Nagata. Interview by Dianne Fukami. Videotape recording. Oakland, Calif., 16 February 1995.

Arimoto, Yoneko (Inouye). Interview by Yasuko "Ann" (Ishida) Ito. Audiotape recording. San Mateo, Calif., 11 February 1996.

Arrington, Leonard J. *The Price of Prejudice*. Delta, Utah: The Topaz Museum, 1997.

Asai, Kiyoshi. "San Mateo Japanese History." San Mateo County History Museum, Museum Archives. Redwood City, Calif., 1940.

_____. "History of the Japanese Pioneers in San Mateo." Unpublished paper written for a course at San Mateo Junior College. San Mateo, Calif. San Mateo County History Museum, Museum Archives. Redwood City, Calif., 1941.

Baba, Haru. Telephone conversation with gayle k. yamada. 7 April 2003.

Edward Norton Barnhart Papers, Japanese American Research Project (JARP) Collection (Collection 2010), Department of Special Collections, Charles E. Young Research Library, University of California, Los Angeles, Los Angeles, Calif.

Beckwith, Jane. "Forty Years Later: Delta High School Students Look at Topaz." *Japanese Americans: From Relocation to Redress*. Edited by Roger Daniels, Sandra C. Taylor, and Harry H. L. Kitano. Seattle: University of Washington Press, 1991.

Benner, Norton, M.D. Interview by Yasuko "Ann" (Ishida) Ito. Audiotape recording. San Mateo, Calif., 24 July 1996.

Biddle, Francis. *In Brief Authority*. New York: Doubleday & Co., 1962. Cited in Michi Weglyn, *Years of Infamy: The Untold Story of America's Concentration Camps*. New York: William Morrow and Company, Inc., 1976.

Bowie, Henry P. *On the Laws of Japanese Painting*. New York: Dover Publication, Inc., 1952.

Buddhist Churches of America. *75 Year History 1899-1974*, Vol. I and Vol. II. Chicago: Nobart, Inc., 1974.

Burton, Jeffrey F., Mary M. Farrell, Florence B. Lord, and Richard W. Lord. *Confinement and Ethnicity: An Overview of World War II Japanese American Relocation Sites*. Washington, D.C.: Western Archeological and Conservation Center, National Park Service, U.S. Department of the Interior, 2000.

Burlingame (Calif.) *Advance-Star*, 17 September 1941. Howard Imada Collection, San Mateo, Calif.

Commission on Wartime Relocation and Internment of Citizens. *Personal Justice Denied*. Washington, D.C.: U.S. Government Printing Office, 1982.

Curtis, Elizabeth Howat. Interview by Yasuko "Ann" (Ishida) Ito. Audiotape recording. San Bruno, Calif., 1 August 1996.

Daniels, Roger. *The Politics of Prejudice: The Anti-Japanese Movement in California and the Struggle for Japanese Exclusion*. Berkeley: University of California Press, 1962.

____. *Asian America: Chinese and Japanese in the United States since 1850*. Seattle: University of Washington Press, 1988.

Daniels, Roger, Sandra C. Taylor, and Harry H.L. Kitano, eds. *Japanese Americans: From Relocation to Redress*. Salt Lake City: University of Utah Press, 1986.

Dewing, Ria Elena. *Heritage of the Wooded Hills: A Belmont History*. Belmont, Calif.: Wadsworth Publishing Company, 1977.

DeWitt, J.L. (General). U.S. Department of War, *Final Report: Japanese Evacuation from the West Coast, 1942*. Headquarters Western Defense Command and Fourth Army, Office of the Commanding General, Presidio of San Francisco, Calif. Washington, D.C., United States Government Printing Office, 1943.

Doi, Amy (Tamaki). Audiotape recording. San Mateo, Calif., 22 February 1994.

Endo, Mariko (Tsuma). Interview by Yasuko "Ann" (Ishida) Ito. Audiotape recording. San Mateo, Calif., 24 February 1994.

Endo, Toshio. Interview by Richard Nakanishi and Shizu "Shazie" (Yamaguchi) Tabata. Audiotape recording. San Mateo, Calif., 1 June 1978.

Enomoto, Edes (Nakashima). Interview by gayle k. yamada. Audiotape recording. Atherton, Calif., 21 October 1997.

Enomoto, William. Interview by Richard Nakanishi. Audiotape recording. Redwood City, Calif., 2 March 1978.

____. Conversations with Richard Nakanishi. 11 January 1981, 25 January 1981.

FTDA Annual Convention 1930, "Japan Day" program. San Mateo County History Museum, Museum Archives. Redwood City, Calif., 1 September 1930.

Fujita, Tad. Interview by Dianne Fukami. Videotape recording. Berkeley, Calif., 1 February 1995.

Fujita, Yuya. Interview by Shizu "Shazie" (Yamaguchi) Tabata. Audiotape recording. San Mateo, Calif., 18 November 1977.

Fukui, George M., Ph.D. Unpublished memoir, 4 June 1997.

Furusho, Shigemi (Saiki). Interview by Yasuko "Ann" (Ishida) Ito. Audiotape recording. San Mateo, Calif., 4 February 1995.

Furusho, Toshio. Interview by Yasuko "Ann" (Ishida) Ito. Audiotape recording. San Mateo, Calif., 4 February 1995.

Grodzins, Morton. *Americans Betrayed: Politics and the Japanese Evacuation*. Chicago: University of Chicago Press, 1949.

Hada, John Juji. Interview by Dianne Fukami. Video-tape recording. San Francisco, Calif., 14 March 1996.

Hapa Issues Forum website, www.hapaissuesforum.org.

Haraguchi, Kazuo. Interview by Yasuko "Ann" (Ishida) Ito. Audiotape recording. San Mateo, Calif., 3 March 1994.

Haraguchi, Tatsuye (Hamasaki). Interview by Yasuko "Ann" (Ishida) Ito. Audiotape recording. San Mateo, Calif., 3 March 1994.

Herzig, Jack. Electronic correspondence to gayle k. yamada, 6 February 2002.

Herzig-Yoshinaga, Aiko. Electronic correspondence to gayle k. yamada. 11 February 2002, 3 April 2002, 9 April 2002.

Herzig-Yoshinaga, Aiko and Jack Herzig. Electronic correspondence to gayle k. yamada, 8 March 2002, 17 March 2002.

Hibi, Hisako. Unpublished children's story. San Francisco, Calif., *circa* 1950-1980s.

Higa, Karin M. "Japanese American Art from the Internment Camps." *Japanese and Japanese American Painters in the United States—a Half Century of Hope and Suffering 1896-1945*. Companion book for traveling exhibit co-organized by the Japanese American National Museum. Los Angeles, Calif., 1995-1996.

Higaki, Harumi "Harry." Interview by gayle k. yamada. Audiotape recording. Hillsborough, Calif., 20 November 1997.

Higaki, Nobuo. Interview by Richard Nakanishi. Translated by Harumi "Harry" and Sachiko Higaki. Audiotape recording. Redwood City, Calif., 4 May 1978.

Higashi, Kenzo. Interview by Yasuko "Ann" (Ishida) Ito. Audiotape recording. San Mateo, Calif., 9 November 1994.

Hirabayashi, Shizu "Sugar" (Mitsuyoshi). Interview by Dianne Fukami. Videotape recording. San Jose, Calif., 6 February 1995.

Hirotsuka, Mitsuye (Yamashita). Interview by Yasuko "Ann" (Ishida) Ito. Audiotape recording. Redwood City, Calif., 1 November 1994.

"History of the San Mateo Labor Association." San Mateo, Calif., 1998.

Hoobler, Dorothy and Thomas. *The Japanese American Family Album*. New York: Oxford University Press, 1996.

Hongo, Florence (Makita). Interview by Dianne Fukami. Videotape recording. San Mateo, Calif., 18 March 1996.

Hoshiyama, Fred. Letter to Lincoln Kanai, Hoover Institution, Stanford University, Palo Alto, Calif., May 1942.

Hosokawa, Bill. *Nisei: The Quiet Americans*. New York: William Morrow & Company, 1969.

Ichihashi, Yamato. *Japanese Immigration: Its Status in California*. San Francisco: The Japanese Association of America, 1913.

_____. "Study of the Situation of the Japanese Nursery and Its Related Business in San Francisco and Bay Region." Unpublished manuscript. Stanford University Archives, Stanford, Calif., 1927-1928.

_____. *Japanese in the United States: A Critical Study of the Problems of the Japanese Immigrants and Their Children*. Stanford, Calif.: Stanford University Press, 1932.

Ichioka, Yuji. *The Issei: The World of the First Generation Japanese Immigrants, 1885-1924*. New York: Free Press, 1988.

Inouye, Hirosuke. Interview by Richard Nakanishi. Audiotape recording. Redwood City, Calif., 20 March 1978.

Irons, Peter. *Justice at War: The Story of the Japanese American Internment Cases.* Berkeley: University of California Press, 1983.

Ishida, Kumiko. Interview by Dianne Fukami. Video-tape recording. San Mateo, Calif., 18 March 1996.

Ishida, Virginia (Sakamoto). Interview by Yasuko "Ann" (Ishida) Ito. Audiotape recording. Belmont, Calif., 17 June 1997.

Ishida, Yoshikazu. Interview by Yasuko "Ann" (Ishida) Ito. Audiotape recording. Belmont, Calif., 17 June 1997.

Ishizaki, Kikue (Fukuichi). Interview by Richard Nakanishi. Audiotape recording. San Mateo, Calif., September 1978.

Ito, Hiroshi. Interview by Richard Nakanishi. Audio-tape recording. San Mateo, Calif., 17 March 1978.

Ito, Kazuo. *Issei: A History of Japanese Immigrants in North America.* Translated by Shinichiro Naka-mura and Jean S. Gerard. Seattle: Executive Committee for Publication of Issei, 1973.

Ito, Yasuko "Ann" (Ishida). Interview by Richard Nakanishi. Audiotape recording. San Mateo, Calif., 17 March 1978.

_____. Electronic correspondence to gayle k. yamada, 31 May 2000.

Iwase, Masako (Hanyu). Interview by Yasuko "Ann" (Ishida) Ito. Audiotape recording. San Mateo, Calif., 22 February 1994.

Japanese American Curriculum Project (JACP). *Japanese American Journey: The Story of a People.* San Mateo, Calif.: JACP, 1985.

Japanese American Research Project (JARP) Collec-tion (Collection 2010), Department of Special Collections, Charles E. Young Research Library, University of California, Los Angeles, Los Angeles, Calif.

Japanese Association of America. *Zaibei Nippon Jin Shi (History of the Japanese in the United States).* San Francisco, 1940.

"Japanese Language School Location Creates Big Stir in San Mateo, New Offer Made." *Burlingame (Calif.) Advance-Star,* 30 September 1930.

Kajiwara, Jim. Interview by Yasuko "Ann" (Ishida) Ito. Audiotape recording. San Francisco, Calif., 26 April 1994.

Kajiwara, Sachi. Interview by Dianne Fukami. Video-tape recording. San Lorenzo, Calif., 2 February 1995.

"Kaoru Okamura Operates Nursery Here 52 Years." *Redwood City Tribune,* 3 August 1961.

Kasai, Yoshio "Yo." Interview by Dianne Fukami. Videotape recording. San Leandro, Calif., 1 Feb-ruary 1995.

_____. Unpublished memoir. San Leandro, Calif., 1994.

Kashima, Hideyoshi "Hid." Interview by Dianne Fukami. Videotape recording. San Carlos, Calif., 19 July 1994.

Kashiwagi, Tomoko. Interview by Richard Nakanishi and Shizu "Shazie" (Yamaguchi) Tabata. Audio-tape recording. San Mateo, Calif., 17 May 1978.

_____. Interview by Yasuko "Ann" (Ishida) Ito. Audiotape recording. San Mateo, Calif., 14 Octo-ber 1993.

_____. Interview by Dianne Fukami. Videotape recording. San Mateo, Calif., 25 July 1994.

Kawaguchi, Gary. *Living with Flowers: The California Flower Market History*. San Francisco: California Flower Market, Inc., 1993.

Kawakita, Sahioye. Interview by Richard Nakanishi and Shizu "Shazie" (Yamaguchi) Tabata. Audiotape recording. San Mateo, Calif., 8 December 1977.

Kawakita, Yoneo "Yon." "The Incarceration of Yoneo 'Yon' Kawakita." Unpublished memoir, San Mateo, Calif., 1997.

_____. Interviews by gayle k. yamada. Audiotape recordings. San Mateo, Calif., 2 March 1998, 12 March 1998.

_____. Electronic correspondence to gayle k. yamada. 4 December 1999, 31 May 2000, 21 November 2001, 28 November 2001, 11 February 2002, 14 February 2002, 15 February 2002, 16 February 2002, 21 February 2002.

Kikuchi, Charles. *The Kikuchi Diary*. Edited by John Modell. Urbana: University of Illinois Press, 1993.

Kimura, Rusty. Interview by gayle k. yamada. Videotape recording. Los Angeles, Calif., 2 February 2000.

Kitashima, Tsuyako "Sox" (Kataoka). Interview by Yasuko "Ann" (Ishida) Ito. Audiotape recording. San Francisco, Calif., 6 April 1994.

Koga, the Reverend Sumio, comp. *A Centennial Legacy: History of the Japanese Christian Missions in North America, 1877-1977, Vol. I*. Chicago: Nobart Publishing, 1977.

Kuwahara, Yuku (Miyazaki). Interview by Richard Nakanishi and Shizu "Shazie" (Yamaguchi) Tabata. Audiotape recording. San Mateo, Calif., 28 October 1978.

Light, Ivan H. *Ethnic Enterprise in America*. Berkeley: University of California Press, 1972.

Lee, Ibuki (Hibi). Electronic correspondence to Dianne Fukami, 5 November 2002.

Maki, Minako. "The History of Japanese Language School in San Mateo County." Unpublished paper written for a California History course. San Mateo County History Museum, Museum Archives, Redwood City, Calif., 1993.

Matsueda, Tsukasa. Interview by gayle k. yamada. Audiotape recording. San Mateo, Calif., 24 October 1997.

Matsuoka, Janet "Inako" (Hirano). Interview by Dianne Fukami. Videotape recording. Oakland, Calif., 17 February 1995.

Meltzer, Milton. *Dorothea Lange: A Photographer's Life*. New York: Farrar Straus Giroux, 1978.

Minami, Dale. Electronic correspondence to Diane Yen-Mei Wong. 10 December 2001, 30 March 2003.

Mineta, Norman Y. Interview by gayle k. yamada. Videotape recording. Monterey, Calif., 1 July 2000.

Miyachi, Hamae (Tanizawa). Interview by Richard Nakanishi and Shizu "Shazie" (Yamaguchi) Tabata. Audiotape recording. San Mateo, Calif., 11 November 1977.

_____. Interview by gayle k. yamada and Yasuko "Ann" (Ishida) Ito. Audiotape recording. Mountain View, Calif., 12 June 1997.

Miyachi, Jubei. Interview by Richard Nakanishi and Shizu "Shazie" (Yamaguchi) Tabata. Audiotape recording. San Mateo, Calif., 11 November 1977.

Miyamoto, Frank S. "Views from Within." Paper presented at symposium on the Japanese American Internment Experience. University of California, Berkeley, Berkeley, Calif., 20 September 1987.

Miyata, Isabel. Unpublished diary. Tanforan, Calif., 1942.

Miyata, Janet. Interview by Yasuko "Ann" (Ishida) Ito. Audiotape recording. San Mateo, Calif., 12 May 1995.

Mizono, Yoshiko "Yoshi" (Sato). Interview by Richard Nakanishi and Shizu "Shazie" (Yamaguchi) Tabata. Audiotape recording. San Mateo, Calif., 15 May 1978.

_____. Interview by gayle k. yamada. Audiotape recording. San Mateo, Calif., 25 March 1998.

_____. Letters to gayle k. yamada. 18 November 1999, 18 May 2000, 27 April 2002.

_____. Telephone conversations with gayle k. yamada. 9 December 2001, 10 December 2001.

Mori, James K. "J. Elmer Morrish," Exhibit for the "Community Story: A History of Japanese Americans in San Mateo County," February-June 2001. San Mateo County History Museum, Redwood City, Calif., 16 February 2001.

_____, compiled. Unpublished list of World War II veterans. Exhibit for "Community Story: A History of Japanese Americans in San Mateo County," February-June 2001. Redwood City, Calif., 2000-2001.

_____. Telephone conversations with gayle k. yamada. 3 February 2002, 3 March 2002.

_____. Electronic correspondence to gayle k. yamada, 29 October 2002.

Mori, Kazuo "Kay." Interview by Dianne Fukami. Videotape recording. San Francisco, Calif., 8 March 1996.

Mori, Kazuye (Honda). Interview by Yasuko "Ann" (Ishida) Ito. Audiotape recording. Redwood City, Calif., 4 April 1996.

Mori, Shigeki. Interview by Richard Nakanishi. Audiotape recording. San Mateo, Calif., 11 January 1978.

Morioka, Frances Kimura. Interview by Yasuko "Ann" (Ishida) Ito. Audiotape recording. San Mateo, Calif., 12 May 1995.

Moriwaki, Suga Ann. Telephone conversation with gayle k. yamada. 7 April 2003.

Mukai, Kyoko Hoshiga. Telephone interview by gayle k. yamada. Audiotape recording. 27 May 1998.

Mukai, Michiko (Takeshita). Interview by Yasuko "Ann" (Ishida) Ito. Audiotape recording. San Mateo, Calif., 20 January 1994.

Mukai, Thomas V. Telephone conversations with gayle k. yamada. 2000-2002.

Nakagawa, Isao. Interview by Yasuko "Ann" (Ishida) Ito. Audiotape recording. San Mateo, Calif., 13 January 1994.

Nakano, Jim Hiroshi. Interview by Yasuko "Ann" (Ishida) Ito. Audiotape recording. San Mateo, Calif., 7 March 1996.

Nakano, Kei. Interview by Yasuko "Ann" (Ishida) Ito. Audiotape recording. San Mateo, Calif., 7 March 1996.

_____. Telephone conversation with Yasuko "Ann" (Ishida) Ito, 5 December 2001.

Nakayama, Keiko. "Japanese Issei's Contribution to San Mateo County During Early 1900's." Unpublished manuscript, 11 December 1989.

Nihonjin-kai. "History of the Japanese Living in the United States." 1940.

Niiya, Brian, ed. *Japanese American History: An A-to-Z Reference from 1868 to the Present.* New York: Facts on File, 1993.

Nosaka, William. Interview by Dianne Fukami. Videotape recording. San Mateo, Calif., 19 July 1994.

_____. Interview by gayle k. yamada. Audiotape recording. San Mateo, Calif., 12 November 1998.

Ohrn, Karin Becker. *Dorothea Lange and the Documentary Tradition*. Baton Rouge: Louisiana State University Press, 1980.

Okamura, Sue Sato. Interview by Richard Nakanishi and Shizu "Shazie" (Yamaguchi) Tabata. Audiotape recording. San Mateo, Calif., 15 May 1978.

Okubo, Miné. *Citizen 13660*. New York: Columbia University Press, 1946.

Onizuka, Stella (Sato). Interview by Yasuko "Ann" (Ishida) Ito. Audiotape recording. San Rafael, Calif., 1 April 1994.

Oshima, Katsuko "Susie" (Endo). Conversation with Yasuko "Ann" (Ishida) Ito, San Mateo, Calif., October 2001.

Ota, Kimiye (Wada). Interview by Yasuko "Ann" (Ishida) Ito. Audiotape recording. San Mateo, Calif., 8 March 1994.

"Pacific Coast Convention of the Anti-Jap Laundry League Proceedings," Bancroft Library, University of California, Berkeley, Berkeley, Calif., 8 December 1908.

"Pioneer Flower Growers Honored After 50 Years," *Redwood City* (Calif.) *Tribune*, 24 February 1959.

Postel, Mitchell. *San Mateo: A Centennial History*. San Francisco: Scottwall Associates, 1994.

"Redwood City's Contribution to San Francisco," *American Florist*, December 26, 1901, Richard N. Schellens Collection, personal clipping file, Redwood City Library, Redwood City, Calif.

Rikimaru, "Joseph" Iwasuke. Interview by Richard Nakanishi. Audiotape recording. San Mateo, Calif., 10 January 1978.

Saito, Kaoru "Ruth." Interview by Yasuko "Ann" (Ishida) Ito. Audiotape recording. San Mateo, Calif., 26 January 1996.

_____. Telephone conversation with Yasuko "Ann" (Ishida) Ito, 19 April 2001.

Sakakibara, Haruko. Electronic correspondence to gayle k. yamada, 1 December 2001.

Sakuma, Masae. Letter. Recipient unknown. 22 March 1978.

Sakuma, Sei (Kashiwagi). Interview by Richard Nakanishi and Shizu "Shazie" (Yamaguchi) Tabata. Audiotape recording. San Mateo, Calif., 17 May 1978.

_____. Interview by Yasuko "Ann" (Ishida) Ito. Audiotape recording. San Mateo, Calif., 14 October 1993.

Sakuma, Tadashi . Conversations with Yasuko "Ann" (Ishida) Ito. 3 April 2002, 21 April 2002.

San Francisco Examiner, 20 May 1909, Richard N. Schellens Collection, personal clipping file, Redwood City Library, Redwood City, Calif.

San Mateo Buddhist Temple: 70th and 75th Anniversaries. Fresno, Calif.: Self-published by the San Mateo Buddhist Temple, *circa* 1986.

San Mateo Chapter, Japanese American Citizens League, *1872-1942: A Community Story*. Palo Alto, Calif., 1981.

San Mateo County. I*ndex to Births 1866-1965, A-K and L-Z*. Office of the Assessor-County Clerk-Recorder, Vital Records, Redwood City, Calif.

San Mateo (Calif.) *News-Leader*. 22 March 1919, 9 April 1919. Richard N. Schellens Collection. Personal clipping file. Redwood City Library, Redwood City, Calif.

San Mateo (Calif.) *Times*. 8 March 1924, 7 May 1942, 8 May 1942.

Sarasohn, Eileen S. *The Issei*. Palo Alto, Calif.: Pacific Books, 1983.

Sasano, Kyoko (Takeshita). Interview by Yasuko "Ann" (Ishida) Ito. Audiotape recording. San Mateo, Calif., 24 January 1994.

Sato, Seishi "Sam." Interview by Dianne Fukami. Videotape recording. San Francisco, Calif., 8 March 1996.

Richard N. Schellens Collection. Personal clipping file. Redwood City Library, Redwood City, Calif.

Segi, Masao. Interview by Richard Nakanishi and Shizu "Shazie" (Yamaguchi) Tabata. Audiotape recording. San Mateo, Calif., 11 November 1977.

Sekerak, Eleanor Gerard. "A Teacher at Topaz." *Japanese Americans: From Relocation to Redress*. Edited by Roger Daniels, Sandra C. Taylor, and Harry H.L. Kitano. Salt Lake City: University of Utah Press, 1986.

Slesnick, Carole. Electronic correspondence to gayle k. yamada, 20 July 2002.

Smith, William C. *Americans in Process: A Study of Citizens of Oriental Ancestry*. Ann Arbor, Mich.: Edwards Brothers, Inc., 1937.

"The Story of the Kiku Matsuri." San Mateo County History Museum, Museum Archives. Redwood City, Calif., 1 October 1931.

Sturge Presbyterian Church. *Fiftieth Anniversary*. San Mateo, Calif., 1973.

Suyeyasu, Rose (Nakagawa). Interview by Yasuko "Ann" (Ishida) Ito. Audiotape recording. San Mateo, Calif., 9 February 1995.

Suyeyasu, Sakai "Sox." Interview by Yasuko "Ann" (Ishida) Ito. Audiotape recording. San Mateo, Calif., 9 February 1995.

Suzuki, Lester E. *Ministry in the Assembly and Relocation Centers of World War II*. Berkeley, Calif.: Yardbird Pub. Co.,1979.

Suzuki, Yasukazu. Interview by Yasuko "Ann" (Ishida) Ito. Audiotape recording. San Mateo, Calif., 13 January 1994.

Svanevik, Michael. Interview by Dianne Fukami. Videotape recording. San Mateo, Calif., 26 July 1994.

Svanevik, Michael and Shirley Burgett. "Henry P. Bowie: The Man Who Loved Japan." *The* (San Mateo, Calif.) *Times*, 23 July 1993.

Tabata, Shizu "Shazie" (Yamaguchi). Interview by Yasuko "Ann" (Ishida) Ito. Audiotape recording. San Mateo, Calif., 14 April 1994.

_____. Interview by Dianne Fukami. Videotape recording. San Mateo, Calif., 26 July 1994.

Takaha, Yoneji. Interview by Richard Nakanishi. Audiotape recording. San Mateo, Calif., 3 October 1978.

_____. Interview by Dianne Fukami. Videotape recording. San Mateo, Calif., 18 March 1996.

Takahashi, Aya (Miyake). Interview by Yasuko "Ann" (Ishida) Ito. Audiotape recording. San Mateo, Calif., 15 November 1994.

Takahashi, Best (Rikimaru). Interview by gayle k. yamada. Audiotape recording. San Mateo, Calif., 11 January 2000.

Takahashi, Ishiye (Baba). Interview by Richard Nakanishi and Shizu "Shazie" (Yamaguchi) Tabata. Audiotape recording. San Mateo, Calif., 16 November 1977.

Takahashi, Jerrold H. "The San Mateo JACL." Unpublished paper written for a Contemporary Asian Studies course. University of California, Berkeley, Berkeley, Calif., 1973.

Takahashi, Kamechiyo (Morishita). Interview by Richard Nakanishi and Shizu "Shazie" (Yamaguchi) Tabata. Audiotape recording. San Mateo, Calif., 8 November 1977.

Takahashi, Shigeharu "Shig." Interview by Dianne Fukami. Videotape recording. San Mateo, Calif., 13 February 1999.

_____. Interview by gayle k. yamada. Audiotape recording. San Mateo, Calif., 11 January 2000.

_____. Telephone conversation with gayle k. yamada, 27 January 2002.

Takahashi, Tomoye "Tami" (Nozawa). Interview by gayle k. yamada. Videotape recording. San Francisco, Calif., 15 April 2002.

Takaki, Ronald. *Strangers from a Different Shore: A History of Asian Americans.* Boston: Little, Brown, 1989.

Takeda, Eiko. "Return Homecoming Exhibition of Friendship Dolls from U.S.A." Translated and edited by Minoru Saitoh. Pamphlet. Tokyo: GOSP, Publishers, 1989.

Tamaki, Mari (Takaha). Interview by Richard Nakanishi. Audiotape recording. San Mateo, Calif., 3 October 1978.

Tamura, Minoru. Interview by Yasuko "Ann" (Ishida) Ito. Audiotape recording. San Mateo, Calif., 16 September 1993.

Tanforan. Lyricist unknown. Tanforan (San Bruno), Calif. *Circa* 1942.

Tanforan Totalizer. 14 May 1942.

Tanouye, Satoye "Sally" (Kawakita). Interview by Yasuko "Ann" (Ishida) Ito. Audiotape recording. Redwood City, Calif., 21 February 1995.

Tatsuno, Dave. Interview by Dianne Fukami. Videotape recording. San Jose, Calif., 5 February 1995.

Taylor, Sandra C. *Jewel of the Desert: Japanese American Internment at Topaz.* Berkeley: University of California Press, 1993.

tenBroek, Jacobus, Edward N. Barnhart, and Floyd W. Matson. *Prejudice, War and the Constitution.* Series: *Japanese American Evacuation and Resettlement, Vol. 3.* Berkeley: University of California Press, 1968.

Texas Legislature. *General Laws, 1921 Regular Session, on Aliens–Amending Act Relating to the Rights, Powers and Disabilities of.* Austin, Texas, 1921.

Togasaki, Chizu. Interview by Dianne Fukami. Videotape recording. Walnut Creek, Calif., 2 February 1995.

Topaz, the Gem of the Desert. Lyricist unknown. Topaz, Utah. *Circa* 1943-45.

Topaz Times. 1 January, 1943.

Tsukushi, George. Interview by Richard Nakanishi. Audiotape recording. Redwood City, Calif., 29 March 1978.

Uchida, Yoshiko. *Desert Exile: The Uprooting of a Japanese-American Family.* Seattle, Wash.: University of Washington Press, 1982.

U.S. Bureau of the Census. *1990 Census of Population, Asians and Pacific Islanders in the United States, CP-3-5.* Washington, D.C., 1990.

U.S. Office for Emergency Management, War Relocation Authority. Topaz files. Record Group 210, National Archives and Records Administration. 4 February 1943.

_____. "Education in Topaz." Topaz files. Record Group 210, National Archives and Records Administration. 1 January 1944.

_____. Topaz files. Record Group 210, National Archives and Records Administration. 25 March 1944.

Valentine, Katherine (Pitcher). Telephone interview by Richard Nakanishi. Date unknown.

Walker, Roger. Interview by Wendy Walker. Delta, Utah, January 1983. Cited in Sandra C. Taylor, *Jewel of the Desert: Japanese American Internment at Topaz*. Berkeley: University of California Press, 1993.

War Relocation Authority. Manuscripts and University Archives. University of Washington Libraries, Seattle, Wash.

Washington Legislature. *Session Laws, 1920 Extraordinary Session, on Aliens*. Olympia, Washington, 1921.

Watanuki, Hasuko (Yamanouchi). Interview by Richard Nakanishi and Shizu "Shazie" (Yamaguchi) Tabata. Audiotape recording. San Mateo, Calif., 11 June 1978.

_____. Interview by gayle k. yamada. Audiotape recording. San Mateo, Calif., 19 November 1998.

Weglyn, Michi. *Years of Infamy: The Untold Story of America's Concentration Camps*. New York: William Morrow and Company, Inc., 1976.

Whitney, Merrill P. Letter. Recipient and date unknown. San Mateo, Calif.

Wilson, Robert A. and Bill Hosokawa. *East to America: A History of the Japanese in the United States*. New York: William Morrow & Company, 1980.

yamada, gayle k. *Uncommon Courage: Patriotism and Civil Liberties*. Television documentary. 2001.

Yamaguchi, Aiko (Inouye). Interview by Richard Nakanishi and Shizu "Shazie" (Yamaguchi) Tabata. Audiotape recording. San Mateo, Calif., 26 January 1978.

Yamamoto, Verlin T. Interview by Shizu "Shazie" (Yamaguchi) Tabata. Audiotape recording. San Francisco, Calif., 26 December 1977.

Yoshifuji, Chiye (Shintaku). Interview by Richard Nakanishi and Shizu "Shazie" (Yamaguchi) Tabata. Audiotape recording. San Francisco, Calif., 12 May 1978.

Yoshifuji, Kaoru. Interview by Dianne Fukami. Videotape recording. San Mateo, Calif., 13 April 1994.

_____. Interview by Yasuko "Ann" (Ishida) Ito. Audiotape recording. San Mateo, Calif., 23 March 1995.

_____. Interview by gayle k. yamada. Audiotape recording. San Mateo, Calif., 11 February 1998.

_____. Telephone conversation with gayle k. yamada, 11 December 2001.

_____. Conversation with Richard Nakanishi, San Mateo, Calif., date unknown.